A COLONIAL ECONOMY IN THE GREAT DEPRESSION

A COLONIAL ECONOMY IN THE GREAT DEPRESSION

Madras (1929–1937)

K. A. MANIKUMAR

Orient Longman

ORIENT LONGMAN PRIVATE LIMITED

Registered Office
3-6-752 Himayatnagar, Hyderabad 500 029 (A.P.), India

Other Offices
Bangalore / Bhopal / Bhubaneshwar
Chennai / Ernakulam / Guwahati / Hyderabad / Jaipur / Kolkata
Lucknow / Mumbai / New Delhi / Patna

ISBN 81 250 2456 5

Typeset by
Vans Information Limited
Mumbai 400 034

Printed in India at
Novena Offset Printing Co.
Chennai 600 005

Published by
Orient Longman Limited
160 Anna Salai
Chennai 600 002

For Jaya

Contents

Tables and Graphs

Tables:

Graphs:

Acknowledgements

This book is an outcome of my thesis for which the University of Madras awarded me a doctorate in 1989. In the initial stage of this work I had the fortune of working with Professor S. Krishnaswamy, who introduced me to the study of the economic history of colonial India at Madras Christian College, Tambaram. Later, when he left for Edmonton I wrote the dissertation under the supervision of Professor C. J. Nirmal. Both provided insights that have been incorporated in the thesis.

A number of scholars read earlier drafts of this work and gave extensive comments. They include Professor K. Nagaraj, Professor Venkatesh B. Athreya and Dr M. S. S. Pandian. I owe my thanks to all of them, and also to the anonymous reviewer for Orient Longman Ltd. Dr A. R. Venkatachalapathy's editing brought greater clarity to this work.

My special thanks are due to the former vice-chancellor of my university, Dr V. Vasanthi Devi, for granting a year's sabbatical leave for revision of my doctoral thesis. The late Professor Sarvepalli Gopal, the late Professor Ravinder Kumar and Professor C. T. Kurien remained constant sources of encouragement.

The librarians and library staff of the following institutions assisted me in collection of data: Connemara Library, Madras University, Tamilnadu Archives, Southern India Chamber of Commerce, Madras Chamber of Commerce and the Madras Institute of Development Studies—all of which are in Chennai—and the Centre for Development Studies in Thiruvananthapuram. Mr P. Pandiaraj helped in word-processing the manuscripts.

My wife Jaya had to bear with many discomforts, caused by my long absences on account of my objectives of leading the state-wide movement of college teachers and carrying on this research project. Our children Vishnu and Charan provided me with support and affection. Even in the hours of neglect, they sustained me and helped to complete the dissertation.

Abbreviations

b.e.	budget estimate
cwt.	hundredweight, 1/20 of one ton
I.C.S.	Indian Civil Service
I.P.S.	Indian Police Service
PMLC	*Proceedings of the Madras Legislative Council*
RBI	Reserve Bank of India
r.e.	revised estimate
Rs. an. p.	rupees, annas and pies
s. d.	shillings and pence
WIMCO	Western India Match Company

Introduction

The Great Depression of 1929 had a profound impact on the world economy. The collapse of export markets, fall in the prices of agricultural and commercial products, and decrease in government revenue from customs, excise, stamps and registration were the marked features of this global phenomenon. India, too, was not exempt from its disastrous effects. However, the fact that India's economy functioned under colonial aegis added further complexity to the whole issue.

In the West, the study of the Great Depression has excited continued interest amongst economists, probably because of the catastrophic economic losses suffered.[1] In India contemporary studies were undertaken by economists such as K. T. Shah, P. J. Thomas and B. V. Narayanaswamy Naidu.[2] However, unlike the USA, where there was continuing interest in study of the Depression,[3] there was no effort in India to have a fresh look at

1 John Kenneth Galbraith, *The Great Crash: 1929*(Australia: Penguin Books, 1969); Charles Kindleberger, *Manias, Panics and Crashes: A History of Financial Crisis* (New York: Basic Books, 1970); Tom Shachtman, *The Day America Crashed: A Narrative Account of the Great Stock Market Crash of October 24, 1929* (New York: G. P. Putnam's, 1975).

2 K. T. Shah, *World Depression* (Madras: National Literature, 1933); P. J. Thomas, *Papers on Currency and Depression* (Madras, 1938), *Papers on Rural Debt* (Madras, 1934), *Papers on International Trade* (Madras, 1933), all published in the Madras University Economics Series; B. V. Narayanaswamy Naidu and P. Vaidyanathan, *The Madras Agriculturists Relief Act: A Study* (Annamalai Nagar: Annamalai University, 1939); B. V. Narayanaswamy Naidu's *Report of the Economist for Enquiry into Rural Indebtedness* (Madras, 1946), *The Co-operative Movement in the Madras Presidency* (Annamalai Nagar: Annamalai University, 1933).

3 John A. Garraty, *The Great Depression* (Florida: Jovanovich, 1986).

its onslaught. Recently, the historian D. Rothermund has attempted an account of India in that period,[4] but hardly any worthwhile regional study has been undertaken so far. C. J. Baker has highlighted[5] the distress caused to the people of the Madras Presidency; yet how each sector and each section of society came to be affected by this economic calamity has not been adequately dealt with. Against this backdrop, this book attempts a detailed study of the Depression.

The Depression, the policy of the colonial state, and the result of their interplay are the three aspects that the study sets out to examine. While conducting this investigation the following questions are posed. Was the incidence of the Depression severe? Did the government evolve any new economic policy to combat it? What kinds of established policies were given up? To what extent did the trade and financial policies pursued by the British add to the Depression and aggravate it? Was the impact uniformly felt or were there sub-regional variations? If so, what were the economic areas in which the impact was different? What was the people's attitude and response? How far did the Depression provide an opportune moment for nationalists to intensify the struggle for liberation?

The area chosen for the study, namely the Madras Presidency, was vast; it included the present Tamilnadu, portions of the present-day states of Andhra Pradesh and Karnataka, and the Malabar region covering some parts of present Kerala and Karnataka. Though we have taken the Presidency as a unit for the study of state policy, the focus of the Depression's impact was Tamilnadu. Madras, Chengalpattu, South Arcot, North Arcot, Salem, Coimbatore, Tiruchirappalli, Thanjavur, Madurai, Ramanathapuram, Tirunelveli and the Nilgiris were the twelve districts that constituted Tamilnadu then. We have excluded the princely state of Pudukkottai. Tables and graphs, drawn mostly from government records, have been compiled based on statistical

[4] D. Rothermund, *India in the Great Depression* (New Delhi: Manohar Publications, 1992).

[5] C. J. Baker, *The Politics of South India (1920–1937)* (New Delhi: Vikas Publishing House, 1976), *An Indian Rural Economy (1880–1955): The Tamil Nad Countryside* (New Delhi: Oxford University Press, 1984).

evidence pertaining to Tamil districts. The period of study pertains to the time when the politics of the Madras Presidency took the form of a keen contest between British imperialism, the nationalist movement and regional politics.

The first chapter of the book is concerned with events from the stock market crash in the US to the outbreak of the Depression, which resulted in disastrous trade returns in the Presidency. Chapter 2 deals with the colonial economy of Tamilnadu on the eve of the Depression. Chapter 3 dwells on how the Depression affected the peasantry and immiserized them. In the fourth chapter, the condition of industry in this period is examined. The financial and monetary policies pursued by the colonial government in the aftermath of the Depression are reviewed in chapter 5, while the sixth chapter discusses the Madras government's response and the remedial measures undertaken. The seventh chapter delineates the repercussions of the Depression on the social life of people and their politics. Finally, the conclusion summarises the discussions in all preceding chapters.

1

The Depression and Its Onset

The economic depression that broke out in 1929 in the aftermath of the US stock market crash was international in character. By far, it was the most severe in the history of capitalism. The entire world was engulfed by this catastrophe, debilitating the economy of all countries. In this chapter we first trace the origin and spread of the Depression. The second section analyses the Depression's onslaught on India. Its impact on external and internal trade of the Madras Presidency under the aegis of British colonialism is dealt with in the third section.

Developments Leading to the Depression

The First World War had stimulated certain industries to their utmost capacity in Europe. The rise in prices, due to this stimulus as well as the gradual inflation of the currency systems, led to expansion of other industries in the belief that the war-time boom would continue indefinitely.[1] However, when the war came to an end, the industries brought into existence because of its requirements had to be abandoned or modified. Stocks of goods and materials had to be liquidated, and a large number of workers had to be diverted from the occupations they had been following during the war.[2] Besides, while the European countries were in conflict, the remaining world had equipped itself to supply the needs of the belligerent countries and to cope with their withdrawal from the international markets. After the war, however, Europe tried to recapture what she had lost.[3] But the

[1] Shah, *World Depression,* 37–50.
[2] *Ibid.*
[3] *The Indian Annual Register* (Calcutta: The Annual Register Office, 1936), 1: 434–35.

task was made harder by the political complications caused by the Treaty of Versailles; it had brought about a new wave of economic nationalism which expressed itself in tariff barriers. Even Great Britain, which for a hundred years had practised free trade, tried to check the inflow of foreign goods with heavy tariff rates. Such tariff barriers erected by nations the world over dampened world trade.

The war also placed a heavy burden of debt on every European country. The British national debts after the war, for instance, amounted to $6.5 billion.[4] The condition of the USA, however, was different because it had entered the war on the side of the Allies and supplied their funds. When the war began the US government owed Europe $5 billion. By the end of the war the tide had turned; Europe now owed the US $10 billion.[5] America was the moneylender to the world and the rest of the world was its debtor. Such was its commanding financial position that America could reduce any of the debtor countries to bankruptcy by merely demanding settlement of debts.

The statesmen of the period called the post-war era "the period of restoration and reconstruction." However, throughout this period the debtors had been paying their debts not out of any real surplus of production over consumption, but because they had creditors to offer them further credit.[6] The debtor countries that were financially in bad shape could have cleared their debts by sending their manufactures to the USA, but its policy of protectionism had raised high tariff walls that the European exporters could not scale. The US government while adopting measures to protect its industries had, however, encouraged the flow of capital into Europe. These flows only helped the European debtor countries to meet interest obligations on existing debt.[7] The capital flow from America also found its outlet in new investments which were no doubt productive and certain to be profitable, but the profits would accrue only after a period.

[4] Jawaharlal Nehru, *Glimpses of World History* (London: Lindsay Drummond, 1949), 885.

[5] *Ibid.*, 896.

[6] Shah, *World Depression*, 37–50.

[7] Nehru, *Glimpses of World History*, 687 and 886.

In the meanwhile, the internally generated slump in the US upset all calculation and forced the government to impose quantitative restrictions on capital expo.ted. American overseas lending began to decline from mid-1928. After reaching a peak of $1,050 million in the first half of that year, it fell to $450 million, both in the second half of 1928 and in the first half of 1929. It fell further to $229 million in the second half of 1929.[8]

The withdrawal of American capital caused decline in the volume and value of exports all over. The effects of this development were accentuated by the US market crash. The American stock market's first huge crash occurred on 24 October 1929. That day 12,894,650 shares changed hands, many of them at prices that shattered the dreams and hopes of those who had owned them.[9] It was the most devastating day in the history of the New York Stock Exchange. There is a general consensus among scholars that the American stock prices were not unreasonably high in 1929, and that the Wall Street collapse had little direct effect on economic activity in the US or anywhere else. But its psychological effect was terrific. The shock of the crash discouraged investors and consumers to such an extent that a recession turned into an economic collapse.[10] The stock market crash prompted more and more people to sell their shares and dispose of their stocks—but there was no buyer for them.[11] The Chicago and Buffalo exchanges had closed. The country witnessed a suicide wave and eleven well-known speculators had already killed themselves.[12]

The market crash and subsequent decline in security prices were followed by the failure of American banks.[13] The American financiers were forced to recall their own funds invested abroad, largely in Germany. As Germany had invested the American money in long-term industrial enterprises, it could meet the demand for repatriation only by fresh borrowing from Britain and its European neighbours. Britain was already experiencing hardships as

[8] Marcello de Cecco, *The International Gold Standard: Money and Empire* (London: Frances Pinter, 1984), 167–68.

[9] Galbraith, *The Great Crash*, 121.

[10] Garraty, *The Great Depression*, 32.

[11] Shachtman, *The Day America Crashed*, 12–13.

[12] Galbraith, *The Great Crash*, 105.

[13] *Ibid.*, 197.

creditors in South America and Asia were pressing for repayment of dues.[14] In the case of European neighbours, the Depression had already had its impact and the price of agricultural produce was crashing. The prices were so low that banks in East Europe could not recover money from their debtors and thus could not pay back the money they had borrowed in pounds and dollars in Vienna.[15] This led to a banking crisis in Vienna, and the greatest Viennese bank, the Credit-Anstalt, failed. Eventually there was no creditor to advance loans to Germany. The stoppage of loans to Germany immediately brought on a crisis and the failure of two large German banks, the Darmstadt and National Bank, and the Dresden Bank. Germany stopped paying reparations and debts. The failure of the Austrian Credit-Anstalt caused serious concern since the Bank of England had lent heavily to that bank and these funds were now "locked-up and frozen."[16]

The Bank of England now found itself in serious difficulty as a result of its liberal credits abroad. It raised its rates of interest by rapid stages from 2.5 to 4.5 per cent in the latter half of July 1931. A credit of fifty million pounds was obtained by the British government from France and the United States of America to overcome the crisis. In the first week of September 1931, a further credit of eighty million pounds was taken and an emergency budget was introduced with drastic taxation and retrenchment.[17] All these measures were of no avail and on 21 September the British decreed a departure from the gold standard.

Almost simultaneously, a great number of countries left the gold standard: the Scandinavian countries of Denmark, Norway and Sweden; Egypt; and practically the whole of the British Empire with the exception of South Africa and Canada. This resulted in the breakdown of the international system of exchange that had guaranteed monetary stability and economic growth for several decades.[18] In an endeavour to protect domestic markets, each nation resorted to a policy of protectionism and competitive

[14] Shah, *World Depression*, 37–50.

[15] Nehru, *Glimpses of World History*, 899–900.

[16] *India in 1931–32* (Calcutta, 1932), 153–54.

[17] *Ibid.*, 154.

[18] *India in 1931–32*, 153–54; D. Rothermund, *The Global Impact of the Great Depression* (New York: Routledge, 1996), 6–8.

devaluation. Such devaluation was often accompanied by suspension of debt service to foreign creditors. The creditors in turn responded by stopping their lending activities. This led to a world-wide credit contraction. Thus the defensive measures initiated by each country to safeguard its internal economic system led to unprecedented decline in world economic activity.[19] Charles Kindleberger thought that the Depression could have been staved off, had there been an international lender. But there was no such lender of last resort. "Exhausted by the war and groggy from the aborted recovery of the 1920s, Great Britain was unable to act in that capacity and the United States was unwilling to do this."[20] Therefore, the 1929 depression was wide, deep and prolonged.

India in the Depression

Britain as colonial power had forced the policy of free trade on India, using India as a supplier of food and raw materials, and as a market for British manufactures. In the beginning of the second decade of the twentieth century, particularly in the context of the First World War, there arose a need to procure a supply of industrial goods from within India. The British government was forced to proclaim a policy to develop India industrially. After the war, on the pretext of respecting the viewpoints of nationalists, Britain gave "discriminating protection" to nine industries in 1923. However, the professed new economic doctrine was only to thwart her competitors in the Indian market.[21] Discrimination in favour of their industries at the expense of indigenous ones was the principle by which the colonial rulers continued to administer India. Imports from countries of the British Empire including Britain were still given preferential treatment. That the policy of protectionism did not help to reduce imports is evident from the trade returns for 1928–29. Out of aggregate trade value of Rs. 2,530 million for that year, the United Kingdom had the lion's share, supporting imports to the value

19 H.W. Arndt, *The Economic Lessons of the Nineteen Thirties* (London: Oxford University Press, 1944), 34.

20 Kindleberger, *Manias, Panics and Crashes,* 4.

21 D. Rothermund, *An Economic History of India* (USA: Croom Helm, 1988), 60.

of Rs. 1,130 million (44 per cent of the total imports)—against Rs. 1,160 million as the value of imports from all foreign countries put together.[22]

The economic policy of the government of India throughout the period of depression was one geared to the policy of preserving the British imperial order. In the name of "sound finance" India was forced to follow deflationary policy ruthlessly. According to Keynes, during a depression fiscal policy calls for government expenditure to exceed tax revenue. This means that the government was expected to increase aggregate spending in the economy; but the colonial government did the very opposite. The orthodox financial policy that the government's expenses should not exceed its income was adopted in India. Therefore the incidence of the Depression was severe.

The price decline in India until October 1931 was 36 per cent, while it was 27 per cent in the UK and 26 per cent in the US.[23] As the fall of prices in India was heavier than in other countries, the internal prices of agricultural products remained higher than the export price and hampered its natural outflow. The peasants in the absence of an export market for their produce found it difficult to meet their commitments such as debt service and land revenue payment. The Depression also dealt a severe blow to the treasury of the government of India. Income under the major heads of revenue declined from Rs. 1,548 million in 1929–30 to Rs. 1,389 million in the following year. It continued to remain at that reduced level for about two years.[24] When the revenue fell the government tried to overcome the crisis by raising taxes and pruning expenditure.

India's foreign trade was severely hit by the Depression. The total value of Indian imports of private merchandise in 1931–32 was lower by Rs. 384 million (23 per cent) as compared with 1930–31, and by Rs. 1,144 million (47 per cent) as compared

22 *The Hindu*, 19 July 1930.

23 R. Krishnamurthy, "India Through Slump and Recovery, 1929–1937: Being a Study of the Trade Cycle in relation to India" (M.Litt. diss., University of Madras, 1940), 14.

24 D. Rothermund, "The Great Depression and British Financial Policy in India, 1929–1934," *The Indian Economic and Social History Review* 18, no. 1, 1981.

with 1929–30. The exports were less by Rs. 651 million (29 per cent) than those in 1930–31, and by Rs. 1,574 million (49 per cent) than those in 1929–30. Both imports and exports were practically halved in three years. As a result, the excess of Indian exports over imports was more than halved. It fell from Rs. 7.7 million in 1929–30 to Rs. 6.09 million in 1930–31, and to Rs. 3.42 million in 1931–32.[25]

The slump in foreign trade was reflected in India's internal trade and transport.[26] A proper study of internal trade during the Depression is severely handicapped for want of regionwise statistics. It was calculated that for every acre of land producing goods for export, eleven acres were being cultivated for local consumption. The huge exports of cotton, jute, rice, wheat, oil seeds and other crops formed only a small proportion of the total internal production that was annually consumed within the country. Some estimated that the proportion of exports to internal trade was 1:16 or 1:11. Professor K. T. Shah estimated the value of India's internal trade to be Rs. 150 million. The impact of the Depression on internal trade is known from the fall in the income of the railway companies. Low prices and consequent constriction of money flow affected the passenger traffic earnings. On the other hand, wagon figures suffered in two ways. Movement to the ports was affected by the collapse of the markets for Indian staples. And movement away from the ports dwindled because imports were checked by the boycott of foreign goods launched as a part of the swadesi (made in India of Indian-produced materials) movement.[27]

Indian railway finances were thrown out of equilibrium by a sudden drop of Rs. 150 million in their traffic receipts in two years of the Depression, 1930–32. By 1932, the reserves accumulated out of the first six prosperous years after the separation of

[25] L. C. Jain, "Economic Depression in India," *Indian Journal of Economics* 13, 1932–33, 370–72.

[26] B. V. Narayanaswamy Naidu, ed., *Indian Trade,* Annamalai University Economic Series no. 9 (Annamalai Nagar: Annamalai University, 1942), 16–17.

[27] *The Hindu*, 7 July 1930.

the railway budget in 1924 had been wiped out.[28] After 1924, the railway finances improved for a time, and the contribution to the general revenues was maintained at an annual average of about Rs. 60 million until the Depression broke out. In the years from 1924–25 to 1929–30, the railways contributed nearly Rs. 360 million to general revenues.[29] In 1930–31, the Depression affected the railway earnings and the contribution was paid entirely from the Railway Reserve Fund. In 1931–32, the crisis intensified further and in spite of retrenchment measures, deficits continued from year to year; the railway budget was only balanced by drawing repeatedly on the Reserve Fund, and after that was exhausted, on the Depreciation Fund.[30] Table 1.1 highlights the crisis of the railway administration in terms of deficits incurred.

TABLE 1. 1: Deficit Finance of Indian Railways, 1930–31 to 1933–34 (for the whole country)

Year	*Deficit finance (in Rs. million)*
1930–31	52 (100)
1931–32	92 (117)
1932–33	93 (180)
1933–34	77 (149)

Note: Figures in brackets give index numbers with 1930–31 = 100.
Source: *Asiatic Review* 29, 1933, 487–88.

As a result of the large shrinkage in the total foreign trade, the balance of trade considerably dwindled. India had to suffer a severe balance of payment crisis and deterioration in the terms of trade. In view of colonialism, the exports had to be much greater in India or the Presidency in order to cover the invisible imports called Home Charges. It was with the help of gold exports that India was able to pay for her Home Charges. The nature of this expenditure is set out in table 1.2.

[28] *The Indian Review* 35, no. 3, 1934, 151.
[29] P. J. Thomas, *The Growth of Federal Finances in India: Being a Survey of Indian Public Finance from 1833 to 1939* (Oxford: Oxford University Press, 1939), 358–59.
[30] *Ibid.*

TABLE 1.2: Home Charges for the Year Ending 31 March 1929

Items	*Pounds (in millions)*	*Percentage of total*
Capital expenditure	10.8	27
Railways	9.0	22
Military services	9.9	24
Debt services	5.6	14
Pension etc.	2.4	6
Civil administration (high commissioner's leave salary)	2.0	5
Others	0.8	2
Total	40.5	100

Source: G. Findlay Shirras, "The Situation in India: A Rejoinder," *The Economic Journal* 42, 1932, 575.

The decline in the volume and value of the seaborne trade is given in table 1.3. The net export (+) or import (-) of gold in each year is also shown so as to indicate the influence of gold exports on the total visible balance of trade.

TABLE 1.3: Seaborne Trade of India (in Rs. million)

Year	*Imports*	*Exports*	*Net exports of merchandise*	*Net export (+) or import (–) of gold*	*Excess of exports*
1928–29	2630 (100)	3390 (100)	+760	-210	550
1929–30	2500 (95)	3190 (94)	+690	-140	550
1930–31	1730 (66)	2260 (67)	+530	-150	380
1931–32	1300 (49)	1610 (47)	+310	+580	890
1932–33	1350 (51)	1360 (40)	+10	+650	660
1933–34	1170 (44)	1500 (44)	+330	+570	900
1934–35	1350 (51)	1550 (46)	+200	+530	730
1935–36	1340 (51)	1640 (48)	+300	+370	670
1936–37	1250 (48)	2020 (60)	+770	+280	1050

Note: Figures in parentheses are index numbers with 1928–29 = 100. Merchandise includes government stores.

Source: Lakshmi Narain, *Price Movements in India, 1929–1957* (Meerut: Shri Prakasham Publishers, 1957), 46.

It is clear from table 1.3 that seaborne trade of India in merchandise declined between 1928–29 and 1933–34. The decline in the case of exports was 55.75 per cent while the imports fell by 55.51 per cent. Until 1930–31, India had a favourable balance of trade out of which it could afford to import gold. But thereafter the balance dwindled to Rs. 10 million in 1932–33. From 1931–32 onwards gold began to leave the country. From table 1.3 it is understood that in six years, 1931–32 to 1936–37, the net exports of gold amounted to Rs. 2,980 million, of which Rs. 2,330 million were in the four years from 1931–32 to 1934–35.[31]

Like all agricultural countries, India also witnessed a serious deterioration in its terms of trade. The prices of its exports fell more heavily than the prices of imports. Between 1927–28 and 1933–34 the index number of export prices fell by 46.7 per cent, while that of import prices declined only to the extent of 30.9 per cent. Most agricultural countries such as Australia, New Zealand, Brazil and Denmark counteracted this worsening of the terms of trade by a depreciation of the exchange rate.[32] An independent India would have responded with a devaluation of the currency as the above countries did. But the colonial India was not allowed to opt for such a course of action.

The Consequences of a Manipulative Currency System

The rupee exchange rate always fluctuated in relation to silver prices in Western countries. When the rupee depreciated, it caused a currency crisis in Britain leading to the outflow of gold and silver to India. In such circumstances the imperial government resorted to a deflationary measure as an antidote. This happened, for example, when the rupee depreciated from 2s. in 1872 to 1s. 25d. in 1893–94. The government of British India closed down the mint and refrained from minting silver coins, which led to constriction of money available for internal credit supply. In an agricultural country like India, this meant undermining of the peasant's holding power in the market, forcing him to sell his produce at the prevailing unremunerative prices. The rural households in the 1890s had no other option but to liquidate their assets, possessed in the form of gold and silver, to finance consumption and settle debts.[33]

31 Narain, *Price Movements in India*, 46.

32 Radha Kamal Mukerjee and H. L. Dey, eds., *Economic Problems of Modern India* (London: Macmillan, 1941), 2:235.

33 G. Balachandran, *John Bullion's Empire: Britain's Gold Problem and India Between the Wars* (London: Curzon, 1996), 178.

In this way, a transfer of liquid resources to Britain was facilitated without any direct steps for gold or silver imports. Whenever Britain was confronted with a currency crisis, it adopted the manipulative technique of making the rupee scarce and forcing the Indian households to sell the precious metals they had saved over time.

The high exchange rate—following an increase from 1s. 4d. to 1s. 6d. in June 1925—meant increase in the value of the fixed commitments of agriculturists such as debt-interest payment, rent and land revenue by 12.5 per cent. Therefore, when prices of agricultural produce fell during the Depression, the higher exchange ratio turned out to be a crushing burden. This forced the peasant households to liquidate whatever assets they had in the form of gold and silver.[34] So the gold that was exported during the Depression came through the distress sales of gold by peasants.

By 1931, about sixteen hundred ounces of gold, mostly in the form of jewellery, were arriving in Bombay every day. As the market price of gold was lower than the official price, much of this gold went to the government's coffer. According to one estimate, by early 1931 the monthly flow of gold into the Bombay mint amounted to nearly one million pounds. The success of the currency policy pursued by the imperial administration during the Depression evoked jubilation in bureaucratic circles. The viceroy, Willingdon, struck a self-congratulatory note.

> For the first time in . . . history owing to the economic situation, Indians are disgorging gold. . . . We have sent to London in the past 2 or 3 months . . . 25,000,000 sterling and I hope the process will continue![35]

The outflow of gold from India provided relief to the Bank of England and prevented it from taking any desperate measures. This prompted Britain's chancellor of the exchequer to rejoice over the development.

> The astonishing gold mine we have discovered in India has put us in a clover. The French can take their balances away without our flinching.

[34] Aditya Mukherjee, "The Rupee Question, 1926–28: Rupee Sterling Ratio and the Gold Standard," *Studies in History* 5, no.1, 1989, 111–13.
[35] *Ibid.*, 181.

> We can accumulate credits for the re-payment of our 80m pound loan and we can safely lower the the bank rate. So, there is great rejoicing in the City.[36]

The nationalists while attacking the government's monetary policy made a plea that the government should intervene to buy gold in the local market to strengthen the resources of the proposed central bank. It was argued that once a central bank was established, the currency system of the country could not be manipulated. But paradoxically, when the Reserve Bank of India was set up, it was not allowed to function independently. The finance member, P. J. Grigg, was dead set to maintain the government's supremacy over the bank. Grigg ruthlessly rejected the proposals of the governor of the RBI, Osborne Smith, "for an expansionary monetary policy." This strained the relationship between the RBI governor and the finance member.

The quarrel between the two ended only when Grigg succeeded in getting rid of Smith through India Office, which pressured Smith to resign. With the resignation and exit of Osborne Smith the RBI was reduced to the status of a mere government department and was thereby denied the authority to initiate action on its own.[37]

The Depression's Onslaught on Madras

By the turn of the century the extension of communication had made the transportation of agricultural produce out of villages possible. The peasant, on account of this new development, began to grow crops that provided him with a profitable market abroad.[38] The production of crops for sale, rather than for one's own consumption, became a widespread phenomenon. This was because of the recurring need of the peasants, under the new system of land tenures, to meet the exacting demands of the state and the landlords.[39] Expansion of railways provided the

36 *Ibid.*
37 Balachandran, *John Bullion's Empire*, 210–15.
38 D. R. Gadgil, *The Industrial Evolution of India in Recent Times* (London: Oxford University Press, 1954), 208.
39 Daniel and Alice Thorner, *Land and Labour in India* (Bombay: Asia Publishing House, 1962), 54.

required stimulus for cultivation of industrial crops in the Madras Presidency. Industrial crops such as cotton, groundnuts, sugar cane and tobacco were more remunerative than food grains, as they had export markets. But it was very expensive to grow these crops. As a majority of the peasants were on the margin of subsistence after paying rent or tax, they could take to commercial crops only with heavy borrowing.[40] The peasants informed the Madras Provincial Banking Enquiry Committee that they undertook cash crops, despite low prices, because of land revenue and debt obligations.[41] The peasants took to borrowing and cultivated the commercial crops hoping that there would be an export market for their produce. But they were ignorant of the fact that if there was a glut in the world market the prices of these crops would crash and they would be economically ruined.

In view of the new trend in favour of commercial agriculture, total acreage under food crops had fallen from 83 per cent of total area in 1905 to 77 per cent in 1929.[42] At the same time the acreage under cotton and groundnut rose by 60 per cent and 160 per cent respectively during 1884–85 to 1925–26.[43] The process of commercialisation of agriculture was rapid, particularly in the 1920s, with production of non-food crops increasing by 35 per cent in the first half of the decade and another 17 per cent during the latter half.[44] The change from cultivation for home-consumption to cultivation for the market had integrated the Madras economy into the world economy. The result was that the prices for cotton, groundnut and other Madras export crops were fixed

[40] Utsa Patnaik, "The Process of Commercialisation under Colonial Conditions," in *Proceedings of the Seminar on Commercialisation in Indian Agriculture* (Thiruvananthapuram: Centre for Development Studies, 1981), 15–16.

[41] *Madras Provincial Banking Enquiry Committee Report* 1, 105–08.

[42] Elizabeth Manak, *Formulation of Agricultural Policy in Imperial India, 1872–1929: A Case Study of the Madras Presidency* (Hawaii: University of Hawaii, 1979), 123.

[43] D. A. Washbrook, "Economic Development and Social Stratification in Rural Madras: The Madras Region, 1878–1929," in *The Imperial Impact: Studies in Economic History of Africa and India*, eds. Clive Dewy and A. G. Hopkins (London: University of London, 1978), 68.

[44] R. Rukmani, "The Process of Urbanisation and Socio-economic Change in Tamilnadu" (Ph.D. diss., University of Madras, 1994), 67.

in the auction markets of the West. Madras was a puny figure in these markets, as the level of her supplies had little effect on the performance of the world market.[45] Without any organisation to support him and with no meaningful credit facilities, the Madras agriculturist could hardly bargain for a fair price when he dealt with the large and powerful trading organisations of European nations. So world-determined prices had to be accepted in Madras. Against this backdrop, let us see what impact a global phenomenon like the Depression had on the Presidency.

The export-import economy of Madras was so heavily dependent on the world market that the effects of the economic depression in the United States and Europe were felt here as early as November 1929. Madras had been involved in two kinds of overseas trade. To the industrial countries of Europe and North America, it was exporting raw materials and importing manufactures from them; to Southeast Asia it exported capital, skills and manufactured goods, and brought back food, raw materials and remittance.[46] The external demands for its staples (textiles and metalware) continued to increase in the 1920s and as a result trade improved. The value of the foreign trade of the Madras Presidency increased steadily and by the late 1920s it had reached a peak of about seven million rupees per year.[47] It was expected that there would be a definite upward movement in the balance of trade and revenues. The outbreak of the Depression belied these expectations.The administrative report for 1929–30 referred to the Depression in Madras and stated that the seaborne trade of the Presidency had decreased by almost two million rupees during the first eleven months of the year.[48] Surveying the conditions of trade and industries for the year 1929, the president of the Southern India Chamber of Commerce in his annual report observed:

> I feel that the conditions of the past year (1929) present a picture of unredeemed gloom in almost all sections of trade, commerce and industry. Whether we look to the Railway earnings or to the clearing

45 Baker, *An Indian Rural Economy*, 121.
46 *Ibid.*,106.
47 Baker, *Politics of South India*, 173.
48 *Report on the Administration of the Madras Presidency*, for 1929 (Madras), x.

house returns, or to the Reports of the Registrar of Joint Stock Companies or to the dividends declared, or to the price index of Indian produce, there are evident signs of stagnation in some cases and of deterioration in others. A most disappointing circumstance during the past year was the continuous fall in prices all around, much more in the case of our export goods than in imported articles.[49]

The history of foreign trade of the Presidency from 1928–29 to 1936–37 provides sufficient testimony to the fact that it was foreign trade which acted as the most effective and disastrous channel through which the world slump transmitted its effects to the Madras economy. In the first year of the Depression, 1929–30, the value of foreign exports fell by 3.5 per cent from Rs. 4.7 to Rs. 4.5 million.[50] During 1930–31, the value of exports to foreign countries dropped further by Rs. 1.3 million or 28 per cent. The value of foreign imports declined by Rs. 0.6 million or 18 per cent.[51] Tables 1.4 and 1.5 show the extent to which the value of some articles of export as well as import declined during the year 1930–31, as compared with the previous year.

TABLE 1.4: Comparative Statement of Prices of Export Items, 1930–31

Principal articles of export	*Value (in Rs. million)*	*Decrease as compared with the previous year (in Rs. million)*	*Percentage decline*
Seeds	81.1	60.1	42.3
Cotton, raw	16.4	28.8	63.7
Leather	56.4	12.9	18.6
Cotton manufactures	17.6	7.5	29.9
Spices	6.1	5.1	45.5
Rubber, raw and manufactures	10.0	2.5	20.00
Postal articles	4.9	2.1	30.00
Coir, raw and manufactures	8.8	1.5	14.6
Oil cakes	2.1	1.5	41.7
Tea	41.2	1.3	3.1

Source: *Report, Administration of Madras Presidency*, 1930–31, 117.

49 *Annual Report of the Southern India Chamber of Commerce*, for 1929 (Madras), 2–3.
50 *Report, Administration of Madras Presidency*, 1929–30, 137–38.
51 *Ibid.*, 117.

TABLE 1.5: Comparative Statement of Prices of Imported Articles, 1930–31

Principal articles of import	*Value (in Rs. million)*	*Decrease as compared with the previous year (in Rs. million)*	*Percentage decline*
Cotton manufactures	19.5	15.4	44.1
Metals and ores	22.3	7.6	25.4
Cotton twist and yarn	8.3	7.6	47.8
Sugar	12.9	5.6	30.3
Vehicles	10.9	4.5	29.2
Machinery and mill work	20.5	3.8	15.6
Rubber, raw and manufactures	4.3	1.9	30.6
Silk, raw and manufactures	3.4	1.8	31.1
Tobacco, raw and manufactures	3.1	1.4	31.1
Manure	3.2	1.4	30.4
Spices	4.5	1.1	19.6
Glass and glassware	2.1	1.0	32.3
Apparel	1.6	1.0	38.5

Source: *Report, Administration of Madras Presidency*, 1930–31, 117.

In the case of exports the worst-hit articles were cotton, spices and oil seeds. As for imports, the worst hit were cotton manufactures and cotton twist and yarn.

The gloom of the Depression had deepened by 1931. The Madras Chamber of Commerce in its annual proceedings for 1931 recorded that "Enormous carryover stocks of staple commodities—cotton, wheat, sugar, rubber and metals—are still in godown, and one may wonder when consumption will overtake production."[52] The administrative report of the Madras Presidency for 1930–31 provides a vivid account of this depression:

> Importers generally suffered a heavy fall in their turnover while European business houses, especially those dealing in piece goods, either suffered heavy losses or fared worse than in 1929–30. Exporters of tanned skins and hides were hard hit by the imposition of an import duty of 10 per cent by the United States of America without a corresponding duty on raw hides. Owing to lack of demand from the continent and the uncertain state of the foreign markets, several tanneries were closed. . . . There was a

[52] *Proceedings of the Madras Chamber of Commerce*, 1931 (Madras), 4.

> heavy fall in the incomes of railway companies. The reason for this fall was mainly the marked fall in the goods traffic — a clear index of the depression in trade. . . . There was little export trade in rice to Ceylon, owing to the continuous fall in the price of paddy and the competition of Burma and Saigon dealers. Several rice mills remained closed for considerable periods on this account. Business in groundnuts also was not generally profitable. . . . Business in cotton, yarn and piece goods suffered severely on account of the big fall in prices and some of the ginning factories had to be closed on account of loss. Lungis [length of cloth worn around the waist] and Madras handkerchiefs showed a considerable decline in exports to the Federated Malay States and West Africa, due to the slump in rubber in the Federated Malay States and to the competition of cheaper mill manufactured goods from Japan and Germany. . . . Weaving and other allied industries were severely affected by the economic depression.[53]

By 1934, the value of exports had declined from Rs. 4.5 million in 1929–30 to Rs. 2.8 million, while the imports had declined from Rs. 3.2 million in 1929–30 to Rs. 1.5 million—a fall of 37 per cent and 51 per cent respectively.[54] The fall in the total volume of exports and imports was reflected in the seaborne trade of the Presidency, which suffered a serious setback. In Madras Harbour the total tonnage of imports registered was 1,007,431 tons in 1928–29, but it was 781,013 tons in 1932–33. The total tonnage of goods shipped amounted to 493,916 tons and 229,377 tons respectively for the said periods. The number of vessels that entered Madras Harbour fell from 896 in 1928–29 to 694 in 1932–33. There was a significant decrease in the gross revenue of Madras Port Trust. Its total revenue receipts in 1928–29 were Rs. 4.96 million; but they had shrunk to 2.99 million in 1932–33.[55]

The basis of the trade surplus, which provided foreign exchange, was exports of raw materials and agricultural produce. The Depression hit these commodities the hardest. The three main export crops of Madras agriculture were rice, groundnut and cotton. The volume of demand for Madras paddy and rice and cotton was severely reduced (tables 1.6 and 1.7).

53 *Report, Administration of Madras Presidency*, 1930–31, 152.
54 *Ibid.*, 1930–31 and 1933–34.
55 *Ibid.*, 1928–29 to 1933–34.

TABLE 1.6: Paddy and Rice Exported, 1929–30 to 1933–34 (in tons)

Year	*Rice*	*Paddy*
1929–30	93,852 (100)	4,265 (100)
1930–31	101,711(108)	4,368 (102)
1931–32	61,175 (65)	2,355 (55)
1932–33	64,894 (69)	2,028 (48)
1933–34	78,262 (83)	1,082 (25)

Note: Figures in brackets give index numbers with 1929–30 as the base.
Source: W. R. S. Sathyanathan, *Report on Agricultural Indebtedness* (Madras, 1935), 29.

TABLE 1.7: Raw Cotton Exported

Year	*Quantity (tons)*	*Value (in Rs. million)*	*Unit value (Rs. / ton)*
1929–30	41,122 (100)	45.24 (100)	1100.24 (100)
1930–31	21,167 (51)	16.4 (36)	774.60 (70)
1931–32	12,264 (30)	7.3 (16)	594.42 (54)
1932–33	10,514 (26)	7.0 (15)	663.88 (60)

Note: Figures in brackets give index numbers with 1929–30 as the base.
Source: *Annual Report of the Department of Industries*, 1932, 12; and 1933, 14.

Groundnut accounted for around 20 per cent of the agricultural income for a year. The condition was so pathetic that the crop had to be exported at whatever prices it fetched. The export of groundnuts declined from 582,963 tons in 1929–30 (valued at Rs. 133.9 million) to 457,204 tons in 1930–31 (valued at Rs. 73.5 million).[56] Its unit value fell from Rs. 229.68 to Rs. 160.76, i.e. by 30.01 per cent. Although exports of groundnuts had increased from 349,912 tons in 1931–32 to 455,337 tons in 1932–33, the value of exports further declined from Rs. 55.99 million to Rs. 54.46 million.[57] The unit value declined from Rs. 160.01 to Rs. 119.61, i.e. by 25.25 per cent. The decline in export volume was 21.57 per cent while the export value fell by 45.11 per cent.

The decline in export earnings was due both to decline in demand and to decline in unit value of export. In many countries import duties were imposed in order to protect the home market

[56] *Annual Report, Department of Industries*, 1933, 17.
[57] *Annual Report, Department of Industries*, 1934, 23–24.

from flooding by foreign goods. Great Britain witnessed the unique phenomenon of the "Buy British" campaign, supported by the people and the government. As a result of the campaign, the influx of exports to that country was very soon checked.[58] In contrast, in India there was no governmental action to check the flooding of products of foreign countries. In the absence of any effective steps on the part of the government to reduce the volume of foreign imports, domestic agricultural products faced severe handicaps. Groundnut was faced with an adverse tariff in France and Germany and with serious competition from substitute products from abroad like soya beans, palm kernels, olives and fish oil. Australian wheat threatened the Indian wheat market.[59] In the case of cotton, the commerce member in 1930 estimated that "approximately 12.5 per cent of the imports of cotton piece goods from the UK, 90 per cent of the imports from Japan, and 40 per cent of those of other countries competed directly with Indian goods."[60] Rice from Burma, Japan, Indo-China and Siam flooded the rice market and depressed the prices of Indian rice further. The import of rice was not a Depression phenomenon. Rice was imported into the Presidency even during the pre-Depression days. This was not due to crop shortfall but because of the practice of free trade policy. During the Depression the same unrestricted flow of foreign rice aggravated the situation (table 1.8).

TABLE 1.8: Rice Imported into Madras Presidency, January to September, 1934

Source	*Quantity in tons*
Siam	1,57,352
Indo-China	27,872
Ceylon	1
Japan	750
Straits	7
Burma (up to May)	5,18,478

Source: *Proceedings of the Madras Legislative Council* (hereafter *PMLC*) 72, 1934, 141 and 254.

58 *The Indian Annual Register* 1, 1933, 378.

59 *G.O. No. 350 (MS) Finance Department*, 29 May 1934.

60 Quoted in Gadgil, *Industrial Evolution of India*, 234.

As regards rice, Madras had already lost many of her export markets to the Burmese producers. The selling price of Burma rice (boiled) per bag of two maunds at Tuticorin was Rs. 6-8-0 (six rupees, eight annas and zero pies), while local rice at Thanjavur cost Rs. 8-12 per bag.[61] Because of this, Burma rice was despatched from Tuticorin to Thanjavur, the very centre of the rice-producing area. This led to accumulation of stocks, which severely affected Thanjavur farmers.

Tanning was one of the principal industries of the Presidency and there was considerable export trade in skins and hides. About 80 per cent of the export business in tanning in the country was carried on in the Madras Presidency. Table 1.9 shows the extent to which total shipments had fallen during this period.

TABLE 1.9: Export Trade in Tanning, 1928–29 to 1931–32

Year	*Quantity (tons)*	*Value (in Rs. million)*	*Unit value*
1928–29	20,949 (100)	80.7 (100)	38.56
1929–30	18,595 (89)	68.9 (85)	37.08
1930–31	16,218 (77)	55.8 (69)	34.43
1931–32	14,560 (70)	47.63 (59)	32.71

Note: Figures in parentheses are index numbers with 1928–29 = 100.
Source: *Annual Report, Department of Industries,* 1931, 18; 1932, 13.

The US had been taking large quantities of leather from Madras. Its enhanced tariff of 10 per cent on all classes of leather in the wake of the Depression adversely affected the industry in the Presidency. The disastrous effect of the American tariff on the local tanning industry is brought out in table 1.10.

TABLE 1.10: Hides and Skins Exported to USA, 1928–29 to 1930–31

Export of tanned hides and skins			
September–January	1928–29	:	Rs. 2.4 million
	1929–30	:	Rs. 1.3 million
	1930–31	:	Rs. 0.2 million
Percentage decline between 1928–29 & 1930–31		=	92.24

[61] *G.O. No. 2142 Ry. (MS) Public Works and Labour Department*, 28 August 1931.

Export of raw skins and hides			
September–January	1928–29	:	Rs. 13.1 million
	1929–30	:	Rs. 13.0 million
	1930–31	:	Rs. 9.3 million
Percentage decline between 1928–29 & 1930–31		=	29.01

Source: *Proceedings, Madras Chamber of Commerce,* 1931, 273.

It is noted that the decline was very sharp in the case of tanned hides—much more so than in raw skin and hides; in other words the high-value-added items were the worst hit.

Madras handkerchiefs and lungis were the two classes of hand-woven goods that constituted the major part of the export trade. While the former was chiefly exported to West Africa, the Indian labourers in the Strait Settlements, Federated Malay States, Ceylon and Java used the latter.[62] The handkerchief trade in Madras suffered from the Depression and exports showed a considerable decline both in quantity and value (table 1.11).

TABLE 1.11: Handkerchiefs Exported, 1929–30 to 1934–35

Year	*Quantity (Numbers)*	*Value (Rs.)*	*Unit value*
1929–30	4,785,914 (100)	4,352,417 (100)	0.91
1930–31	2,607,279 (54)	2,142,105 (49)	0.82
1931–32	3,503,338 (73)	2,257,240 (52)	0.64
1932–33	5,073,829 (106)	3,630,361 (83)	0.72
1933–34	3,463,173 (72)	1,840,719 (42)	0.53
1934–35	1,310,034 (27)	1,245,468 (29)	0.95

Note: Figures in parentheses are percentages of the corresponding figure for 1929–30.
Source: *G.O. No. 1699 (MS) Development Department,* 4 December 1935.

It is interesting to note that in the period 1933–35 there was a sharp decline in the number of handkerchiefs exported but the unit value increased. This may be due to the mass market being wiped out but some specialised market remaining. There was also considerable reduction in the shipment of lungis. Table 1.12 shows the extent to which the lungi business was ruined by the onset of the Depression.

[62] *Annual Report, Department of Industries,* 1933, 18–19.

TABLE 1. 12: Lungis Exported, 1928–29 to 1934–35

Year	Quantity (Yards)	Value (Rs.)	Unit value
1928–29	26,122,914 (100)	13,427,804 (100)	0.51
1929–30	25,717,587 (98)	13,570,377 (101)	0.53
1930–31	19,202,916 (74)	9,762,842 (73)	0.51
1931–32	15,148,495 (58)	7,588,806 (57)	0.50
1932–33	13,639,802 (52)	6,518,623 (49)	0.48
1933–34	5,599,444 (21)	2,779,070 (21)	0.50
1934–35	6,594,260 (25)	3,346,724 (25)	0.51

Note: Figures in parentheses are percentages of the corresponding figures for 1928–29.

Source: *G.O. No. 1699 (MS) Development Department*, 4 December 1935.

As shown in the table there was not much of a decline in the unit value, though the quantity of exports fell sharply. The total output would probably have declined, coupled with a fall in wage earnings. It is evident that decline in unit value, decline in demand, and heavy competition from other countries led to decline in both quantity exported and a much sharper decline in value of exports.

The fallout of the slump in internal trade told upon the railway finance. The Madras and Southern Mahratta Railway, and the South Indian Railway both experienced dire financial straits. In 1930–31, as compared with the previous year, the total number of passengers decreased by 5,956,200 in the case of Madras and Southern Mahratta Railway, and by 1,270,400 in the case of the South Indian Railway.[63] Similarly, the decline in the earnings was also striking (table 1.13).

TABLE 1. 13: Gross Earnings of Madras and Southern Mahratta Railway

Head	1930–31 (Rs.)	1931–32 (Rs.)	Difference (Rs.)	Percentage Decline
Coaching	30,308,410	28,823,621	1,484,789	4.90
Goods	50,125,820	48,536,647	1,589,173	3.17
Total	80,434,230	77,360,268	3,073,962	3.82

Source: *G.O. No. 2184 Rys. (MS) Public Works and Labour Department*, 18 October 1932.

[63] *Report of the Railway Board on Indian Railways*, for 1930–31.

The fall under the heading "goods" was due to diminution in the transport of grains and pulses. For instance, the earnings obtained by the Madras and Southern Mahratta Railway from the transport of oil seeds were Rs. 12,748,000 in 1928–29. But in 1931–32 the earnings stood at Rs. 8,954,000—a decline of 29.76 per cent.[64]

The total earnings of the two railways between 1929–30 and 1935–36 are shown in table 1.14.

TABLE 1.14: Total Earnings of the Presidency Railway System

Name of railway	*1929 –30*	*1930 –31*	*1931 –32*	*1932 –33*	*1933 –34*	*1934 –35*	*1935 –36*
Madras and Southern Mahratta Railway	89.7 (100)	79.8 (89)	71.5 (80)	66.6 (74)	68.4 (76)	67.2 (75)	62.5 (73)
South Indian Railway	63.3 (100)	58.0 (92)	53.0 (84)	55.1 (87)	51.4 (87)	52.5 (83)	50.0 (79)

Note: Figures in parentheses are index numbers with 1929–30 = 100.
Source: *Report, Railway Board on Indian Railways,* 1929–30 to 1936–37.

In Madras, too, the prices of exports fell more heavily than the prices of imports. By 1932 the imports and exports of merchandise had become practically balanced. Exports of merchandise in the Presidency declined from Rs. 447.2 million in 1929 to Rs. 259.8 million in 1932, while the imports fell from Rs. 268.8 million to Rs. 155.8 million (table 1.15). The decline in both cases was of 42 per cent.[65] This made the payment of Home Charges problematic. The imperial government handled the crisis by deflating the economy and thereby facilitating export of gold. Between 1932–33 and 1934–35 Madras made a net export of treasure to the extent of Rs. 86 million. The net export (+) or import (-) of gold from and into the Madras Presidency is shown in table 1.15.

[64] *G.O. No. 2184 Rys. (MS) Public Works and Labour Department*, 18 October 1932.
[65] *Report, Administration of Madras Presidency*, 1929–30 to 1931–32.

TABLE 1.15: Seaborne Trade of the Madras Presidency in Private Merchandise, Excluding Stores (in Rs. million)

Year	*Imports*	*Exports*	*Net exports of merchandise*	*Gold Export (+)*	*Gold Import (-)*	*Excess of Export*
1929–30	268.8	447.2	+ 178.4	–	47.2	131.2
1930–31	207.0	320.1	+ 113.1	–	34.3	78.8
1931–32	155.8	259.8	+ 104.0	+ 5.3	10.6	98.7
1932–33	168.6	235.5	+ 76.4	+ 42.0	5.2	113.2
1933–34	148.1	246.4	+ 98.3	+ 33.3	5.0	126.4
1934–35	173.5	250.9	+ 77.4	+ 10.7	3.6	84.5
1935–36	157.1	269.1	+ 112.0	+ 4.7	3.2	113.5
1936–37	152.6	362.4	+ 209.8	–	2.3	207.5

Source: *Report, Administration of Madras Presidency*, 1929 to 1937.

Summary

The Depression starting from the Wall Street collapse in October 1929 spread from country to country until the whole world was enveloped in it. Foreign trade provided the channel through which the effects of the Depression were transmitted to India. India as a colony of Britain experienced the Depression in an unprecedented way. The colonial state's policy—which sought to resolve its financial crisis by transferring the burden to its empire colonies, particularly to India—accentuated the situation. As Madras had been linked to the global market through trade it began to feel the impact within a month's time. The market for the main export crops of the Presidency such as rice, groundnut and cotton collapsed. Spices and oilseeds were other export articles which had a dwindling market. There was a considerable decline in the exports of Madras handkerchiefs and lungis. The export trade in tanned skins and hides, cotton piece goods and cotton manufactures declined to a great extent. The Depression in internal trade lowered the finances of the railways. The Madras and Southern Mahratta Railway, and the South Indian Railway suffered falls in their incomes.

The decline in volume of export trade affected the Presidency's balance of payment position so seriously that the provincial government had to meet its overall external obligations such as payment of Home Charges by exporting gold from the Madras Presidency and elsewhere. In the normal course of trade, a country's imports of merchandise should be balanced by its exports. It was not by exporting goods but by exporting gold that Madras paid its dues in London, which was tantamount to living on capital.

A brief account of the economic condition of the people of Tamilnadu will provide background knowledge to grasp the gravity of the Depression's onslaught. We turn our attention to this now.

2

Tamilnadu on the Eve of the Depression

In the second decade of the twentieth century Madras was considered to be the most economically backward of all provinces. In fact, Lord Willingdon, governor of Madras (1919–24), called it the "Cinderella" province,[1] as industrial growth was hampered by a paucity of natural resources. The indigenous capital was reluctant to enter industry because there was competition not only from goods from England but also from India-based European enterprises like Binnys, Harveys and Parrys.[2] During the swadesi phase of Indian nationalism some indigenous interests set up factory industries in the Presidency, but they could not survive due to lack of state patronage.[3]

Albert Chatterton, the director of the newly started Department of Industries, as a strong advocate of state aid to industrial development demonstrated the commercial viability of producing aluminium ware by utilising water power. He proved his point that given state aid, industrial growth was bound to occur. But the success of the aluminium project of the Madras School of Arts, as well as the provincial government's undertaking of

1 Quoted in Manak, *Agricultural Policy in Imperial India,* 4.

2 Raman Mahadevan, "The Development of Modern Entrepreneurship in the Chettiyar Community of Tamil Nadu: 1900–1930," in *Essays in Modern Indian Economic History,* ed. Sabyasachi Bhattacharya (New Delhi: Munshiram Manoharlal, 1987), 225.

3 Lord Pentland, the governor of Madras, told Montague in 1917 that he believed "We ought to play with them (Indians), humour them in politics and discuss with them industrial development, education and social reform; but there is no necessity for doing anything." Montague's note in his diary is cited in D. H. Buchanan, *The Development of Capitalistic Enterprise in India* (London: Frank Cass, 1966), 193.

tannery, evoked protests from the European traders who were organised in the Madras Chamber of Commerce. At the industrial conference held at Uthagamadalam in 1908 Simpson, representing the Madras Chamber, objected to the initiative of Chatterton in industrialising the Province:

> By starting a tanning factory, Government will necessarily compete with existing factories, if not in Madras, at any rate in Cawnpore. If it is Government's object to improve the system of tanning, I think they should confine their efforts to research and experimental work, such as can be carried on in a laboratory, and technical training.[4]

Later, the European trade interests represented to the secretary of state for India that the effort of Alfred Chatterton was tantamount to state participation in industrial development and pleaded for his intervention to stall the "pioneer industries." The secretary of state succumbed to the pressure of the Madras Chamber and issued instructions for the abolition of the Department of Industries of the Madras government in 1910. Thereafter, the government's endeavour was restricted to "provision of technical and industrial education" in the Province.[5]

In Madras Province there were tea and coffee plantations, a few cotton mills, some engineering establishments, rice mills and cotton gins. Barring a few exceptions, these enterprises were controlled by British businessmen. In addition to the above there were handloom factories and a few cottage industries. The outbreak of the First World War had stimulated certain industries, and in 1914 the Department of Industries had been re-established. It undertook manufacture of soap, ink and adhesives—and specialised in paper making, oil pressing, fruit processing and the decorticating of groudnuts. Yet the Presidency on the whole remained industrially backward. On the eve of the Great Depression Madras was thus, pre-eminently agricultural. To understand the full gamut of the Depression's effect on the

[4] Quoted in Padmini Swaminathan, "State Intervention in Industrial Development: A Case Study of the Madras Presidency," *Proceedings of the Seminar on South Indian Economy 1914–1945* (Tiruvananthapuram: Centre for Development Studies, 1985), 1:14.

[5] *Ibid.*

agricultural sector, background knowledge of peasant conditions is crucial.

Landholdings

According to the census report of 1921, 71 per cent of the total population was engaged in agriculture.[6] The Presidency had 57 million acres of cultivable land,[7] of which an area of 38.29 million acres was under cultivation in 1925–26.[8] The average holding in Madras was small, and this rendered impossible an update of technology through the use of modern agricultural implements. The average size of holdings was 148 acres in the USA and 62 acres in England, while in Madras it was only 3 to 4 acres.[9]

The smallness of the units that were contributing to the peasants' subsistence needs could possibly have tempted them to take to cash-cropping at a time when it turned out to be profitable.[10] However, compared to other countries the yield per acre in India was very low. The average yield of paddy per acre in Madras was 1,392 lb, while it was 3,920 lb in Japan and 2,350 lb in the USA. With regard to industrial crops like cotton and sugar cane, the average yields per acre in the Province were 161 lb and 6,305 lb, respectively; but it was 207 lb in the USA and 540 lb in Egypt with regard to cotton, and 49,625 lb in Canada and 35,447 lb in America in the case of sugar cane.[11] The Indian Central Banking Enquiry Committee estimated the average income of an agriculturist in British India to be about forty-two rupees or a little over three pounds a year. The average income per head in England was ninety-five pounds in 1922—a striking contrast which the Simon Commission recorded in its report.[12]

6 Narayanaswamy Naidu, *Report of Economist, Rural Indebtedness,* 6.
7 *PMLC* 61, 1932, 2:658.
8 Narayanaswamy Naidu, *Report of Economist, Rural Indebtedness,* 10.
9 Narayanaswamy Naidu and Vaidyanathan, *Madras Agriculturists Relief Act,* 2.
10 Neil Charlesworth, *Peasants and Imperial Rule: Agriculture and Agrarian Society in the Bombay Presidency, 1850–1935* (Cambridge: Cambridge University Press, 1985), 7–10.
11 Narayanaswamy Naidu, *Report of Economist, Rural Indebtedness,* 10.
12 B. V. Narayanaswamy Naidu and V. Venkataraman, "The Problem of Rural Indebtedness," *Journal of the Annamalai University* 4, no. 2, 1935, 194–95.

There were three land tenure systems in the Presidency: the *ryotwari*, under which assessments are made on individual land holdings; *zamindari*, under which a system of revenue farming is used; and *inam*, an estate gifted by the king. The ryotwari system was the principal tenure of the Province. Under this system the peasant was the proprietor and taxpayer of the land, and the government dealt with him directly, without the intervention of a middleman or a tax-farmer. He was entitled to remain in possession of land acquired by him so long as he paid the land revenue. In case of default—apart from eviction—attachment of livestock, household property or personal belongings was resorted to.[13] According to the theory of the ryotwari settlement, the government assessed the revenue of each cultivated field. This assessment was reviewed once in thirty years, to take account of changes in prices, marketing opportunities, irrigation facilities and other such factors.[14] The ryotwari system introduced the phenomenon of private property in land; the individual holders were registered and permitted to sell, lease, mortgage or transfer their right over the land.[15]

The zamindari land system was an eventual outcome of revenue farming during the Mughal period, when the revenue collection of a particular region was "put out to tender." In course of time, the zamindars, who were originally tax collectors, acquired hereditary rights over such land. When the Madras government introduced the system of permanent settlement, it gave the zamindar a title to his estate in return for payment of a fixed sum of revenue each year. The system suited the British since much of the burden of policing and administering the tracts within these estates could be left to the zamindars. Nearly one-third of the total area of the Presidency was under such tenure, much of it in the Telugu coastal districts. There were altogether fifteen hundred zamindars in the Presidency. They controlled nearly thirteen million acres of cultivable land.[16] The cultivator in a zamindari tract was called a tenant, while such a peasant in a ryotwari tract was called a *ryot*.[17]

13 Narayanaswamy Naidu, *Report of Economist, Rural Indebtedness*, 7–8.
14 Baker, *Politics of South India*, 7.
15 Thorner and Thorner, *Land and Labour in India*, 54.
16 *PMLC* 1 & 2, 1937, 243.
17 *PMLC* 78, 1935, 609.

The tenant in the permanently settled zamindari areas had occupancy rights, but could be evicted for non-payment of rent.[18] The zamindars derived from these tenants a total revenue of around Rs. 20 million, of which they paid Rs. 4.7 million as *peshkush* (land revenue collected from a zamindar) to the government.[19]

The rent of certain lands in zamindari areas averaged from Rs. 50 to Rs. 60 per acre, while the rate of rent in the ryotwari villages did not exceed Rs.13 or Rs.14 per acre.[20] Despite this, the irrigation sources in zamindari areas were not properly maintained. Further, securing credit in these estates was more difficult than in ryotwari tracts; tenures, sub-tenures and mortgages within the estates were so complicated that a moneylender could lend money only at personal risk. A moneylender who lent on the security of grain had to compete with the local zamindar, who since the passage of the 1908 Estates Act had "first charge on the harvest."[21] Suspension and remission of land revenue granted by the government in times of natural calamities like floods and famines did not apply to zamindari tracts.[22]

A large number of holdings were under inam (gift) tenure. These inams or *manyams* were granted mostly by the earlier governments on specific conditions "that they should not be alienated without the prior consent of the Government, that they would escheat to the Government in the absence of male heirs in the direct line and they would be annulled for lapses."[23] Inams were given for religious and state services. The beneficiaries of this tenure were mostly village officers, temples and charitable institutions. There were 7.75 million acres of inam in the Presidency, of which religious and charitable inam constituted only a quarter; the remainder was personal inam.[24]

[18] Narayanaswamy Naidu, *Report of Economist, Rural Indebtedness,* 6.

[19] *PMLC* 1 & 2, 1937, 243.

[20] *Ibid.,* 250.

[21] Baker, *Politics of South India,* 205–06.

[22] *Andhra Patrika,* Madras, 11 January 1936, in *Confidential Report on Native Newspapers Examined in the Fort St. George Secretariat* (hereafter *Report on Native Newspapers*), no. 1, 1936, 28.

[23] Narayanaswamy Naidu, *Report of Economist, Rural Indebtedness,* 12–13.

[24] Eric Stokes, *The Peasant and the Raj* (Cambridge: Cambridge University Press, 1978), 46–48.

In the Presidency a substantial number of privileged members of society such as the relatives and the dependants of big zamindars held land under intermediary tenure, called *jagirs*. The other registered landholders were classified as the big, the medium-sized and the small. The first category included holdings of twenty-five acres or more, regardless of their being irrigated or not. A medium-sized farm was one with less than twenty-five acres but more than five acres. Farms of less than five acres constituted the category of small holdings.[25] Apart from the registered landholders, there was a considerable section of the rural population that cultivated land without owning it. They were landless cultivating tenants making a livelihood by tilling the soil. And last of all there was a large section that neither owned nor cultivated land held on lease, whose members remained mere wage earners in the agricultural sector. They were the agricultural labourers.[26] The existence of such a variety of relationships between the owner and the actual cultivator further complicated an already complex problem.

Land Revenue System

Traditional land tenures in Madras were at variance with the revenue policies of the West. The colonial government treated land revenue as rent and not as tax. The government of Madras frequently stated in the Legislative Council in the 1920s that it was the land that paid the revenue and not the cultivator.[27] The government's whole system of resettlement did not take into account the fall in prices at all. In their calculation cultivation expenses were conveniently omitted. The assessment rate fixed at the time of resettlement on the basis of prevailing prices was then applied for the subsequent thirty years.[28]

The government had no concern for the economic well-being of the peasant. As was natural with any colonial state, it held the

[25] Narayanaswamy Naidu, *Report of Economist, Rural Indebtedness*, 12–13.
[26] *Ibid.*
[27] *PMLC* 74, 1935, 34–35.
[28] *Swarajya*, Madras, 30 May 1931, in *Report on Native Newspapers*, no. 23, 1931, 732.

view that out of land it was entitled to extract a certain sum of money as rent. As early as 1919 the government of British India had appointed a Joint Parliamentary Committee to have a fresh look at the land revenue system of the country. The Committee found the system inequitable and recommended to the government the enactment of a comprehensive land revenue law to rectify the anomalies.[29] The Indian Taxation Enquiry Committee had recommended a flat rate of 25 per cent of the produce as taxation. But all these recommendations had been conveniently put in cold storage. *Andhra Patrika*, a Telugu newspaper in the Presidency, wrote on the question of land revenue policy:

> It would have been advantageous to the cultivator had he been liable to pay towards assessment of specific proportion of the produce raised in his land. Instead of adopting such a method the Government entrusted the responsibility of assessment to certain officials who took into account the maximum yield per acre and fixed the assessment in coin.[30]

After the peasant paid the land tax there was practically nothing left for the maintenance of his family. He had to secure loans at heavy rates of interest to meet his family expenses. Though the main problem of the Madras Presidency was peasant indebtedness, the government deliberately ignored it. The colonial administration in Madras defended its policy of non-intervention in the matter, claiming that it had always been a staunch supporter of freedom of contract, and any legislation aimed at providing relief to the distressed agriculturists would infringe on that freedom. But the concern voiced by the government was mainly to ensure the continuation of the role of moneylenders in guaranteeing prompt payment of land revenue.[31] As Daniel and Alice Thorner observed:

[29] *Swadesamitran*, Madras, 9 August 1935, in *Report on Native Newspapers*, no. 9, 1935, 524.

[30] *Andhra Patrika*, Madras, 24 January 1931, in *Report on Native Newspapers*, no. 6, 1931, 189.

[31] D. Rothermund, *Indian Economy under British Rule and Other Essays* (New Delhi: Manohar Publications, 1983), 128–29.

Although in pre-British times the local moneylender extended casual credit to meet occasional needs of the villages he occupied a subordinate place in the economy of the countryside. The new forms of land holding, land revenue system, legal procedures and commercial agriculture of the nineteenth century, however, opened up a golden age for the moneylender. The demand for his services became an inescapable part of the peasant's life; to the state the moneylender was of invaluable aid in converting the peasants' crops into cash and passing on the land revenue due to the Government. The moneylender was encouraged to expand his activities by the fact that under the new order of things he could make a good and secure profit. If the peasants defaulted he could use the new legal procedure to attach their lands, livestock and personal possessions.[32]

Organisation of the Credit System

The government's failure to arrange cheap credit facilities contributed to the volume of indebtedness in the Presidency. Agriculturists, traders, merchants and small industrialists had to depend largely on indigenous bankers and moneylenders for banking facilities. While *taccavi* (government agricultural loans) and co-operative societies accounted for only 7 per cent of the total debts, the moneylenders were responsible for 93 per cent of the debts.[33] The co-operative credit societies were formed under the aegis of the Co-operative Credit Societies Act (1904). The village-level primary credit societies that formed the base of the co-operative financial structure were monitored and administered by an apex bank in Madras, the Madras Central Urban Bank, with its affiliates in the districts.[34] With the introduction of dyarchy in 1919, co-operatives had become a provincial subject in the charge of a popular minister, and the co-operative movement was expected to gain momentum during the period. In 1925 the government had approved the organisation of land mortgage banks on a co-operative basis. The primary object was to tackle agricultural indebtedness—especially of

[32] Thorner and Thorner, *Land and Labour in India,* 55.

[33] Narayanaswamy Naidu and Venkataraman, "Problem of Rural Indebtedness," 5.

[34] Bruce L. Robert Jr., "Agricultural Credit Co-operatives in Madras, 1893–1937: Rural Development and Agrarian Politics in Pre-Independence India," *The Indian Economic and Social History Review* 16, no. 2, 1979, 173.

small holders—by providing loans for the redemption of mortgages on agricultural lands, and the discharge of prior debts not secured by mortgages. But these banks were unable to float debentures and obtain capital locally. In order to resolve this problem the government sanctioned the establishment of a Central Land Mortgage Bank. The Central Bank was allowed to float debentures on the assets transferred to it by primary land mortgage banks and finance the latter out of the proceeds of such debentures.[35]

In view of the popular support extended, the co-operative credit societies that numbered about 3,676 during 1918–19 had increased to 14,878 by 1930.[36] There were nearly one million members involved in thirty-seven different types of co-operative activities with an aggregate working capital of approximately Rs. 1.8 billion.[37] Yet their loans amounted to only a very small fraction of the total flow of credit in the Province. The Indian Central Banking Enquiry Committee Majority Report presented figures which were revealing in this connection. In Bombay, where the financial requirement of the agricultural population was Rs. 325 million, the co-operative organisations supplied about Rs. 22 million (6.77 per cent). In Bengal the short- and medium-term loan need was Rs. 960 million, with Rs. 40 million supplied (4.17 per cent).[38] In Madras no provincial estimate was available. In its absence the estimate of Tanjore District Delta Mirasidars' and Landowners' Association helped to arrive at an idea: the cost of one crop of paddy in the wet delta area was Rs. 35 million. The co-operative societies supplied Rs. 1.075 million (3.1 per cent).[39]

The Royal Commission on Agriculture in India held the view that the greatest hope for the salvation of the rural masses with regard to debt lay in the growth and spread of a well-organised co-operative movement. But the working of the co-operatives was far from satisfactory. The co-operatives were originally designed to meet the credit need of tenants, labourers and small

[35] *G.O. No. 1450 (MS) Development Department*, 9 November 1932.

[36] *Annual Report on the working of the Madras Co-operative Societies Act for 1930*, 5.

[37] Robert, "Agricultural Credit Co-operatives in Madras," 183.

[38] *Indian Annual Register* 1, 1936, 79.

[39] *Ibid.*

farmers; but these very people were excluded from effective participation in the movement.[40] The credit societies in most cases were controlled by rich landlords and moneylenders.[41] A government report noted:

> *Benami* [illegal ownership under a false name] transactions are by no means scarce. In many societies, the Secretary or President, or both, are men who wield great influence and completely dominate the remaining Panchayatdars [members of a village council]. Such influential men unfortunately often enter the movement not to help the poor and needy, but solely to enrich themselves by all manners of means. Loans are first taken by such men in their own names, then in the names of their friends or relations and others, whom they can dominate. The money does not go to those who ostensibly take the loans. I was told by the Secretary of a co-operative society, who spoke openly in a large gathering of people that benami loans often amount from 30 to 40 per cent of the total amounts lent out. The unscrupulous and influential President or Secretary gets the thumb-impressions of himself and his followers on to numerous loan applications, which are promptly granted, as he is a virtual dictator in the society.[42]

Colonial Agrarian Policy

The agrarian situation was further worsened by the colonial state policy. The sorry state of affairs prevailing in the latter half of the nineteenth century was exposed by no less a person than the collector of Coimbatore, F. R. Nicholson. Irked by the advice of the government of India to spend public money for agricultural experiment only under exceptional circumstances, Nicholson wrote a strong-worded rejoinder to the government in which he criticised the colonial state policy on agriculture.

> Experiment was subsequently abandoned in favour of enquiry; enquiry has largely dwindled to the collection of statistics; positive improvement barely exists; the only considerable operations are against cattle disease which is described . . . as insufficient and inefficient

40 Robert, "Agricultural Credit Co-operatives in Madras," 171–72.

41 P. J. Thomas and K. C. Ramakrishnan, *Some South Indian Villages: A Resurvey* (Madras: University of Madras, 1940), 52–54.

42 Sathyanathan, *Report, Agricultural Indebtedness,* 62.

and a disgrace to a civilised country. . . . [A Department] conceived in error, born by chance, bred by accident, developed in starvation, guided by change, never had any vigorous vitality.[43]

Agricultural matters were dealt with in four separate departments. The Agriculture Department looked after crops, the Board of Revenue was responsible for survey, irrigation was overseen by the Public Works Department, and agrarian credit by the Development Department. There was no coordination between one department and another. The Agriculture Department consisted only of British officials ignorant of agriculture in India. The Royal Commission on Agriculture in India was stunned when the Head of the Madras Agriculture Department failed to answer elementary questions about crops, tenures and agricultural practices in the Province.[44] Paddy or rice was the main crop of the Presidency and the staple diet of the population. The Province could produce a considerable exportable surplus of rice annually. In such a situation it would be difficult for foreign rice to secure a foothold. Yet because of the policy of allowing free import of foreign rice into the country, the governments of Japan, Burma, Indo-China and Siam were exporting rice into Madras.[45]

The average farmer in the Madras Province was also seriously handicapped in marketing his agricultural produce. The middlemen and the indigenous bankers undertook the financing of the peasant, with the result that the peasant's margin of profit was next to nil. Lack of funds handicapped the peasant not only as a purchaser but as a seller as well; if he was in debt to the middlemen, he was compelled to sell his produce immediately after harvest when prices were low. Often he was in need of money even to cart his produce to a central market.[46] The bigger landlord-moneylenders acquired much of the village crop not only by taking from their debtors but also by buying from other cultivators who were forced to sell immediately at harvest to

[43] Quoted in Manak, *Agricultural Policy in Imperial India*, 31.

[44] *Report of Royal Commission on Agriculture in India* (Madras, 1928), 2: 270–303.

[45] *Swarajya*, Madras, 30 May 1931, *Report on Native Newspapers*, no. 23, 1931, 732.

[46] Sathyanathan, *Report, Agricultural Indebtedness*, 12.

pay their land revenue or to pay off other loans. If the landlord-moneylender stored the grains in his barn or pit for four months or so, he could expect the price to rise, and then could either sell the grain back to other villagers, or take it to the local market.[47] The report on marketing of agricultural produce by T. Adinarayana Chettiyar, M.L.C.—an early member of the Congress Party and critic of the government policy on agriculture and co-operatives—throws light on this pattern:

> That the average farmer is unfitted by education and upbringing to fight against the organised, clever and resourceful buyer is only a truism. One can see in any weekly market a bag of onions being sold for four annas or even less and a bunch of about 150 bananas for 2½ or three annas not as a rare occurrence but as a daily fact. Want of marketing intelligence, the smallness of the farmers' output, the absence of access to the markets, the perishable nature of his produce and above all his want to financial position to hold out for better prices—all these combine to produce this unfortunate result. [48]

Condition of Peasants

The conditions under which agricultural production took place were pitiable. Madras agriculture was mainly dependent on rainfall, but the rainfall in the Presidency varied from year to year and place to place. The southwest monsoon in early June and northeast monsoon between October and December brought rain. The northeast monsoon, on which Tamilnadu was dependent for the most part, was erratic and unreliable. Tamilnadu's rivers were mostly filled by the monsoons. The river Kauveri derived water from areas covered by the southwest monsoon and hence was useful as a river system. Of the four other river systems, Palar, Ponnaiyar and Vaigai—with the exception of perennial Tamiraparani—remained dry outside the monsoon months. These rivers were prone to flooding if the monsoon rain became excessive. Absence of water storage facilities in several parts of the Province further worsened the situation. There were huge reservoirs in Chengalpattu district and some minor irrigation tanks

[47] *Madras Provincial Banking Report* (Madras, 1930), 2: 210.
[48] Quoted in Sathyanathan, *Report, Agricultural Indebtedness,* 20.

in other agricultural regions. But the maintenance of tanks was utterly neglected.[49] A government report noted, "The monsoon may fail, or what is more likely near the hills the rain may come at the wrong time, or a river may rise and sweep away harvest, hamlet and herd."[50] It was reckoned that a cycle of five years would give one good year, one bad year and three years that were neither bad nor good.[51] In Tamilnadu, Thanjavur was the only district immune to famine, as it was protected by irrigation works which afforded an assured water supply to large areas of paddy lands. The districts of Tirunelveli, South Arcot and Tiruchirappalli were generally secure, though to smaller degrees. The remaining districts of Tamilnadu were more or less prone to famine.[52]

In the first twenty-six years of the twentieth century, Tamilnadu had experienced seven years of famine.[53] The non-official members in the Madras Legislative Council made pointed reference to the operation of the governmental machinery under distressing famine conditions. Moving resolutions on the conditions of poor peasants, the members often pointed out how grave the situation was in their district, and how indifferent the officials were to the public's suffering. A few of them through cut motions passed for reduction of land tax as a permanent solution to check the recurrence of famine. Intervening in the deliberations of 15 March 1927, the revenue member said that under the existing system of dyarchy, the Legislative Council did not have such a power because of limitations imposed by the 1919 Act.[54]

The government paid scant attention to repairs of irrigation channels. If any channel was repaired, ten or fifteen rupees were invariably demanded from the peasant. The officials threatened not to repair the tank or channel if he was not prepared to pay; the peasant had no option but to acquiesce.[55] Unexpected devastation by floods or absence of water in the irrigation canals in

[49] Baker, *An Indian Rural Economy,* 23, 24, 464, 465 and 467.

[50] Sathyanathan, *Report, Agricultural Indebtedness,* 12.

[51] *Ibid.*

[52] S. Y. Krishnaswamy, *Rural Problems in Madras* (Madras: Superintendent, Government Press, 1947), 104.

[53] *PMLC* 35, 1927, 132.

[54] *Ibid.*

[55] *PMLC* 74, 1935, 405.

proper seasons had been recurrent in Tamilnadu, adding to the difficulties of the peasant. In times of famine and scarcity he could not even recover his cultivation expenses and the costs of labour. The government investigated this issue and in one of its pronouncements stated that it was aware of the very serious losses that the peasant was put to because of famine. It however regretted that it was able to give nothing by way of relief because even a total remission of the assessment would not be sufficient to meet those losses.[56] The peasant also incurred serious losses on account of insects, pests and rats; in any particular year these losses could come to 25 per cent of the entire produce.[57]

In a province where water was scarce and the monsoon erratic, the proportion of peasants at the mercy of moneylenders was bound to be large. Sowcars, moneylenders from Rajasthan, advanced money to agriculturists during famines and floods or at the beginning of the agricultural season, to be repaid in cash or kind after the crop was harvested. Indigenous bankers known as *shroffs*, belonging to the Marwari, Multani and Sindi communities, were found practically in all the important markets in India. In Madras, in addition to these there were two classes of indigenous bankers, the Nattukkottai Chettiyars and Kallidaikurichi Brahmins.[58] Besides, there were also a number of independent merchants who financed smaller traders. A number of them were wholesalers in agricultural produce such as cloth, chilli and gram.

There were periodical migrations of Afghan moneylenders to various parts of India every year. They lent out money to indigent illiterate people in villages across the country at exorbitant rates of interest and recovered their loans by resorting to extra-legal methods. Such incidents were reported on a large scale in Coimbatore and Madurai districts. In response to a query raised in the Legislative Council, the registrar of co-operatives officially explained the practices of the Kabuli moneylenders.

[56] *PMLC* 61, 1932, 36.

[57] *Ibid.*, 34–35.

[58] B. V. Narayanaswamy Naidu, *The Economics of Indian Agriculture* (Madras: Rochouse and Sons, 1943), 72.

> The Afghan moneylenders are carrying on a moneylending business in all the districts of Ramnad, Trichinopoly, Tanjore, North Arcot, Chittor, Salem, Malabar and South Canara. They do not generally lend more than Rs.50/- to an individual at a time and their customers are usually drawn from the poorer class of wage earners. The rate of interest charged by them varies from one anna to two annas per rupee per mensem [per month] generally; in rare cases the interest rates go up to 3 or 4 rupees per mensem. The interest is invariably deducted at the outset from the principal amount lent.[59]

At the start of every agricultural year, cultivators went to moneylenders to borrow money for farming expenses. The dry land cultivators in particular had to depend solely on such advances. The Madras Provincial Banking Enquiry Committee was informed that the peasants who held a minimum of twenty acres of dry land were in a position to take their crops to the market.[60] The security for such a loan was generally that year's crop. The moneylender collected his principal and interest in kind on the threshing floor itself. The Madras Provincial Banking Enquiry Committee observed:

> It is usually the Sowcar who buys the crops and sometimes specific conditions are entered by which the cultivator is bound to measure the crop to the Sowcar in kind for the discharge of the loan. The Sowcar, who is better informed about market prices, buys the crop at a price advantageous to him. If the Sowcar does not purchase the crop himself he arranges for its sale so as not to lose sight of the crop till his amount is realised.[61]

The failure of a peasant to repay the debt during droughts would raise his burden of debt with the accumulated interest. So he was left with no choice but to convert the pro-note debt into a mortgage debt, which eventually led to the creditor taking possession of a portion of the peasant's land.[62] During the investigation in some villages of Cuddalore *taluk* (an administrative district for taxation purposes), B. V. Narayanaswamy Naidu

[59] *Letter No. 2325 (MS) Law (General) Department,* 8 November 1934.

[60] Washbrook, "Economic Development and Social Stratification," 72.

[61] *Madras Provincial Banking Report,* 2: 45.

[62] Narayanaswamy Naidu and Venkataraman, "Problem of Rural Indebtedness," 3.

found that the Sowcars of Kurinchipadi who provided credit to the villagers usually charged six *pies* (one-twelfth of an anna) for a rupee per month, or 37.5 per cent per year; but nine pies or 56.25 per cent per year was not uncommon.[63] Such usurious rates of interest charged by moneylenders increased the volume of debt. To illustrate the evil effect of higher rates of interest, Narayanaswamy Naidu quotes a case where the amount borrowed was Rs. 40. In a period of twenty years, the debtor was made to pay Rs. 360, for which he had to dispose of his only house.[64] The most serious obstacle to the clearance of indebtedness was the existence of a large volume of inherited ancestral debt. The Indian Central Banking Enquiry Committee Majority Report said,

> Children born in debt are making every feasible effort to pay the debt of fathers and forefathers. The social tradition and the custom of succeeding generations acknowledging and paying the debts of forefathers have been exalted into a legal doctrine of the pious obligation to pay ancestors' debt, enforceable in courts of law. Even when no assets pass and debts are legally inherited, the debt is generally treated by the son or the heir as a debt of honour by force of tradition.[65]

The Royal Commission on Labour pointed out, "Many, indeed, are born in debt, and it evokes both admiration and regret to find how commonly a son assumes responsibility for his father's debt, an obligation, which rests on religious and social but seldom on legal sanctions."[66]

The provincial government had passed the Agriculturists Loan Act (1884) and Usurious Loans Act (1918) to protect the agriculturist from the extortion and oppression of the moneylender. The Royal Commission on Agriculture reviewed these legislative measures and adjudged most of them comparative failures.[67] The indebtedness of the rural population had been estimated at different times. In 1895, Frederick Nicholson estimated the rural

[63] Narayanaswamy Naidu, *Report of Economist, Rural Indebtedness,* 201–03.
[64] *Ibid.*
[65] *Indian Annual Register,* 1937, 1: 21.
[66] *Report of Royal Commission on Labour in India* (Calcutta, 1931), 224.
[67] *Report, Royal Commission on Agriculture,* 462.

debt of Madras Presidency to be Rs. 450 million. The Banking Enquiry Committee found it to be Rs. 1,500 million in 1928. The volume of debt had grown threefold in thirty-three years.[68] The Royal Commission on Agriculture had sounded a serious note of warning on the growth of rural debt by saying that "the worst policy towards debt is to ignore it and do nothing."[69] Unfortunately, the colonial administration chose to ignore the Commission's utterances.

Summary

Complex land tenures, exploitative revenue policies, scarcity of credit, narrow markets and the colonial nature of the state—all combined to have a ruinous effect on the peasantry. The erratic and usurious rates of interest kept the peasants in perpetual debt, while the legislative measures adopted were woefully inadequate. Let us see what impact the global depression had on Tamilnadu in such a trying situation.

[68] K. A. Manikumar, "The Impact of Great Depression on the Social Life of the Tamils," *Artha Vijnana* 38, no. 3, 1996, 262.

[69] Findlay Shirras, "Situation in India," 577.

3

Agriculture

This chapter seeks to study the effects of the Depression on the agricultural economy of Tamilnadu. The first section explains how the slump in agricultural prices debilitated the entire peasantry. The second section describes the shrinkage of the credit market due to the fall in agricultural prices. Special attention is devoted to the collapse of the co-operative credit societies, which proved unequal to the task of resolving the credit crisis. The last section discusses the effects of the slump on land revenue. It is argued that the intransigence of the colonial government regarding remission aggravated the misery of the peasantry, resulting in large-scale land alienation.

Impact on Agricultural Prices and Incomes

Before the Depression, with rising crop prices and the resultant increase in farm incomes, a substantial number of cultivators entered the land market. As a result, they borrowed at high rates of interest. Both creditors and debtors believed in the high value of land. The lender thought that he had security and the debtor thought that he had a wide margin after paying the debt.[1] With the Depression came disillusionment. The Depression was preceded by a good monsoon and the agricultural output was impressive. But marketing became difficult, due to the slump in prices (table 3.1). The peasant was dismayed to find that "his crops were fetching less and less in terms of money; his commitments to Government and others in terms of money become harder and harder to meet as he was obliged to sell more and more and

[1] C. S. Subramanyam and N. Sundaram, "The Moratorium Bill," *Indian Review* 38, no. 10, 1937, 753–55.

yet more of his crops to get the money required; the value of land declined steeply and there were no purchasers even at low current market prices."[2]

Towards the end of October 1929, there were floods in Thanjavur, Tiruchirappalli and Coimbatore districts, which caused widespread damage to standing crops and irrigation works. This was followed by a cyclone, accompanied by heavy rains in the Chengalpattu, South Arcot and North Arcot districts.[3] In Thanjavur, owing to floods, supplies were short. *Mirasidars* (holders of heritable and transferable rights in land) and merchants held back their stocks, hoping that prices would rise. But with the onset of the Depression prices fell drastically. Eventually they had to dump their stocks at the time of the next harvest, which further pulled the prices down.[4] The special officer appointed by the government to study rice production and trade in the Presidency wrote in his report that

> A large number of big mirasidars and rice traders in Cauvery Delta came to grief during the early part of the Depression period as there was no rise in prices subsequent to the stocking of the produce. This business has now gone down considerably and the landlords do not take any risks by handling any more stock than they themselves produce.[5]

By 1931 three-fourths of the rice mills in the Kauveri Delta remained closed.[6] Thanjavur district, being the largest paddy-producing district in the Presidency, was seriously affected by the fall in the prices of paddy. The enhanced resettlement rates, brought into force in anticipation of a rise in the prices of food-grain, added to the misery of the Thanjavur peasants. Referring to the complaint of the peasants of Thanjavur that the enhanced resettlement rates had been pressing very hard upon them, *Andhra Patrika* recommended that the rates be reduced by 50 per cent.

2 Sathyanathan, *Report, Agricultural Indebtedness*, 28.
3 *Report, Administration of Madras Presidency*, 1929–30, x.
4 Baker, *An Indian Rural Economy*, 251–52.
5 C. R. Srinivasan, *Report of the Rice Production and Trade in the Madras Presidency* (Madras, 1934), 71.
6 Baker, *An Indian Rural Economy*, 251.

The paper regretted the government's refusal to comply with the request of the peasants for a 25 per cent reduction.[7] The government seemed to have little inclination to understand the problems posed by the Depression.

The Thanjavur district had also been affected by the new government orders reclassifying the irrigation sources consequent to the Kauveri-Mettur Project. Unfortunately, this scheme began to operate in a period of acute crisis, which entailed an additional levy of Rs. 540,354 on the district.[8] The Tanjore District Delta Mirasidars' and Landowners' Association submitted memoranda to the government, setting forth the grounds on which the district required a different treatment and a larger relief than others. But the government refused to make any distinction between one district and another.[9] The prices of agricultural products fell drastically (table 3.1).

TABLE 3.1: Wholesale Price Index of Agricultural Products in Madras Presidency, 1928–37

Year	*Rice*	*Groundnut*	*Cotton*
1928–29	100	100	100
1929–30	90(-10.00)	85(-15.00)	85(-5.00)
1930–31	72(-20.00)	55(-35.29)	62(-7.06)
1931–32	60(-16.67)	63(+14.55)	56(-9.68)
1932–33	56(-6.67)	59(-6.35)	57(+1.79)
1933–34	48(-14.29)	39(-33.90)	58(+1.75)
1934–35	56(+16.67)	57(+46.15)	63(+8.62)
1935–36	59(+5.36)	58(+1.75)	62(-1.59)
1936–37	56(-5.08)	62(+6.90)	60(-3.23)
Percentage change between 1928–29 and 1933–34	-52	-61	-42

Note: Figures in brackets give the percentage change over the previous year.
Source: P. J. Thomas, "Agricultural Depression in Madras Presidency," *The Hindu*, 28 January 1938.

7 *Andhra Patrika*, Madras, 9 January 1933, in *Report on Native Newspapers* 1, 1933, 416.

8 *Mirasidar*, Mayavaram, 2 November 1936, in *Report on Native Newspapers* 10, 1936, 633.

9 *Ibid.*

As evidenced by the figures above, in the years 1928–31 the prices of cash crops fell more steeply than the price of rice. During this period the price of rice fell by 28 per cent, while the prices of groundnut and cotton fell by 45 per cent and 38 per cent respectively. The census officer observed this trend in 1931 in his report:

> The decade from a cultivation sense closed gloomily as the price of the industrial crops which have become so popular and from which many ryots look to pay the land assessment had fallen enormously; particularly in groundnut, no sale was possible even at low prices. The grower of food crops was in a better position because these can always be sold in a country which does not produce enough to feed itself but the returns were disappointing.[10]

While unsold rice could be used for household consumption, groundnut and cotton were fully dependent on the market. This had a crippling effect on the peasants.

The recovery in groundnut started from 1931–32. As for rice, revival of the market occured a little later. This was probably due to the unloading of stocks on the market by the agriculturists who had hoarded the stock in the vain hope that the prices would rise. Cotton continued to remain depressed throughout the period.

The harvest price per imperial maund of 82.28 lbs prevailing in each district then indicated how the prices of agricultural produce declined by about 50 per cent (table 3.2).

As the figures indicate, Tiruchirappalli seems to have been worst hit. In the case of rice, Tiruchirappalli, Salem and Thanjavur districts suffered greatly due to the fall in price. As regards cholam, Tiruchirappalli, Coimbatore and Tirunelveli were severely affected. The fall of prices in ragi and cumbu affected Tiruchirappalli, Thanjavur and Madurai more severely than other districts. The slump in the price of rice probably resulted in greater consumption of rice, and consequently, less demand for cholam, cumbu and ragi. This explains the fall in prices of the latter.

While the Depression began to recede in Europe and elsewhere by 1932, agricultural prices continued to decline in India, particularly in the Madras Presidency (table 3.3).

[10] *Census of India 1931*(Madras), vol. 14, part 1, 23–24.

TABLE 3.2: Decline in Agricultural Prices in Madras Presidency, 1928–29 to 1933–34

Districts	*Rice*			*Cholam*			*Ragi*			*Cumbu*		
	1928–29 Rs. an.	1933–34 Rs. an.	*Percentage fall*	1928–29 Rs. an.	1933–34 Rs. an.	*Percentage fall*	1928–29 Rs. an.	1933–34 Rs. an.	*Percentage fall*	1928–29 Rs. an.	1933–34 Rs. an.	*Percentage fall*
Chengalpattu	5.15	3.30	46.32	--	--	--	4.11	2.10	44.00	--	--	--
South Arcot	7.60	3.20	57.63	--	--	--	3.80	2.40	35.71	4.12	2.70	48.68
North Arcot	7.30	3.10	57.39	--	--	--	4.11	2.60	49.33	4.40	2.40	47.05
Salem	8.12	3.40	62.86	4.60	2.10	40.00	4.50	1.14	56.52	4.12	2.40	52.63
Coimbatore	7.90	3.14	48.76	5.20	2.00	60.98	4.13	2.50	51.95	5.50	2.10	50.59
Tiruchirappalli	8.40	3.10	62.88	4.60	1.10	62.86	5.00	1.12	65.00	5.90	2.90	53.93
Thanjavur	7.11	3.10	60.16	--	--	--	5.40	1.13	65.48	--	--	--
Madurai	6.11	3.30	52.34	4.12	2.00	57.89	4.15	1.12	64.56	5.80	2.30	60.22
Ramanathapuram	6.12	2.14	57.41	4.30	1.15	53.73	3.11	1.14	49.15	4.14	2.90	47.44
Tirunelveli	6.70	3.40	49.51	3.15	1.80	61.90	3.13	1.10	57.38	5.20	2.80	51.22
The Nilgiris	7.11	--	-	--	--	--	5.13	--	--	--	--	--

Note: Prices are per imperial maund of 82.28 lbs.
Source: Sathyanathan, *Report, Agricultural Indebtedness*, 29–31.

TABLE 3.3: Prices of Agricultural Commodities, 1932–34

Commodities	*1932–33*	*1933–34*		*Percentage fall*
	Rs. an. p.	Rs. an. p.		
Cotton–Cambodia	154-8-0	115-0-0	per *candy* of 520 lb	32.04
Cotton–Karungani	144-0-0	105-0-0	per candy of 520 lb	27.08
Groundnut	40-8-0	22-10-0	per candy of 531 lb	44.14
Paddy	4-7-6	3-1-2	per bag of 170 lb	31.48
Rice	7-2-0	5-6-9	per bag of 170 lb	23.25
Copra	73-8-0	50-0-0	per candy of 605 lb	31.97
Coconut oil	111-8-0	76-2-0	per candy of 605 lb	31.73

Source: Annual Report, Department of Industries, 1934, 9–10.

The prices of all major commodities, as seen from the above table, continued to fall even after 1932. In the case of groundnut, the initial recovery, as seen in table 3.1, was offset by a subsequent fall in price.

As the farmers strove to counteract the fall in prices by increasing their produce the agricultural depression became more intense and lasting. The farmers found it difficult to market their produce even at such low prices, as they were handicapped by the heavy railway freight. The fall in prices of agricultural commodities called for revision of railway rates on freight charges. The Southern India Chamber of Commerce in a memorandum to the viceroy highlighted this problem. But the viceroy replied, "The proposal to reduce the railway freight on agricultural products has been thoroughly investigated and the resulting benefit to the ryots has been found to be negligible; for example, statistics have shown that the price of Burma rice governs the price of local rice even in a district producing such a large quantity as Tanjore."[11] The heavy railway freight crippled the movement of paddy and

[11] *Report, Southern India Chamber of Commerce,* 1931, 99–100.

GRAPH 1: Wholesale Prices of Rice, Groundnut and Cotton in Madras Presidency

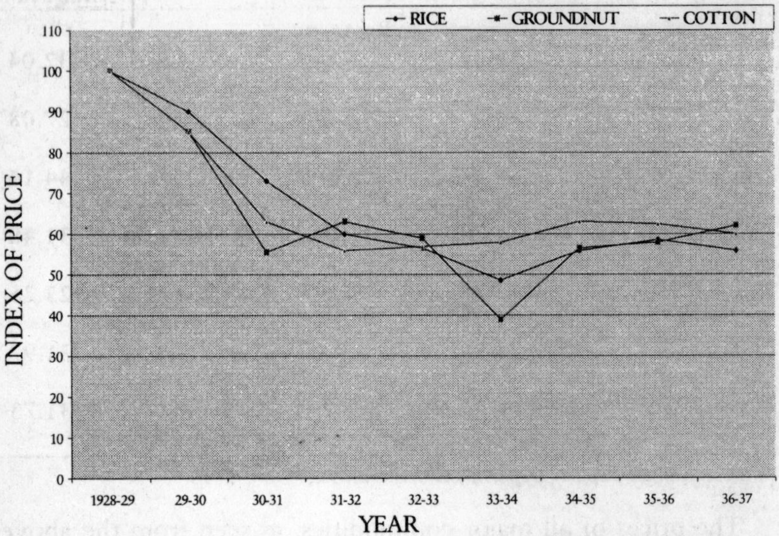

Note: The index for each crop is set at 100 for the wholesale price prevailing for that crop in 1928–29.

rice and depressed their prices further. In 1934 it was reported in the Legislative Council that "there was a time when a *garce* [a measure of capacity: 185 feet or 320 cubic inches] of paddy was sold at Rs. 100 or Rs. 120; and now the same quantity is sold at Rs. 40 or 42; and there is not even sufficient demand for the price."[12] A Tamil newspaper observed that paddy which was selling at Rs. 7 per bag before the Depression set in was available for Rs. 2-8-0 per bag. But demand was low even at this price.[13]

The collapse of foreign markets and the fall in price resulted in a definite drop in the acreage under cultivation. M. P. M. Ramalinga Mudaliyar of Alwarkurich informed the Madras Provincial Banking Enquiry Committee that "The sudden fall in price of paddy without any corresponding reduction in the price of all other cereals and pulses has benumbed the enthusiasm of the agriculturists

[12] *PMLC* 72, 1934, 302–03.

[13] *Tamil Nadu*, Madras, 30 May 1934, in *Report on Native Newspapers* 6, 1934, 346.

to spend more on cultivation."[14] The area and the yield of groundnuts had been estimated at 2,707,500 acres and 1,257,600 tons respectively during 1931–32, as against 3,571,987 acres and 1,764,940 tons in the preceding year. The fall of 24 per cent in acreage was the result of the fall in the price of groundnuts.[15] Over one-third of the groundnut acreage disappeared between 1928–29 and 1934–35.[16] The groundnut acreage in South Arcot almost halved.[17] The district of South Arcot represented 10.1 per cent and Coimbatore 5.3 per cent of the total area under groundnut in the Presidency during 1933–34. K. W. Chakrapani Marar, assistant marketing officer for oil seeds, went on a tour to South Arcot and Coimbatore districts. He visited Cuddalore, Tindivanam, Villupuram, Tirukoilur, Kallakurichi, Virudhachalam and Pollachi, and recorded the opinions of many groundnut producers, merchants, oil mill owners and others involved in the groundnut industry. He reported to the government that there was a reduction of groundnut area in the 1931–32 and 1932–33 seasons owing to the heavy fall in prices and stoppage of flow of credit.[18]

In view of the above developments the income of the peasant was reduced. B. V. Narayanaswamy Naidu, professor of economics at Annamalai University, worked out the per capita income of the agriculturist to be Rs. 20 per annum in 1928–29. During the Depression, with a 47 per cent fall in prices, he calculated that the per capita income had fallen to Rs. 7.60.[19] In 1934 T. A. Ramalingam Chettiyar, M.L.C., introduced a debt conciliation bill in the Madras Legislative Council. In connection with this bill the government in November 1934 appointed W. R .S. Sathyanathan, I.C.S., a member of the Board of Revenue, as special officer to enquire into agricultural indebtedness in the Province.[20] The terms of reference were: the extent to which indebtedness prevailed among agriculturists; how the Depression in terms

[14] *Madras Provincial Banking Report*, 1930, 2: 387.

[15] *Report, Administration of Madras Presidency*, 1931–32, 14.

[16] Baker, *An Indian Rural Economy*, 262.

[17] *Ibid.*

[18] *G.O. No. 1523 (MS) Development Department*, 1 November 1935.

[19] Narayanaswamy Naidu and Venkataraman, "Problem of Rural Indebtedness," 194–215.

[20] *G.O. No. 3295 Law (General)*, 20 November 1934.

of value of land and the fall in prices had affected them; how far compulsory recovery of debts through courts had affected the position of agriculturists who had incurred debts; what facilities were afforded by land mortgage banks and co-operative societies to farmers; whether conciliation in the matter of discharge of debts was being resorted to, and if so, to what extent property had been mortgaged; how much land had changed hands during the last four years and how much thereof went to the non-cultivating classes; whether legislation for the establishment of conciliation boards was really necessary for the relief of agriculturists, and if there was any demand for such legislation by them; and if so, should the scope of legislation be limited only to debts on land or include all debts of agriculturists; whether such legislation was likely to curtail the facilities that existed for borrowing; and finally, in case legislation was considered unnecessary, was there any other possibility of affording relief to farmers in debt.[21]

The special officer who enquired into the agricultural indebtedness put the per capita income at Rs. 15.[22] Commenting on the calculation of Professor Narayanaswamy, he said, "I believe that Rs. 7 an. 8 is too low a figure. My figure of Rs. 15 per head may perhaps be too optimistic, but it is safer to err on the right side and I am positive that my estimate can not possibly be attacked as being too low."[23] The agricultural income of the Presidency, as shown by official figures supplied by the finance member at the time of budget session in 1933, had been reduced from Rs. 1,800 million in 1928–29 to Rs. 990 million in 1932–33.[24] The peasant who cultivated between five and ten acres received very little income to live upon. In former days he was dependent on the subsidiary industries such as hand-spinning and hand-weaving. But with the Depression affecting these industries too, the peasant had to depend entirely on agriculture. Given his dependence upon agriculture for his livelihood, the peasant became captive in the situation.[25]

21 *Ibid.*
22 Sathyanathan, *Report*, *Agricultural Indebtedness*, 11–12.
23 *Ibid.*, 12–13.
24 *Report, Southern India Chamber of Commerce,* 1933, v–viii.
25 *PMLC* 56, 1931, 40.

Shrinkage of Credit

The Depression also hit the bankers and moneylenders hard. As N. G. Ranga observed,

> The first to take fright were the marwaris and other private moneylenders, who lost their nerves at the first signs of Depression and who exaggerated the importance of the reminders sent to them by the Imperial and other Banks. These people began to scrutinize, for the first time, the liquid and solid assets of their customers and on finding a few hopeless cases, lost all sense of proportion and began to harass every one of their debtors without any discrimination. Many of them have proceeded to invoke the aid of the courts and made good their threats by getting the properties of their debtors attached and sold for nominal prices. These mad doings of these people have helped very largely to bring down the prices of land, to undermine the solvency of many a thrifty ryot, to ruin a large number of decent peasants and, to bring every ryot's assets into the boiling pot of ruination.[26]

The Marwari moneylenders withdrew a large part of their capital and some of them even closed down their business on account of heavy loss.[27] K. S. Srinivasa Ayyar, an advocate from Thanjavur, reported to Madras Provincial Banking Enquiry Committee that "the old Nattukottai Chetti is practically a vanishing factor in this business."[28] The failure of a number of indigenous banking firms was brought to the notice of the Banking Enquiry Committee.[29] The landlord moneylenders in villages, who had earned huge profits during times of famine and scarcity in the past, found to their dismay that things were different now. As C. J. Baker remarks:

> In the past half century by controlling the flow of capital and the access to markets in the village, the big landlord moneylenders had insulated their poorer neighbours from many of the effects of economic change, and had taken most of the profits from the new crops and new market opportunities for themselves; now in the 1930s, they found that the full effects of the slump were visited on them rather than their neighbours. The men who were worst hit were

[26] N. G. Ranga, *The Kisan Speaks* (Madras: Kisan Publication, 1937), 76.
[27] *Report, Administration of Madras Presidency*, 1934–35, 159.
[28] *Madras Provincial Banking Report*, 2: 364.
[29] Baker, *An Indian Rural Economy*, 297.

those who had sunk capital in agriculture, particularly in the cultivation of cash crops, and this meant the rural elite.[30]

The moneylenders controlled most of the credit in the rural economy. When they were hit hard by the Depression, they curtailed their lending activities; consequently, the flow of credit stopped. As N. G. Ranga observed contemporaneously, "Anyone who knows anything about the credit market in the Madras Presidency is aware of the fact that none of the usual institutions which supply credit for current purposes is today willing to advance any credit to the peasants. Every one of them is still busy, in its own way, scraping up every pie that can be tapped from the ryots."[31] The value of the crops of the agriculturist was sufficient only to meet the tax of the Government. He had to raise loans for the maintenance of his family and was therefore unable to repay even a pie towards old debts. Moneylenders, in a panic reaction, rushed to the court of law to attach the land. Even the moneylending community of Nagarathars (Nattukkottai Chettiyars), who were quite prosperous and the largest moneylenders of the Province, had to seek the protection of insolvency courts, since their debtors could not pay their debts in time.[32] Consequently, cases of insolvency increased (table 3.4).

TABLE 3.4: Cases of Insolvency in Madras Presidency, 1930–32

Year	*Traders*	*Cultivators*	*Land holders*	*Total*
1930	49 (100)	28 (100)	27 (100)	104 (100)
1931	75 (153)	46 (164)	41 (152)	162 (156)
1932	71 (145)	71 (254)	49 (181)	191 (184)

Note: Figures in brackets give index numbers with 1930 = 100.
Source: PMLC 69, 1934, 528.

The sharpest increase in insolvency was among the cultivators. Sathyanathan, the special officer appointed by the government to investigate agricultural indebtedness, reported the problem of moneylenders in the following words:

30 Baker, *Politics of South India*, 175.
31 Ranga, *Kisan Speaks*, 79.
32 *PMLC* 74, 1935, 347.

> All lands are now either attached or mortgaged to moneylenders. . . . There is a network of cross sureties taken for pro-notes. The money-lender wants a stay of all proceedings against land for a definite period for recovery. He is eager for a settlement of debts, for he has learnt a bitter lesson.[33]

Sathyanathan cited the case of an agriculturist moneylender of Ramanathapuram district to prove that moneylenders to a great extent tried to avoid settlement of debt in insolvency courts.

> He is a Nadar by caste. He has lent over two Lakhs. He now finds great difficulty in getting back even interest. He lends at 9 to 12 percent and tries his best to avoid civil courts. He negotiates privately with debtors and tries to buy their lands in discharge for debts. He leaves a bit of land over for debtors. When he gets lands, he leases them out or leaves them waste. He does not generally lease out to the ex-debtors. He buys land at the present market rate. He prefers cash to land. He will forego interest if he can get back the principal in cash.[34]

The paralysing effects of indebtedness touched the very agencies which were intended to relieve indebtedness; co-operative organisations, too, were not exempt from the disastrous consequences of the Depression. D. R. Gadgil's general analysis of the situation in India holds good for the Madras Presidency also:

> The co-operative movement in India was very much severely tried by the impact of the Depression. Even in countries where it had previously been organised on very sound lines, co-operation experienced some setback during this period. It should suffer especially severely in India. An added consideration was that while the agriculturist and co-operative societies were almost everywhere else helped by the State to weather the storm, in India no such help was forthcoming and everybody was left much to his own devices. The result was that, especially in those provinces in which the organization had previously been built up in a defective manner or where its financial strength was low, the movement virtually broke down. Everywhere a number of the weaker units had to be liquidated, the recoveries declined and the overdues increased in alarming proportion.[35]

33 Sathyanathan, *Report*, *Agricultural Indebtedness*, 16–17.
34 *Ibid.*
35 Gadgil, *Industrial Evolution of India*, xi.

In the Madras Presidency depressing features such as "overdues, mortality in the number of societies, increase in the number of moribund or bad societies, liquidation etc., became prominent in the working of co-operative organisation."[36] Co-operative societies caused concern to those involved in their administration. The report of the registrar of co-operative societies for the year 1932–33 showed that 63 per cent of the long-term overdues, 50 per cent of the short-term dues, and 15 per cent of the interest dues were in arrears.[37] The Committee on Co-operatives noted in its report that on 30 June 1939 the total amount of loans outstanding against members of all primary agricultural credit societies was Rs. 35.35 million—while the corresponding amount on 30 June 1915 had been merely Rs. 5.8 million.[38] While the individual borrowers were not able to repay their loans to the primary societies, the primary societies in turn found it difficult to meet their liabilities to the central institution.[39] The cooperative credit societies, too, had to join other credit agencies in their rush to realise the loans. But the elected representatives in central banks found it difficult to take strong action against defaulters. The registrar of co-operative societies recommended to the government that the duty of recovery and strong action against defaulters be laid on paid officers appointed by the banks, and that these officers should be invested with complete powers to enable them to take such action.[40]

In consequence, *panchayat*s (village councils) which held supervisory authority over the societies were replaced by government officers.[41] In order to extract overdue loans properties of the defaulters were attached or auctioned. In the case of arrears owed by public servants to the co-operative societies, the government passed an order that for money due because of an award made under the rules of the Co-operative Credit Societies Act,

36 *Report of the Committee on Co-operation in Madras*, 1939–40, 14–15.

37 *Indian Express*, Madras, 22 April 1934, in *Report on Native Newspapers*, no. 3, 1934, 132.

38 *Report, Committee on Co-operation in Madras*, 17.

39 *Indian Annual Register*, 1934, 1: 375.

40 *G.O. No. 426 (MS) Development Department*, 19 March 1935.

41 Robert, "Agricultural Credit Co-operatives in Madras," 182.

the salary of public servants could be attached.[42] Table 3.5, on sale of land effected in North Arcot district for arrears due to the co-operative credit societies during 1932–35, gives an idea of the severity of the measures taken by the government.[43]

TABLE 3.5: Land Sales in North Arcot District, 1932–35

Name of taluk	*Number of sales made*
Arkonam	45
Arni	27
Chengam	16
Cheyyar	60
Gudiyattam	46
Polur	54
Tiruppathur	30
Tiruvannamalai	50
Vellore	48
Wallajah	35
Wandiwash	80
Total for the district	491

The staff of the co-operative department devoted more attention during the period to the weeding-out of bad societies than to the organisation and registration of fresh ones. Table 3.6 is illustrative of the striking decline in the number of societies registered in Madras Presidency from 1928–29 to 1932–33.

TABLE 3.6: Societies Registered in Madras Presidency, 1928–29 to 1932–33

Year	*Number of societies registered*
1928–29	726 (100)
1929–30	534 (74)
1930–31	320 (44)
1931–32	127 (17)
1932–33	107 (15)

Note: Figures in brackets give index numbers with 1928–29 = 100.
Source: G.O. No. 426 (MS) Development Department, 19 December 1935.

42 *G.O. No. 3753 (MS) Land Revenue and Settlement Department*, 12 December 1932.
43 *PMLC* 78, 1935, 341–42.

In the years 1931–32 and 1932–33, 1,383 societies had been wound up, 3,453 classified as bad and 5,447 remained in dormant state, out of a total of 15 238.[44] The number of societies liquidated in each year during 1930–38 gives an idea of the progressive increase in liquidation (table 3.7).

TABLE 3.7: Co-operative Societies Dissolved in Madras Presidency, 1930–31 to 1937–38

Year	*Number of societies in liquidation at the beginning of the year*	*Number cancelled during the year*	*Total*	*Number of societies liquidation of which was completed during the year*	*Number pending at the end of the year*
1930–31	612	516	1,128	452	676
1931–32	676	629	1,305	394	911
1932–33	911	691	1,602	449	1,153
1933–34	1,153	462	1,615	294	1,321
1934–35	1,321	281	1,602	235	1,367
1935–36	1,367	334	1,701	247	1,454
1936–37	1,454	195	1,636	270	1,366
1937–38	1,366	235	1,601	225	1,376

Source: Report, Committee on Co-operation in Madras, 1939–40, 66.

The bankers scrutinised the loan applications more carefully than before, and hence there was a decrease in the number of people coming forward to obtain loans. The demand for loans decreased, and large sums of money lay idle with the central banks.[45] The amount lent every year by an agricultural primary society per member was Rs. 36.6 for Madras in 1928–30. During the period 1934–35 to 1937–38 the average loan disbursed varied from Rs. 19 to Rs. 21.[46] The instances of loans issued kept decreasing in the case of agricultural credit societies (table 3.8).

[44] *Annual Report, Working of Madras Co-operative Societies Act*, for 1931–32 and 1932–33.

[45] *Swadesamitran*, Madras, 1 February 1933, in *Report on Native Newspapers*, no. 1, 1933, 87.

[46] Narayanaswamy Naidu, *Economics of Indian Agriculture*, 115.

TABLE 3.8: Value of Loans Issued by Agricultural Credit Societies

Year	Loans not exceeding Rs. 50	Loans exceeding Rs. 50 but not Rs. 100	Loans exceeding Rs. 100 but not Rs. 250	Loans exceeding Rs. 250	Total Loans
1929–30	3,500,854	4,143,063	6,059,520	12,376,227	26,079,664
1930–31	2,458,934	2,665,871	3,834,128	7,391,222	16,350,155
1931–32	1,269,602	1,516,119	2,193,869	4,763,140	9,742,730
1932–33	1,210,012	1,352,102	1,968,857	4,706,108	9,237,079
1933–34	1,150,646	1,239,596	1,805,002	5,020,520	9,215,764
Percentage decline between 1929–30 and 1933–34	67.13	70.0	70.21	59.43	64.66

Source: S. S. Santhanam, "Rural Co-operation in Madras," *Indian Journal of Economics* 22, 1941–42, 795.

The registrar of co-operative societies suggested to the societies that penal interest be waived in cases where overdues were paid before the close of the year 1933–34. The suggestion was implemented but the concession was not availed of to any great extent during that year. The registrar advised the societies to extend the concession during 1934–35. An amount of Rs. 75,000 under penal interest was waived by societies in 1934–35.[47] But such small relief did not help to relieve the situation. By 1936–37 the number of societies had fallen to 12,927 from 15,238 in 1929–30, and the membership declined from 974,919 to 897,128.[48] The special officer, W. R. S. Sathyanathan, noted in his report that, "There were 64 primary land mortgage banks in the Presidency at the end of 1933–34. Very severe test had to be passed by the borrower before he was given a loan. They lent loans to 40 per cent of the market value of the hypothecation."[49] According to the special officer's observation, small and medium landholders and cultivating tenants were hit hard by the government's new deflationary credit policy.[50]

47 *G.O. No. 97 Development Department*, 27 January 1934.
48 Narayanaswamy Naidu, *Economics of Indian Agriculture*, 103.
49 Sathyanathan, *Report*, *Agricultural Indebtedness*, 67.
50 *Ibid.*, 43.

Impact on Land Revenue

The absolute fall in income had a direct bearing on the debt, interest, land revenue and other such financial burdens of the agriculturists. The drastic fall in the prices of agricultural produce called for a remission of land revenue. Land revenue in India was much heavier in its incidence than other taxes. In a memorandum submitted to the government the Thanjavur Mirasidars' Association maintained that an owner of one acre of land, according to the tables prepared by the settlement officers, got Rs. 7-8-8 for the first *taram* (quality) and Rs. 1-5-0 for the last taram as income, while the government revenue demand for the same, were Rs. 16-10-0 and Rs. 3-8-0, respectively.[51] Of the million acres in Thanjavur district, the great majority constituted sixth, seventh and eighth tarams. For the said tarams the incomes per acre were Rs. 1-16-10, Rs. 0-5-1, and Rs. 1-0-4; the government demand for these tarams was Rs. 8-4-0, Rs. 7-2-0, and Rs. 5-15-0, respectively.[52] Despite the hardships faced by the peasants in the wake of the Depression, the government resorted to arrest warrants, auctions and attachments to collect its dues (table 3.9).

The number of attachments was largest in the South Arcot district. This was probably due to the fact that South Arcot was a groundnut-growing area, and the fall in the price of groundnut was much greater than that of other agricultural produce. This prompted Professor B. V. Narayanaswamy Naidu to make a study in the district, from which the figures in table 3.10 are taken.

Land was auctioned on a large scale to realise land revenue. In the absence of any bidder the government purchased the land (table 3.11). The property fetched much less than the estimated value. The *jamabandhi* (annual settlement of land revenue with the cultivators) report of the Presidency for 1931–32 recorded that property worth about Rs. 68,000 fetched only Rs. 11,300 in the sales.[53]

51 *PMLC* 68, 1933, 302–03.
52 *Ibid.*
53 *Navyuga*, Mangalore, 25 April 1933, in *Report on Native Newspapers*, no. 4, 1933, 201.

TABLE 3.9: Coercive Measures in Madras Presidency, 1929–30 to 1932–33

Coercive process	*Fasli 1339 (1929–30)*	*Fasli 1340 (1930–31)*	*Fasli 1341 (1931–32)*	*Fasli 1342 (1932–33)*
Demand notice	765,749 (100)	1,014,321 (132)	972,681 (127)	1,174,528 (155)
Distraint or attachment notice	49,646 (100)	82,873 (167)	89,745 (181)	132,310 (267)
Sale notice	38,036 (100)	57,036 (150)	66,881 (176)	82,048 (216)
Sales (number of defaulters)	4,868 (100)	6,795 (140)	10,062 (207)	11,244 (231)

Note: Figures in brackets give index numbers with 1929–30 = 100.
Source: *Report on the Settlement of the Land Revenue of the Districts in the Madras Presidency,* for Faslis 1339 to 1342.

TABLE 3.10: Coercive Measures in South Arcot District, 1928–29 to 1931–32

Year	*Notice of demand*	*Distraint or attachment*	*Sale notices*	*Sales/number of defaulters*
1928–29	19,933(100)	13,299(100)	12,468(100)	592(100)
1929–30	21,523(108)	10,538(79)	8,907(71)	932(157)
1930–31	36,127(181)	27,314(205)	16,702(134)	1,092(184)
1931–32	36,046(181)	23,885(180)	19,424(156)	3,391(573)

Note: Figures in brackets give index numbers with 1929–30 = 100.
Source: Narayanaswamy Naidu and Venkataraman, "Problem of Rural Indebtedness," 196–97.

With prices of agricultural produce going down by about 50 per cent, the burden of the agriculturist with regard to his debts incurred in the pre-Depression period had practically doubled in real terms. This made it difficult for the debtor to pay his debts. N. G. Ranga's observation is illuminating in this context:

> The ryots who have stored their grain in anticipation of rising prices have lost very heavily and are today entangled in their agreements with the Banks, from which they have borrowed money on godown

TABLE 3.11: Land Sold for Realising Land Revenue in Madras Presidency (in Acres)

Year	*Dry land*		*Wet land*	
	Private buyers	*Government*	*Private buyers*	*Government*
1929–30	8,483.70 (100)	3,669.48 (100)	1,181.92 (100)	1,056.75 (100)
1930–31	24,588.89 (290)	19,427.12 (529)	2,009.64 (170)	1,215.94 (115)
1931–32	12,628 (149)	8,486 (231)	4,919 (340)	2,189 (207)
1932–33	9,107 (107)	9,739 (265)	3,719 (315)	2,963 (280)

Note: Figures in brackets give index numbers with 1929–30 = 100.
Source: Report, Settlement of Land Revenue, Faslis 1339 to 1342.

security. The others who have purchased, though in small quantities, grain and other agricultural produce, in the hope of being able to supplement their scanty earnings have burnt their fingers very badly and are, as a consequence, hopelessly indebted to Banks. It is indeed sad to see these people being harassed everyday by the Bankers for the repayment of the money owed by them, in spite of their sound and honest protestations to meet the demands a little later. . . . Those peasants who have borrowed money from various kinds of people, in order to finance their agricultural operations or improve their lands or augment their landed properties, with a view to repay such sums in a period of three years have also found themselves in a hopeless condition for, little did they imagine that the present dreadful agricultural Depression would come upon them so suddenly and in such a serious manner, bringing in its train the inevitable though suicidal frantic pressure from their creditors for the immediate repayment of their loans. There are again those peasants who have borrowed large sums with a view either to liquidate old debts or to purchase lands, in the hope of repaying them with the sale proceeds of their old lands, whose prices were high until quite recently. But they are now cursing their fate for having left them in the sea of bankruptcy as they are obliged to lose the old as well as the new lands.[54]

Debating the issue of debt, a member pointed out in the Madras Legislative Council that Rs. 100 borrowed before the Depression fetched 100 sacks of rice, but during the Depression it

[54] Ranga, *Kisan Speaks*, 73–74.

required 200 sacks of rice to repay Rs. 100.[55] Highlighting the burden of debt during the Depression, *The Hindu* wrote:

> A good proportion of accretion of the debts has been due to the fact that the monetary mechanism suffered a sudden and revolutionary change. There has been a cataclysmal [*sic*] fall in prices with the result that the relationship between the debtors and the creditors has sustained a violent change. Suppose a ryot had borrowed Rs. 20 in 1929 with which to purchase a bull. What had happened is that two years later, the money values so changed that to repay that Rs. 20 he had not only to sell, not one bull or two, but perhaps his whole herd of cattle.[56]

The aggregate debt of the Madras agriculturists, compounded with interest that remained unpaid, gradually rose from Rs. 1.5 billion to Rs. 2 billion, as calculated by the special officer in 1935.[57] While endorsing the calculation of the special officer, Professor Narayanaswamy Naidu, however, added that "with the 47 per cent fall in prices the real burden would be nearly three hundred million rupees."[58] Thus the burden of indebtedness during the Depression was roughly twice as heavy as in 1928–29.

Narayanaswamy Naidu made an intensive study of fifty family budgets belonging to two villages in Chidambaram taluk—namely Sivapuri and Gavarpet—in January 1935. He found that only four families were completely free from debt. The total amount of debt of the remaining forty-six families was Rs. 44,129-7-0. According to Narayanaswamy it worked out to a debt of Rs. 882-6-0 per family of five, and to a per capita debt of Rs. 180 (table 3.12).[59]

To quote from Narayanaswamy's analysis of the figures, "The sufferings of the agriculturists are clearly indicated by the steady growth of the debt burden during the period of Depression, 1930–1934. Debts incurred during this period accounted for 64.54

55 *PMLC* 3, 1938, 61–62.
56 *The Hindu*, 16 March 1934.
57 Sathyanathan, *Report*, *Agricultural Indebtedness*, 41.
58 Narayanaswamy Naidu and Venkataraman, "Problem of Rural Indebtedness," 200–02.
59 *Ibid.*, 204–06.

TABLE 3.12: Debt Pattern in Chidambaram, 1935

Age of debt		*Value in Rs.*	*Percentage of total*
One year	-	10,345	23.44
Two years	-	4,625	10.48
Three years	-	8,100	18.35
Four years	-	640	1.46
Five years	-	800	1.81
Six years	-	4,219	9.58
Seven years	-	25	0.06
Eight years	-	2,900	6.57
Nine years	-	1,900	4.42
Ten years	-	300	0.68
Eleven years	-	100	0.23
Twelve years	-	4,100	9.29

Note: Debt pertains to fifty families in Sivapuri and Gavarpet villages in Chidambaram taluk.

Source: Narayanaswamy Naidu and Venkataraman, "Problem of Rural Indebtedness," 204–06.

per cent of the total debts. If to these are added the current interest charges we see that the real debt burden of the Depression period is 78.19 per cent of the total debts."[60]

C. Basudev, labour leader and a nominated member of the Madras Legislative Council, while pleading for protection for debtors narrated an instance in the Legislative Council to highlight the magnitude of the problem. Sundaresan, an officer in the Postal Audit Department, borrowed Rs. 600 from a Gujarathi moneylender, and after paying about Rs. 6,000 by way of interest had to be adjudicated for a further sum of Rs. 7,500.[61] In consequence of such ruination, land changed hands from the cultivating class to the non-cultivating class.

The Depression had brought down the value of land and prices of commodities to half of what they were before. The land which was valued at Rs. 3,000 per acre before the Depression could not be sold even for Rs. 500.[62] In 1934, it was informed in the Legislative Council that land worth Rs. 50,000 had been sold for

[60] *Ibid.*
[61] *PMLC* 72, 1934, 288.
[62] *G.O. No. 350 (MS) Finance Department*, 29 May 1934.

Rs. 2,000.[63] But it has to be kept in mind that the value of money had doubled itself during this period. If a creditor had lent Rs. 1,000 in 1927, he had a legal claim to Rs. 1,000 plus interest. With his Rs. 1,000 he could now buy twice as much land or commodities as in 1927.[64] However, the point is that the debtors were becoming bankrupt and so the creditors found it extremely difficult to recover the money lent. Sathyanathan, the special officer who investigated 541 landholding families, found that their landed property, consisting of 12,663 acres of wet land, 16,406 acres of dry land and 108 acres of garden, was worth Rs. 15,700,000 before the Depression. But the value of the same property, as stated by them, was found to be Rs. 1,402,000 at the time of the enquiry. This showed that the relation of debt to value of landed property before the Depression was 9 per cent, but at the time of the special officer's investigation it was 20 per cent.[65]

As Sathyanathan noted, there was a steady increase in the total area that had changed hands (table 3.13).[66] He recorded increased instances of absentee landlordism in various parts of Tamil districts. According to his estimate, about 10,362,000 acres of ryotwari lands had passed from the ryots into the hands of rich mirasidars, big moneylenders, lawyers and high-ranking government officials. This led to absentee landlordism and loss to the ranks of peasant proprietors.[67] On absentee landlordism the special officer made the following observation:

> Absentee landlordism is steadily on the increase. It is especially increasing among those who lend money to agriculturists, whether professional moneylenders or agriculturists or trader moneylenders. . . . We have absentee landlords among Government servants, lawyers and retired men. Professional moneylenders and traders and agriculturists who lend money are gradually turning out to be big absentee landlords. When their loans are not returned, they eventually take

[63] *PMLC* 69, 1934, 170.

[64] Sathyanathan, *Report*, *Agricultural Indebtedness*, 51.

[65] *Ibid.*, 43.

[66] *Ibid.*, 32–87.

[67] Narayanaswamy Naidu and Venkataraman, "Problem of Rural Indebtedness," 203–04.

TABLE 3.13: Land Sold and Mortgaged in Madras Presidency (in Acres)

	Total land that changed hands			*Net land sold by agriculturists to non-agriculturists*			*Net acres sold*			*Net mortgages by agriculturists to non-agriculturists*		
Years	*Dry & garden*	*Wet*	*Total*	*Dry & garden*	*Wet*	*Total*	*Civil courts*	*By private sales*	*Total*	*Dry & garden*	*Wet*	*Total*
1930	3,896	1,229	5,125	505	267	772	181	4,944	5,125	2,652	691	3,343
1931	3,858	1,682	5,540	1,033	335	1,368	203	5,337	5,540	1,800	844	2,644
1932	3,631	2,098	5,729	512	405	917	354	5,378	5,732	1,762	843	2,605
1933	4,934	1,735	6,669	1,049	357	1,406	489	6,179	6,668	1,639	914	2,553
1934	4,095	1,899	5,994	748	333	1,081	496	5,497	5,993	1,501	796	2,297

Note: A statement prepared taking two villages for each district in the Presidency excepting the districts of North & South Malabar and South Kannara.

Source: Sathyanathan, *Report, Agricultural Indebtedness*, 32.

> the land of their debtors in full or part payment. It being impossible for them to cultivate this growing volume of landed property themselves the land is let out on lease to tenants. This tendency of land to pass into the hands of those who will not or cannot cultivate in person has been much aggravated by the economic Depression.[68]

For instance, in Dusi village in North Arcot district, which was first surveyed by G. Slater in 1916 and resurveyed by P. J. Thomas in the late 1930s, it was found that from about eight absentee landlords the number had increased to 107.[69] Similarly, in Eruvelipet in South Arcot district, between the two surveys the number of non-cultivating landlords had risen from nil to nineteen, and the proportion of land leased out from a negligible amount to a quarter of the total area cultivated.[70] In Palakurichi of Thanjavur district, there were only three absentee landlords in 1916, but by 1936 there were ninety non-cultivating landlords.[71] In Gangaikondan of Tirunelveli district, the tenants who were under *kuthagai* (lease) formed an insignificant proportion. But twenty years later they constituted over half of the agricultural population.[72]

The peasant who held land on lease had no permanent interest in it, with the result that he cared very little to improve it; consequently, lands were becoming barren. Reacting to the situation, a vernacular newspaper wrote, "When such a situation like this arose in France and other countries laws were enacted prohibiting alienation of lands by peasants. Even the Land Alienation Act of the Punjab in 1900 was meant for the same purpose. But the Madras government was apathetic to this national calamity."[73]

68 Sathyanathan, *Report*, *Agricultural Indebtedness*, 4.

69 Gilbert Slater, *Some South Indian Villages* (Oxford: Oxford University Press, 1918), 86; Thomas and Ramakrishnan, *South Indian Villages*, 188.

70 Thomas and Ramakrishnan, *South Indian Villages*, 153.

71 *Ibid.*, 121–22; Slater, *Some South Indian Villages*, 78.

72 Slater, *Some South Indian Villages*, 57; Thomas and Ramakrishnan, *South Indian Villages*, 71.

73 *Prajamitra*, Madras, 1 August 1934, in *Report on Native Newspapers* 8, 1934, 426.

Summary

The Depression had a devastating effect on the agricultural economy of the Madras Presidency, primarily because the prices of cash crops fell more steeply than the prices of food grains. Of all the Tamil districts, Tiruchirappalli was the most affected. The other districts to suffer were Salem and Thanjavur. A new government order imposing an additional levy on Thanjavur district, following the completion of Kauveri-Mettur Project, added to the misery of ryots there.

Contrary to the situation in Western countries, where recovery had set in by 1932, the prices of all major agricultural products in Madras Presidency continued to fall even after 1932.

The fall in prices of agricultural commodities called for a revision of railway freight charges. Pleas to this effect were made by the Southern India Chamber of Commerce and the agriculturist lobby in the Madras Legislative Council. The colonial government not only turned this down, but, as we will see, aggravated conditions by permitting import of rice from Burma and Siam. Fall in agricultural prices, collapse of internal trade, and absence of an export market contributed to a substantial drop in the acreage under cultivation.

The fall in the income of peasants was reflected in their debt, interest and land revenue burdens. It became extremely difficult for the peasants to meet their land revenue commitment, which had been fixed on the basis of prices prevailing during the pre-Depression period. The government treated land revenue as the sheet anchor of provincial finance, and resorted to coercive measures like arrest warrants, auctions and attachments. The district worst affected was South Arcot. Being mainly a groundnut cultivating area, the peasants had invested in groundnut cultivation; with the crash in cash crop prices, they came to grief.

The cases of insolvency of cultivators increased during the Depression. Consequently, the bankers and moneylenders suspended their lending activities, which resulted in shrinkage of credit. The co-operative credit societies also had to join other private lending agencies in recovering overdue loans. The properties of the defaulters were either attached or auctioned. Consequently, instances of absentee landlordism increased. There were repeated requests by the nationalists for the passing of a law similar to the Punjab Land Alienation Act (1900) for the Madras Presidency. But the government turned a deaf ear.

It is rather difficult to assess the differential impact of a global phenomenon like the Depression on the peasantry. A government report in 1934 stated that those who had invested money in land, as distinguished from the cultivating tenants and labourers, were the worst sufferers.[74] The special officer appointed by the government to investigate agricultural indebtedness of the Presidency, however, asserted that the small and marginal farmers and cultivating tenants were the hardest hit of all the agricultural classes.[75] This aspect deserves a separate study.

74 *Season and Crop Report of the Government of Madras for 1933–34.*

75 Sathyanathan, *Report, Agricultural Indebtedness*, 42.

4

Industry

The Depression affected not only agriculture and trade, but also industry. Industrial production in the world decreased almost without a break from the last quarter of 1929 to the middle of 1932. But in India, the Depression did not have the same effect on industry as in many industrial countries. In fact it had a positive effect on certain industrial sectors. During this period, industrial production in India did not contract but, on the contrary, increased in some cases. At the national level, cotton, sugar, steel and cement industries expanded rapidly, while in Madras, cotton, sugar and banking were growth industries. But the same was not the case with small-scale and cottage industries. Hosiery, tanning, matches and handlooms had to face rough weather in this period.

Period of Industrial Expansion

The impact of the Depression on industry was different from its impact on agriculture. Speaking in the Legislative Assembly, the finance member asserted that the period of world depression had actually been a period of industrial expansion in India.

> As regards textiles, for the ten months of 1933, while the United Kingdom, the United States of America and France all showed a fall ranging up to 25 per cent, India showed in the same period an increase of 41 per cent, as compared with an increase of 34 per cent in Japan. Taking steel production as another illustration, while the United States in 1933 showed a reduction of 30 and 20 per cent respectively, India showed an increase of 75 per cent as compared with an increase of 55 per cent in Japan. Indian Stores Department reported that marked developments are going on in Indian industries manufacturing a wide range of articles such as electric lamps and all kinds of electrical

appliances, rubber tyres, water softening plant, cooking stoves, asbestos, cement products, paints and enamels, to mention a few.[1]

P. J. Thomas, an economist in the University of Madras at that time, noted that the period 1928–29 to 1936–37 was one of great industrial activity, with production of cotton piece goods increasing by 89 per cent, sugar by 1,016 per cent, pig iron by 213 per cent and steel by 151 per cent.[2] D. R. Gadgil also observed this phenomenon: "Indian capital has become distinctly bolder during the period [1929–39] and with large investment facilities available, more of it is being sunk in industrial enterprises."[3]

The striking industrial growth of this period can be attributed to a variety of causes. The most important is the discriminating protection given to a select number of industries. On the basis of the recommendations of the Tariff Board set up in 1923, the government had granted specific protection to nine industries, namely, steel, cotton textiles, sericulture, paper, sugar, silver thread and wire, magnesium chloride, heavy chemicals and matches. This protective measure was considered to have paved the way for a marked growth in industrial sectors, but the available studies indicate that hardly any Indian firm gained from it. Besides, industrial development of colonies was still anathema to the British government, as it was beginning to feel threatened by the reports of such development in the wake of the Depression. The statement of Neville Chamberlain, Chancellor of the Exchequer in 1934, testifies to this:

> While it was improbable that West Africa would set up factories to compete with these at home (England), there was a real and serious danger of such factories being established in Malaya and possibly other parts of Colonial Empire, and we might well be faced with very serious developments of a problem of industrial competition of which we had already had some experience in the case of India.[4]

1 Extract from the speech by the finance member, made while presenting proposals for 1934–35, *G.O. No. 350 (MS) Finance Department,* 29 May 1934.

2 Thomas, *Papers on Currency and Depression*, 241.

3 Gadgil, *Industrial Evolution of India,* 304.

4 Gotfried Haberler, *Colonialism and Development: Britain and Its Tropical Colonies, 1850–1960* (London: Routlege, 1993), 170.

Thus there was no change of policy until 1939, and imperial interests continued to govern England's policy towards colonies. Sir Henry Moore, assistant secretary at the Colonial Office, addressed a letter to the colonies in 1939 that is revealing in this context:

> At present any proposals for the creation of secondary industry in the Colonial Empire are received with a marked lack of enthusiasm, if not with suspicion. The reason for this, I suggest, appears to me to be found in the more or less unwritten rule that any proposals, whether in the field of industry or tariffs, which give rise to any conflict of economic interest, should be approached from the stand-point of, the United Kingdom trade interests must rank first, Dominion trade interests second, and those of the Colonial Empire last.[5]

Therefore, any industrial growth in the Presidency occurred mainly because of certain special conditions created by the Depression. First, owing to the steep fall in prices of agricultural goods, raw materials were available at very low prices. Second, faced with all-round unemployment, the labourer was willing to work for subsistence wages. Third, money was available at low rates of interest, as funds lying with banks sought outlet. The bank rate stood at 8 per cent in November 1931; by March 1932 it had fallen to 6 per cent and by February 1933 to 3.5 per cent.[6] A further condition, which we shall discuss later, was that the rupee's high exchange rate enabled the manufacturers to obtain machinery and other essential imports at comparatively cheap prices; this was especially at a time when the global demand for producers' goods was at an all-time low. Finally, the real income of fixed-income groups, such as rented classes, high government officials and chieftains of the princely states had increased greatly—due to the Depression and the fall in prices. They were able to save a larger amount of their income and invest it in banks and industries.[7]

The boycotting that accompanied the Swadesi Movement provided a favourable climate for the growth of the cotton industry. It was the economic manifestation of the political movement that had been going on since the Depression started.

5 *Ibid.*, 172–76.

6 Thomas, *Papers on Currency and Depression*, 240.

7 Narain, *Price Movements in India*, 34–35.

It remained in active operation until March 1931 when the Gandhi-Irvin Pact came into force, and was called off along with the Civil Disobedience Movement. The boycott was directed against any foreign cloth and all British goods. Goods whose production was completed in India, but with the use of foreign materials, were also boycotted. Thirdly, the movement was directed against all those mills—generally European-managed—which did not satisfy certain conditions laid down by the Congress as to management, share capital, encouragement of swadesi etc. Congress had a list of fifty-six such proscribed mills, of which twenty-four were in Bombay. Therefore, the conditions prevailing in Bombay were harsh. By October 1930 lockout had been declared in twenty-four mills, throwing about sixty thousand workers out of work. In Bombay, Currimboy Mills worked a smaller number of looms and the Dhanwal Mills had to shut a section of them.[8] The spirit of swadesi and boycott of foreign goods helped some industries to market their products in the vast home market.

Interestingly, although Binnys experienced considerable resistance in many parts of India, in Madras they convinced the Congress that their goods were swadesi. If the Madras and Bangalore mills had come to a standstill, some eighteen thousand workers would have been rendered jobless. In 1931, Munilal Mehra, head of the indentor firm of Brij Mohan Krishna Prashad in the Punjab, visited Gandhi's ashram at Sevagram (Wardha) in the Central Provinces, and got from him a certificate to the effect that Binnys should be treated as a swadesi enterprise.[9] The boycott movement, thus, did not hit the European mills in the Madras Presidency, though some of them were included in the Congress list.[10]

There was a remarkable increase in the production of cotton piece goods. In 1929–30, 44 per cent of the total amount of cotton piece goods consumed in India came from outside, but by 1933–34 the proportion had fallen to 20.5 per cent.[11] Vera Anstey observed

[8] G. D. Karwal, "The Political Factor in Indian Economic Depression," *Indian Journal of Economics* 13, 1932–33, 382–83.

[9] F. Desouza, *The House of Binny* (London: Inchcape, 1969), 228–29.

[10] *Proceedings, Madras Chamber of Commerce*, 1930, 253–54.

[11] Thomas, *Growth of Federal Finance in India,* 365.

that production of cotton piece goods increased by 41 per cent between 1928 and 1934.[12] As regards sugar, P. J. Thomas wrote, "As late as 1925–26, hardly one-tenth of the sugar consumed in the country came from Indian factories; but in 1934–35 India produced as much as 74 per cent of the total Indian consumption."[13] Before 1932 the sugar-refining industry in India employed 15,000 workers in 30 factories and produced about 16,000 tons of sugar, against an import of 600,000 tons. Within the next five years the industry grew at a very rapid rate. The number of operating factories rose to 137, employment exceeded 75,000, annual output averaged about 1,000,000 tons, and imports declined to 140,000 tons. The proportion of cane crop used for factory output rose to 18 per cent of the total cane crop, in contrast to less than 5 per cent in 1931–32. By 1938–39 the factory sugar industry ranked "third among all organised industries in total capital and fourth in fixed capital."[14] The number of modern factories crushing cane in 1930–31 was only 29, whereas in 1934–35 it had increased to 142, of which 15 were in Madras.[15] In the case of cement, India produced 263,746 out of a total consumption of 387,982 tons in 1924 (68 per cent). In 1933, India produced 625,860 out of 689,515 tons (91 per cent) consumed.[16]

However, even within the industrial sector, those linked to the world market suffered very badly. The Depression had an adverse effect on jute. The jute industry catered chiefly to foreign markets. As the demand from foreign markets declined the industry suffered. The coal industry also faced the severity of the Depression—firstly on account of diminishing demand from the jute mills and railways, and secondly due to competition from substitutes like oil and electricity.[17]

[12] Vera Anstey, *The Economic Development of India* (London: Longman, Green and Co.,1936), 488.

[13] Thomas, *Growth of Federal Finance in India,* 366–67.

[14] George Rosen, *Industrial Change in India: Industrial Growth, Capital Requirements and Technological Change (1937–1955)* (Bombay: Asia Publishing House, 1959), 32–33.

[15] *Justice,* 21 June 1935.

[16] Anstey, *Economic Development of India,* 488.

[17] *Ibid.*

Industrial Development in the Presidency

In the Madras Presidency, under the system of dyarchy industry had become a provincial subject, which enabled the government to actively participate in industrial enterprise. The introduction of cheap electric power through hydroelectric schemes, such as the Pykara Hydroelectric Scheme and Mettur Project, helped the industrialists who already had an abundant supply of cheap labour. During the Depression the wage rates were very low on account of falling prices, and there was flooding of the labour market with workers repatriated from Burma, Malaya and Ceylon.[18] Another factor that encouraged the growth of industry was the agricultural depression leading to an extreme degree of indebtedness of peasants. Many men with liquid capital to employ found lending to peasants risky and thus transferred their attention to industry.[19] "Land as investment ceased to be attractive since much of the produce of such land could not be easily sold at a profit. Landlords and others began to invest increasingly in industry, especially in sugar and cotton, the Chettiyars and Naidus diversifying from trading and indigenous banking into cotton mills."[20]

The census of India in 1931 noted the industrial developments that were taking place in the Madras Province: "Signs of industrial development are appearing and cotton mills are springing up at small country centres supplied by the cotton growing areas they adjoin."[21] The companies to come up first were those set up for the transmission of electricity to the towns of the Province. Then came the petroleum distribution companies, banks, insurance companies, cotton, sugar and jute mills, and cinema enterprises.[22] While the Depression was paralysing agriculture and trade in the Presidency, the number of industrial undertakings registered kept increasing every year. The aggregate joint-stock capital in the Province grew by 37.2 per cent between 1935 and 1940, five

18 Baker, *Politics of South India,* 184.

19 Amiya Kumar Bagchi, *Private Investment in India (1900–1939)* (New Delhi: Orient Longman, 1982), 210.

20 B. R. Tomlinson, *The Political Economy of the Raj 1914–1947: Economics of Decolonisation in India* (London: Macmillan, 1979), 43.

21 *Indian Annual Register,* 1933, 2: 419.

22 Baker, *Politics of South India,* 186.

times faster than over the previous twenty years. The newly registered joint-stock companies in Madras between 1928–29 and 1936–37 are shown in table 4.1. Cotton and sugar industries recorded remarkable growth during the period. In 1929–30 there were only nineteen spinning and weaving mills in the Presidency, with 697,564 spindles and 5,039 looms at work. But by 1937 there were forty-seven mills at work with 1,134,222 spindles and 5,866 looms.[23]

TABLE 4.1: Industrial Development in Madras Presidency, 1928–37

Year	*Total*	*Banking & credit*	*Insurance*	*Transport*	*Trade & manufacture*	*Percentage of total*	*Cotton mills*	*Other mills*	*Sugar mills*	*Others*
1928–29	64	9	5	9	20	31.25	4	3	-	14
1929–30	98	32	18	8	19	19.39	3	4	-	14
1930–31	109	27	7	11	40	36.70	-	5	-	19
1931–32	93	27	10	7	38	40.86	2	3	-	6
1932–33	146	38	33	6	8	32.33	5	3	-	13
1933–34	159	34	24	6	61	38.86	3	8	4	19
1934–35	189	44	12	17	86	45.50	8	9	2	11
1935–36	174	34	4	5	75	43.10	14	5	3	34
1936–37	235	39	8	10	112	47.66	4	8	2	52

Note: Of the 1,267 companies registered, banking and insurance accounted for 284 (22.42 per cent) and trade and manufacture for 499 (39.38 per cent).
Source: Baker, *Politics of South India*, 187.

The history of the textile industry in Madras dates back to the latter half of the nineteenth century. But the greatest expansion of the industry seems to have taken place during the nineteen thirties, as the equipment of the mills and the labour force employed increased (table 4.2).

[23] *Annual Report, Department of Industries*, 1929 to 1937.

TABLE 4.2: Progress of Textile Industry in Madras Presidency

Year	No. of mills	Capital (in Rs. million)	Looms	Spindles	Labourers
1929–30	20 (100)	24.62 (100)	5,039 (100)	697,564 (100)	34,513 (100)
1930–31	22 (110)	29.61 (120)	5,033 (100)	753,520 (108)	34,670 (107)
1931–32	24 (120)	27.65 (112)	5,143 (102)	714,404 (102)	37,872 (116)
1932–33	23 (115)	28.33 (115)	5,137 (102)	794,564 (114)	38,769 (119)
1933–34	29 (145)	30.30 (123)	4,083 (81)	846,230 (121)	41,208 (127)

Note: Figures in parentheses are percentages of the corresponding figure for 1929–30.

Source: N. C. Bogendranath, *Development of the Textile Industry in Madras (up to 1950)* (Madras: University of Madras, 1957), 52.

The number of looms remained constant up to 1932–33 and then declined. It can be seen from the table above that on the whole the textile industry was thriving in the Madras Presidency even during the period of acute depression.

The story of the textile industry in other parts of India was different. In Bombay, for instance, it was the industry most affected. *The Indian Year Book 1934–35* reported:

> Several cotton mills in Bombay were closed down, some of them permanently and their machinery was scrapped. The failure of Messrs. Currimboy Ebrahim & Sons who controlled ten mills aggravated the position and tens of thousands of workers were thrown out of employment as a consequence of the closure of the mills under this agency. In many other cases the alternative to closure was reduction of wages of the operatives.[24]

[24] *Indian Year Book 1934–35*, 21: 471.

The wages in Bombay mills were always higher than in other centres of India. This was because of the strong presence of organised labour there. Attempts to reduce wages and retrench labour in 1929, therefore, caused working-class agitation in Bombay.[25] The large number of mills and other businesses under the umbrella of the same managing agents led to inadequate attention being paid to individual mills. Besides, in Bombay there were combined spinning and weaving establishments and hence the size of the mills was greater. Whereas in South India pure spinning mills were established which were favoured by nearness to markets, raw materials and the cheapness of electric power.[26] The economist P. S. Loganathan examined the correlation between size and profit in mills.

> When the earning capacity of mills of different size was compared, an investigation covering the working of 53 mills in India for 15 years led to the striking result that small mills having spindles less than 30,000 and very large mills having more than 75,000 did not do as well as those in the intermediate scale. There seemed to be some correlation between size and profits up to a certain point after which size became uneconomical.[27]

In the Presidency, the town of Coimbatore grew into a major cotton-manufacturing centre in the 1930s, profiting from protective duties, the Swadesi Movement, low wages and hydroelectricity. The first mill in Coimbatore, the Coimbatore Spinning and Weaving Mill, was established in 1888 by a local British trading firm named T. Stanes. In 1919 Stanes controlled three of the four mills in the town. The other mill at that time was the Kaleeswarar Mill, managed by a Nattukkottai Chettiyar. Due to high land prices, no further mills could be started.[28] Drastic decline in land value in the Depression years facilitated expansion of mills in the town. Twenty-nine mills and ginning factories were floated in the Coimbatore area during 1929–37. Sri Sarada Mills, Palani Andavar Mills, Sri

[25] Bagchi, *Private Investment in India,* 248.
[26] *Ibid.,* 248–51.
[27] P. S. Loganathan, "Major Industries in India: An Examination of Their Structure," *Justice,* 30 August 1935.
[28] Eamon Murphy, *Unions in Conflict: A Comparative Study of Four South Indian Textile Centres, 1918–1939* (New Delhi: Manohar Publications, 1981), 25.

Renganathan Mills, Pulicar Mills, Trimurthy Mills, Kumaran Mills, Vimla Mills, Vasantha Mills, Coimbatore Cotton Mills, Indian Mills Ltd., Pankaja Mills, Sri Venkatesa Mills and Rajalakhsmi Mills were some of them.[29] Mahalakhsmi Mills in Madurai (1929), Sri Sankar Mills in Salem (1936) and Rajapalayam Mills in Ramanathapuram district (1936) were also established during this period.[30] Coimbatore began to function as the chief centre of the cotton textile industry in Madras. As the number of cotton mills in Coimbatore increased, several adjoining towns also registered growth. Tirupur, for instance, emerged as the major cotton mart in Coimbatore district.[31] Two cotton mills, namely Sri Ramalinga Choodambigai Mills and Dhanalakshimi Mills Limited, had come into being in Tirupur during the Depression.[32]

The Depression acted as an incentive for the growing of cane in the place of paddy, as the latter's price was falling rapidly. A few units were established for manufacturing sugar with the aid of power-driven machinery. In 1932, the Tariff Board recommended, and the government of India adopted, a protective tariff for the sugar industry. Within the next five years the industry grew at a very rapid rate. The number of sugar factories in the Province rose from two to eleven between 1931 and 1936, and output rose from 29,000 tons in 1934–35 to 67,000 tons at the end of the decade.[33] In Tamilnadu, the Coimbatore Laxmi Sugar Mill, an old sugar refinery at Podanur, which had long been in existence but had not been worked for several years, was reconstructed during 1933–34 and re-equipped with a cane-crushing plant, sulphuring apparatus and other machinery. During 1936–37, the Southern India Sugar Company Ltd., in the Karur area and the Srimathi Sugar Mills Ltd., in the Lalgudi area of Tiruchirappalli district were started.[34]

A cement factory started at Madukkarai in Coimbatore district in 1932 gave fillip to the cement industry in the state.[35] The Mettur

29 *Annual Report, Department of Industries,* 1929 to 1937.
30 *Ibid.*
31 Baker, *Politics of South India,* 190.
32 *G.O. No. 1193 (MS) Development Department,* 29 August 1935.
33 Baker, *Politics of South India,* 187.
34 *Annual Report, Department of Industries,* 1933–34, 23; *ibid.,* 1936–37, 34.
35 K. V. Natarajan, "Economic and Financial Condition of the Residuary Madras State" (M.Litt. diss., University of Madras, 1956), 76.

Chemical and Industrial Corporation Ltd., established in 1937, undertook the production of caustic soda.[36] The Indian Steel Rolling Mills started at Nagapattinam for the manufacture of steel was considered the most noteworthy registration in 1933–34.[37] Apart from factory industries yet another prominent avenue of investment for merchants, moneylenders and rich agriculturists was the cinema industry. Some of the first cinema companies were started in the 1930s by Nattukkottai Chettiyar bankers who had returned from Burma, and by Coimbatore mill owners.[38] Of the 174 companies registered in 1935–36, 26 were cinema enterprises.[39]

There was also a proliferation of oil mills in the 1930s. The number of oil presses in the Province increased from 34 to 238 between 1931 and 1938.[40] A survey undertaken in 1939 found 153 full-time groundnut dealers in the groundnut-cultivating areas. These dealers who survived the crash invested in groundnut-decorticating plants. In Salem there was an enormous increase in the construction of groundnut-decorticating mills. C. J. Baker noted the industrial development of Salem when he wrote: "In the Southern part of Salem, for instance, there had been two new mills built every year in the 1910s and three a year in the 1920s; in 1929 twelve were built, in 1930 nineteen, in 1931 nine, in 1932 eleven and in 1933 nine."[41] The level of investment and the number of freelance stockbrokers rose so rapidly in the 1930s that a Madras Stock Exchange Association was founded in 1937.[42]

There was expansion of the banking sector in the 1930s. The share of Indian joint-stock banks in total deposits had increased from about 31 per cent in 1930 to about 40 per cent in 1936.[43] In the Madras Province seven new banks were founded in the 1930s. The Chettinad Bank, floated by a leading member of the

36 *Ibid.*
37 *Annual Report, Department of Industries,* 1933–34, 14–15.
38 Baker, *An Indian Rural Economy,* 389.
39 *Annual Report, Department of Industries,* 1935–36, 23–24.
40 Baker, *An Indian Rural Economy,* 373.
41 *Ibid.*, 264.
42 Baker, *Politics of South India,* 186.
43 A. G. Chandavarkar, "Money and Credit, 1857–1947," in *The Cambridge Economic History of India, 1757–1970*, eds. Dharma Kumar and Tapan Raychoudhari (New Delhi: Orient Longman, 1984), 2: 782.

Nattukkottai Chettiyar community, became operational in 1929; with ten million rupees of paid-up capital it had become the second biggest of the joint-stock banks in the Tamil districts.[44] Some leading North Indian indigenous bankers of Madras City started the Bank of Hindustan. Its paid-up capital was one million rupees, and it was the third biggest of the joint-stock concerns. By 1939 it had fetched deposits for an amount of five million rupees.[45] The Indian Overseas Bank Ltd., with the authorised capital of five million rupees was established during 1936–37.[46] Around this time, two insurance companies, the South Indian Fire and Chemical Insurance Company, and the Indian Circular Insurance Company Limited, were founded in Madras.[47]

An important development following the growth of banking institutions was the founding of the Reserve Bank of India in 1935. Up to the mid-thirties the British government had blocked the recommendations of various commissions to form a unitary bank. In view of the changed situation, the British financiers now found it necessary to form a central banking institution that would enable them to retain their grip over currency circulation, and the growing indigenous and foreign banks in India.[48]

Crippling of Small-Scale and Cottage Industries

The Depression, however, had its negative impact on small-scale and cottage industries.[49] In 1929–30 there were twenty hosiery mills in the Presidency; in 1935 only seven organised factories

[44] Baker, *An Indian Rural Economy,* 315–16.

[45] *Ibid.*

[46] *Annual Report, Department of Industries,* 1936–37, 26–27.

[47] *Annual Report, Department of Industries,* 1934–35, 18–19; *ibid.*, 1935–36, 23–24.

[48] A. I. Levkovsky, *Capitalism in India: Basic Trends in its Development* (Bombay: People's Publishing House, 1966), 130–31.

[49] A cottage industry is an industry which can be carried on in or near one's own residence, in a town or village habitation, in which the operations are carried out by members of the family, but with permanent or semi-permanent hired labour, either as a full- or part-time occupation. A small-scale industry is defined as one which is operated mainly with hired labour—usually ten to fifty hands. Natarajan, "Economic and Financial Condition, Residuary Madras State," 39.

had survived the onslaught of the Depression.[50] Japanese knitted goods crippled the industry further. The products of small industries in the Presidency were exposed to the competition not only of Japan, but also of other foreign countries. There was, for instance, the competition from Britain with regard to soap, earthenware, and umbrella fittings—and of Czechoslovakia in glass bangles.[51] There was an alarming increase in imports of Japanese rubber and canvas shoes and boots. The imports were found to have increased from 78 thousand pairs in 1921–22 to over 10 million pairs in 1930–31.[52] Japan very nearly eliminated her competitors in a single year. In 1928–29 out of about 3 million pairs imported into India, more than half a million pairs (16.67 per cent) came from Japan, while in 1929–30 she accounted for no less than 4 million pairs out of about 6.3 million (63.49 per cent). Japan's success was due to low prices with which neither British nor American manufacturers could compete.[53] Thousands of cottage workers and small traders were seriously affected by these large-scale imports, while in the larger factories a great deal of machinery had to be kept idle as a result of curtailment of production.

The export market for tanned skins and hides collapsed, and the competition from foreign interests in the Indian home market of raw materials and in the leather market abroad became too stiff for the tanning industry. Therefore, to protect it from foreign competition and to facilitate the export of skins in tanned form, rather than in raw form, a sufficiently high export duty on raw skins and hides was considered necessary. A 5 per cent duty was levied, but this did not give adequate protection to the industry, which demanded further increase of duty. However, some foreign interests pressurised the government and got the export duty on raw hides and skins totally abolished, in utter disregard of the industry's demand for protection and a strong public opinion in its favour.[54] The abolition of export duty on raw skins affected

50 *Annual Report, Department of Industries,* 1929 to 1935.
51 *Report, Southern India Chamber of Commerce,* 1936, 51.
52 *Ibid.,* 1931, 74–75.
53 *Modern Review* 68, 1930, 478–79.
54 *Report, Southern India Chamber of Commerce,* 1933, xii–xv.

the economy of the Presidency, as tanning was its premier industry. The finance member, however, defended the taxation measure, saying that by removing the export duty the government wanted to accelerate the exports of the country. Jamal Mohamad, representing the interests of the tanning industry in the Province, refuted the argument advanced by the finance member:

> The reasons given by Hon'ble the Finance Member for removing the export duty on raw hides and skins are unconvincing, incorrect and misleading. He says that the exports of the country are to be accelerated, rightly so in a general way. But what he is doing in this particular case is to encourage the export of produce of the country in a raw form rather than in a manufactured state. This is surely not in the interest of the country. We of course want to export the skins as far as possible; but want to export them in a manufactured form as tanned skins as much as possible, particularly so when there is an established industry in the country which is well capable of expansion and in view of the fact that the world cannot afford to ignore the huge supply of Indian skins which is 30 to 35 per cent of the world supply. Encouragement given . . . in aiding the export of raw materials as against manufactured articles will only add to the already acute trade Depression and unemployment problem.[55]

The oil milling industry was hit in view of the low prices prevailing for all varieties of vegetable oils. Several mills either stopped working or reduced their output considerably. The price of coconut oil declined from Rs. 387 to Rs. 287 per ton in 1931.[56] There was a large influx of coconut oil from Ceylon, which owing to its cheapness had almost displaced Malabar coconut oil in the markets. Timber, coir and tiles industries were severely affected. In their anxiety to find outlets for stocks by securing orders, the manufacturers had to cut down prices.[57]

Match factories also ran into rough weather. The Swedish Match Company, which was doing business in India under the name of Western India Match Company (WIMCO), had posed

[55] *The Tragedy of the 18d Rupee: Speeches and Writings on the Currency and Exchange Question of M. Jamal Mohamad Saib* (Madras: R. J. Ram, 1937), 78.

[56] *Annual Report, Department of Industries,* 1931, 11–12.

[57] *Ibid.,* 1933, 24.

a serious threat to the existence of Indian match factories. WIMCO had about eleven factories by April 1931, and was manufacturing matches on a large scale. It had reduced the prices of matches in the wake of the Depression, as a result of which the indigenous match factories were unable to compete and were faced with extinction.[58] Several match factories establised at Sattur and other places in Ramanathapuram district, and Vellore, Vaniyambadi and Gudiyatham in North Arcot district faced closure; labourers working there were thrown out of employment.[59]

Britain's protective tariffs, though imposed only in sectors where no imperial interests were involved,[60] led to a fall in imports and decline in customs revenue. This along with dwindling return of the railways prompted the government to look for other sources of revenue. The choice naturally fell on excise. The Madras government passed the Match Excise Duty Act which came into force on 1 October 1934. The duties of Rs.1 per gross of boxes containing forty sticks, and Rs. 1.8 per gross of boxes containing sixty sticks, and Rs. 2 per gross of boxes containing eighty sticks worked havoc on small establishments.[61] The remarks of the director of industries illustrate the government's callousness to the misery caused to thousands of people employed in the match sector, on account of the newly levied excise duty.

> It is expected that the excise duty on matches will drive off the market products of very inferior quality and it is probable that only the very efficient units of the cottage industry will be able to continue the manufacture of matches once the full force of the excise duty is felt

58 *Swadesamitran*, 23 April 1931, in *Report on Native Newspapers* 18, 1931, 594.

59 *Dinamani*, 27 July 1935, in *Report on Native Newspapers* 7, 1935, 445.

60 Bombay mill owners demanded protection for their textile industry against Japanese competition. England gave protection because there was no competition between Indian and British mills, as the former concentrated on production of coarse yarn and piece goods while the latter specialised in finer varieties. Similarly, when the Indian sugar manufacturers wanted import duty on Japanese sugar, protective tariff was imposed. See Rothermund, *Economic History of India*, 248.

61 *Report, Southern India Chamber of Commerce,* 1934, 16–17.

> upon the industry. This would counteract to some extent the continued heavy overproduction, which at present exists.[62]

The effect of the excise duty on matches was disastrous. It was informed in the Legislative Council, to a question raised by Avinashilingam Chettiar, that as many as 132 cottage match factories had been closed in a year as a result of the new duty.[63] The provincial government through the Match Excise Duty Act made it incumbent on those who had match factories to obtain a licence. If any work was done in a house for a match factory, that house was also declared a factory under the act and a licence had to be obtained. As a result, matches ceased to be manufactured in houses of villagers and thousands of labourers engaged in such places were rendered jobless.[64] *Jaya Bharathi,* a Tamil newspaper, commented that "if the Government are to derive a revenue of three and a half crores of rupees from the tax on matches, 125,000 poor persons will be thrown out of employment."[65]

Apart from the excise duty on matches, an excise duty of Rs. 1-5-0 per hundredweight was imposed on factory-made sugar. The Madras Chamber of Commerce opposed the duty on sugar because since its imposition in April 1934, there had been a steady increase in the import of sugar. In April 1934 the volume of import was 11,765 tons, in May it was 17,069, and in June it increased to 21,273 tons.[66] The government then classified tobacco as an article of luxury and levied a tax on it. This raised acrimonious debate in the Legislative Council. But the revenue member argued that the tax on tobacco would affect only the shopkeepers. *Dinamani* disputed this.

> The tax proposed, as per the Madras Tobacco Bill, will affect the people alone. The beedi industry and the scented tobacco industry are providing work to thousands of persons in our country. The bill will only result in depriving these people of their livelihood. It will

[62] *Annual Report, Department of Industries,* 1934, 28.
[63] *Indian Review* 36, no. 5, 1935, 279.
[64] *Ibid.*
[65] *Jaya Bharathi,* 27 November 1935, in *Report on Native Newspapers* 12, 1935, 709.
[66] *Proceedings, Madras Chamber of Commerce,* 1934, 229.

> also deprive thousands of petty shopkeepers who are eking out their livelihood by selling beedies and tobacco.[67]

The handloom industry faced a serious crisis in the context of dwindling demand for its products in foreign markets. The government by its taxation policy helped only to exacerbate the situation. An excise duty of 3.5 per cent on mill products, which was in force until 1926, afforded no great assistance to the handloom sector. The removal of this duty after 1926 proved to be a setback to the handloom weavers, while it provided relief to the Indian mills.[68] Similarly, the imposition of the import duty on yarn, intended to keep out foreign yarn and give fillip to the Indian spinning industry, hit the handloom industry as it consumed the great bulk of the imported yarn. The Indian mills taking advantage of the protection began to produce yarn on a large scale, and the handloom weaver had to buy this yarn at a higher price than he would otherwise have had to.[69] The mills not only produced yarn but also began to produce cloth, which was previously the preserve of the handlooms. As the mills produced cloth out of their own yarn, the handloom weavers found themselves further handicapped—they had to use the same expensive mill yarn, making their products still costlier. Apart from the price competition from the mills, the handloom weavers had to face foreign competition that affected many of the handloom fabrics, especially lungis and muslin, and even *dhoti*s (a loincloth worn by male Hindus). Artificial silk yarn and manufactured goods imported into India from Japan also posed a threat. Owing to the depreciation of the yen, their prices had fallen drastically after 1931. This too, hit the handloom industry.[70] In most of the centres the weavers were thrown out of employment, and those in employment were getting a poor wage. Messrs. W. A. Beardsell & Co. Ltd., a Madras firm which had a long experience of the export trade

[67] *Dinamani,* 30 October 1935, in *Report on Native Newspapers* 11, 1935, 671.
[68] *Report of the Fact-Finding Committee (Handlooms and Mills)* (Calcutta, 1942), 13.
[69] *Ibid.,*14.
[70] *Ibid.,*18.

in handloom cloth, highlighted the plight of handloom weavers to the Tariff Board in 1935:

> The cumulative effect of the various factors operating against the handloom weaver is that today he is in a most precarious position. There is no continuity of work. He has to change from the weaving of saris to the weaving of may-be [*sic*] exportable articles. But however hard he may try he can never get more than a starvation wage under the present conditions.[71]

Because of the slump in the export market and consequent fall in the value of handloom products, a large number of weavers were either rendered jobless or received lower wages. Weaving rates were reduced to such a level that many weavers were working at an average rate between five and six rupees per loom per month. The Salem weavers who used to get eighteen rupees for a sari before the Depression got only nine rupees.[72]

In December 1933 a strike broke out in all the districts where Madras handkerchiefs were woven. The strike also spread to the districts that wove lungis. The strike continued until the end of the year, but weavers involved in the agitation did not get any relief.[73] Masses of handloom weavers were thrown out of employment and riots broke out in Coimbatore, Gudiyatham and Komarapalayam. There was a large riot of the unemployed weavers of Komarapalayam (Salem district). In Gudiyatham (North Arcot district), a crowd of 500 weavers who had gathered to ventilate their grievances turned violent and attacked the police.[74] At Salem and Rasipuram (Salem district) there was looting of grain shops, and at Kollegal (Coimbatore district) *shandy* (market) carts carrying grain were attacked and looted.[75] The outbreak of riots in areas where handloom weaving was undertaken was suggestive of the acute distress experienced by the handloom weavers.

[71] *Ibid.*, 22–24.

[72] Eugene F. Irschick, *Tamil Revivalism in the 1930s* (Madras: Cre-A, 1986), 132.

[73] *Annual Report, Department of Industries*, 1934, 17–18.

[74] Baker, *An Indian Rural Economy*, 401.

[75] *Report on the Administration of the Police of the Madras Presidency*, 1934, 15.

Dissonance in Industrial Relations

Depression in industry led not only to high levels of unemployment, but to wage reductions. There was some unrest in the labour force, but it was unable to defend itself effectively against the erosion of its standard of living in the 1930s. As Gadgil observed, "Since 1929 there had been a distinct fall in the number and intensity of labour disputes as a result of the utterly helpless position to which the vastness of unemployment had reduced the working class."[76] Strikes of comparatively short duration broke out in a few industrial establishments in protest against cuts in wages. But the fear of unemployment sent the workers back to work within a few days.

In the cotton industry, intense Japanese competition forced the Indian mills to cut prices to uneconomic levels in an effort to survive in the business. The mill owners endeavoured to cover part of the losses by cuts in wages and retrenchment in other forms. This resulted in strikes in certain mills.[77] In 1930, Harveys led the way in cutting mill wages. On 3 February 1930 the workers in Harvey Cotton Mills in Papanasam (Tirunelveli district) struck work. On 11 February, the management put up the following notice at the mills:

> Trade, which has been depressed for a considerable period, has now reached a stage that the managers are forced with much regret to close down the mills. This takes immediate effect and will remain in force until such time as trade shows signs of revival.[78]

Harveys remained stubborn and the government refused to intervene. On 14 April, the management posted another notice at the mills:

> The management hereby gives notice that as trade conditions have shown slight improvement recently, they are prepared to start the new mill on Wednesday 16th April provided sufficient workers present themselves for re-employment on that date. It is regretted that conditions do not permit of the old mill being restored meantime.[79]

76 Gadgil, *Industrial Evolution of India,* 277.
77 *Annual Report, Department of Industries,* 1934, 17–18.
78 *Administration Report of the Labour Department* (Madras), 1929–30, 7.
79 *Ibid.*

The mill reopened but no concessions were made. By 19 April, only about 300 out of 1,543 workers were on strike. Eventually they were also forced to return, although many of them were dismissed when they turned up to work.[80] The strike at the Papanasam Mills ended in complete defeat for the workers. The same was the case with workers of Choolai Mills, Madras in 1930. In both cases the management resorted to lockouts and dictated their own terms for the reopening of the mills.[81]

The mill owners in Coimbatore reduced wages by one-third because they claimed "the Depression forced them to cut back on labour cost."[82] There were strikes in two cotton mills in Coimbatore district. About half of the 1,716 employees of the Kaleswarar Mill went on strike against pay cuts imposed on them. At about the same time 600 workers in the Vasantha Mills also struck work. But the strike was easily broken and a majority of them had to return to work.[83] On 16 May 1936, about a 100 labourers struck work at the Loyal Mills, Kovilpatti. The strike fizzled out on 18 May as fear of starvation undermined their spirit of struggle.[84]

The Western India Match Company (WIMCO), Thiruvottiyur, proposed to retrench 40 per cent of its workers. The workers went on strike in May 1931. The strikers could only make the management accept their demand for payment of gratuity to the retrenched workers.[85] The workers renewed their agitation in May 1932. In response the management threatened to terminate the services of all the workers, about 800, and to re-employ only a section of the workers on new terms and conditions. A notice to the above effect was issued in order to discourage workers from pressing demands which had been put forward to the management previously. Despite a long-drawn-out struggle the workers had to return to duty unconditionally in the end.[86]

80 Murphy, *Unions in Conflict,* 118–19.
81 *Fortnightly Reports* (from the chief secretary of the Madras government to the secretary of the government of India), second half of April 1930.
82 Murphy, *Unions in Conflict,* 143.
83 *Fortnightly Reports,* second half of February 1934.
84 *Ibid.,* second half of May 1936.
85 G.O. *No. 2158-L (MS) Public Works and Labour Department,* 15 October 1932.
86 G.O. *No. 1354-L (MIS) Public Works and Labour Department,* 23 June 1932.

The management of the Standard Oil Company discharged 107 of their workers on 22 July 1932, giving them a month's salary in lieu of notice. In protest, all the workers, numbering about 300, downed tools the next morning. However they had to resume work unconditionally in a week.[87] Minor strikes occurred in the Madras Pencil Factory and in Addison & Co.'s workshop in Madras. But they were all settled without any benefit to the strikers.[88] Workers in the seven tanneries of Madhavaram struck work on 19 August 1934, demanding enhanced wages; but they returned to work unconditionally on 27 August 1934.[89] About 450 out of 500 employees in Roshan and Company's tannery at Meenambakkam struck work on 8 February 1935, demanding, amongst other things, increase in wages and a reduction in workload. The strike lasted for two days and on the third day the strikers returned to work unconditionally.[90]

In the railways, when the administration proposed retrenchment, the All-India Railwaymen's Federation demanded that a board of conciliation be constituted to examine policies relating to retrenchment measures contemplated by the government. This, they said, was to avoid the discharge of the staff at the lower level.[91] But the railway administration went ahead with its own programme of retrenchment and refused to discuss it with the union. The Madras and Southern Mahratta Railway Employees' Union was sore over the attitude of the railway administration; in its annual conference, held at Bangalore on 4 and 5 April 1931 under the presidentship of V. V. Giri, it passed a resolution condemning the retrenchment policy of the railway administration.[92] The government took no action, stating that under Section 3 of the Indian Trade Disputes Act 1929, where

[87] *Fortnightly Reports,* first half of June 1932.

[88] *Ibid.,* first half of August 1932.

[89] *Report, Administration of Madras Presidency,* 1934–35, 115.

[90] *Ibid.*

[91] *Indian Annual Register* 2, 1931, 67.

[92] G.O. *No. 1060-L (MS) Public Works and Labour Department,* 17 April 1931.

the employer was a railway company, it was only the governor-general in council who had the authority to refer a dispute to a court of enquiry or a conciliation board.[93]

The general trend was in favour of a direct action programme. The Railway Employees' Union authorised its president, V. V. Giri, to get the decision ratified by the All-India Railwaymen's Federation that was to hold a convention at Simla towards the end of June 1931.[94] On 16 June the railway administration precipitated the matter by dismissing 50 workers of the Perambur workshop with 24 hours' notice, and with "a month salary in lieu of notice as a measure of retrenchment."[95] There were 6,100 employees in the workshop. Those who had not been dismissed went to the workshop as usual on 17 June but refused to work, in protest against the dismissals. The following day each worker was asked to sign a declaration saying either that he was willing to work or that he was unwilling. But those who signed the declaration in the affirmative staged a *dharna* (demonstration) on being admitted to the workshops. So on 19 June the workers were refused entry into the work spot. Negotiations were held between the Union office-bearers and the management. The management regretted its inability to take back the dismissed workers, as dismissal was pursuant to a nationwide retrenchment policy. The workers resumed work on 23 June without achieving their demand.[96]

The governor-general in council in the meanwhile had appointed a court of enquiry to investigate the dispute that had arisen. But without waiting for the recommendation of the Court of Enquiry, the Railway Board decided to discharge 10,000 more railway employees.[97] Besides, the Railway Retrenchment Committee had recommended cuts in the salaries of railway employees. The members of Madras and Southern Mahratta Railway Union refused to receive their pay for December 1931

93 *Ibid.*
94 *Fortnightly Reports,* first half of June 1931.
95 G.O. No. *1686-L (MS) Public Works and Labour Department,* 2 July 1931.
96 *Fortnightly Reports,* second half of June 1931.
97 *Ibid.,* second half of October 1931.

and January 1932 in protest against the wage cut.[98] In an opinion poll held among the members of the Union at Perambur workshop on the question of a general strike almost all workers who voted were in favour of a strike.[99] A special convention of the All-India Railwaymen's Federation, held in Madras on 2 and 3 September 1932, decided to postpone the proposed general strike in view of "the incompleteness of the preparation."[100] However, the fresh proposal of the Madras and Southern Mahratta Railway to retrench 473 workers precipitated the situation.[101]

Thereupon the Madras and Southern Mahratta Railway Employees' Union gave a call for a strike in the Perambur workshop from 23 September 1932.[102] Work in Perambur workshop came to a standstill. The workers of the Arakonam engineering workshops joined the strike on 3 November 1932. On 18 December 1932, the sheriff of Madras formed a committee consisting of prominent citizens of Madras, in order to effect a settlement.[103] The Citizens' Committee, presumably without consulting the management, gave an assurance to the Union that their demand would be conceded. The strike was called off. When the workers returned to duty, sixty-three of them had been permanently replaced. This had a demoralising effect on the workers, causing them to believe that the strike was a total failure.[104]

Consideration of a few major strikes in the Depression years indicates that in establishments where labour unrest erupted, the management could force the workers to submit by declaring a lockout or by holding a threat to wind up the factory. Protests by the unions were of little avail. The Madras Labour Union, the leading trade union in Tamilnadu, experienced great difficulty in enrolling members during the Depression.[105] B. Shiva Rao's attempts to start textile workers' unions evoked no response in Tirunelveli district. No mill

98 *Fortnightly Reports,* second half of January 1932.
99 *Ibid.,* first half of May 1932.
100 *Ibid.,* first half of August 1932.
101 *Ibid.,* first half of December 1932.
102 *Report, Railway Board on Indian Railways,* 1932–33, 1: 66–67.
103 *Ibid.*
104 *Fortnightly Reports,* first half of January 1933.
105 Murphy, *Unions in Conflict,* 125.

worker attended the meeting he convened at Tuticorin. Even his efforts to organise a meeting of workers at Kovilpatti ended in failure.[106] The general secretary of the Indian National Congress in his annual report for the year 1936 wrote, "The labour movement in India before it could attain any measure of maturity and strength suffered from the recent acute trade and industrial Depression."[107]

Summary

The economic area where the impact of the Depression turned out to be different was industry. The industries which served the home market protected by the government's tariff measures thrived. But the industries that relied on the export market came to grief. Conditions created by the Depression in the Presidency, such as availability of raw material at low prices, cheap labour, and low rates of interest for the money lent by banks, proved to be conducive to the growth of certain industries. Cotton, sugar and banking industries registered commendable advances during this period. Coimbatore emerged as an important textile centre in South India. As the banking institutions multiplied in the Province, a Central Bank came into existence to monitor them.

Though the Presidency witnessed industrial development, handloom, cottage and small-scale sectors had a trying time. The government's taxation policy turned out to be disastrous to those sectors. When the tanners were demanding high export duty on raw skins and hides, the government abolished the duty —much against Indian interests. An excise duty levied on matches crippled the industry, and the government's protective tariffs extended to Indian textile mills affected the handloom sector. A large number of weavers in handloom centres and labourers in small industrial establishments lost their jobs. In large factories, the workers had to suffer wage cuts. Instead of taking the offensive, the working class, in the face of acute crisis, remained passive. Even the strikes and struggles launched by the organised labour unions were of short duration, fizzling out in the end.

[106] *Fortnightly Reports,* second half of January 1932.

[107] A. M. Zaidi and S. G. Zaidi, eds., *The Encyclopaedia of the Indian National Congress, 1930–1935* (New Delhi: Chand, 1968), 11: 223.

5

Fiscal and Monetary Policy of the Colonial State

As we saw in chapter 1, the Depression initially manifested in disastrous trade returns. The decline in exports and the resultant fall in the prices of agricultural products (chapter 3) led to a steady diminution of government revenue. In response, the government attempted to stabilise its revenue by levying additional taxes and collecting land revenue, the mainstay of government finance, through coercive measures. Drastic retrenchment of expenditure was also effected simultaneously. Notwithstanding the budgetary equilibrium maintained by the colonial government, the Depression caused great hardship to all sections of the populace. In this chapter we first discuss the impact of the Great Depression on Madras's economy, highlighting the response of the government as well as the reactions of the press, the business class, and the people's representatives in the Legislative Council. Second, the emergency fiscal measures—with heavy accent on retrenchment of expenditure—adopted by the provincial government, and their fallout are analysed. Third, the implications of the monetary policy pursued by the imperialist government are assessed. Finally, the government's strict adherence to the principle of a "balanced budget" is reviewed.

Budget Crisis

Excise and land revenue occupied crucial places in the revenue structure of the Madras government. These two heads were "the sheet anchor of provincial finance," and in 1929–30, when the revenue of Madras was at its zenith, they accounted for 72.69 per cent of it.[1] Stamps followed excise and land revenue. Revenue from stamps and excise always reflected the economic conditions prevalent in the country.[2] The fall in the prices of agricultural and commercial products in the wake of the Depression, and the resultant decline in the economic prosperity of the community, led to a fall in the revenues from excise and stamps. The revenues of the Madras government fell from Rs. 180.88 million in 1929–30 to Rs. 168.39 million in 1930–31—a decrease of Rs. 12.49 million.[3] The budget estimate for the year 1930–31 anticipated a deficit of Rs. 1.66 million in the revenue accounts,[4] but in fact the year closed with a deficit of Rs. 10.57 million.[5] Excise revenue decreased from Rs. 52.43 million to Rs. 42.58 million in 1931–32.[6] The receipts under stamps fell from Rs. 25.30 million in 1930–31 to Rs. 23.88 million in 1931–32.[7] Registration was yet another head on which the Depression had its impact: its revenue dropped from Rs. 3.26 million in 1930–31 to Rs. 2.95 million in 1931–32.[8]

In April 1931, the government of India asked the provincial governments to prepare reviews of their financial positions and prospects, to be discussed at a conference in May 1931. At the conference the provincial representatives gave their latest appraisal of financial prospects, indicating that the outlook was worse than had been expected in their earlier reviews.[9] In view of such a fluctuating trend, the hopes on which the government of Madras had framed the budget estimate for 1931–32 proved to be too "sanguine" —a comparison of the budget and the revised estimates brings this out clearly (table 5.1).

1 T. Meenakshi, "The Finance of Madras Government since 1919" (M.Litt. diss., University of Madras, 1950), 56–79.

2 The provincial tax structure was so lopsided that the entire burden of taxation was borne by the people in rural areas. It was they who paid land revenue, excise—by consuming country liquor—and stamp duty by involving themselves in litigation. Meenakshi, "Finance of Madras Government," 69.

3 *Ibid.*, 53–63.

4 *Report, Administration of Madras Presidency*, 1930–31, xxxxi.

5 *The Hindu*, 25 February 1933.

6 *Report, Administration of Madras Presidency*, 1931–32, 79.

7 *Ibid.*, 136.

8 *Ibid.*, 53.

9 *G.O. No. 692 (MS) Finance Department*, 6 November 1931.

TABLE 5.1: Budget and Revised Estimates of 1931–32

Principal heads	Budget estimate (b.e.) (in Rs. million)	Revised estimate (r.e.) (in Rs. million)	Difference (in Rs. million)	r.e. as percentage of b.e.
Taxes on income	0.50	0.45	- 0.05	90.00
Land revenue	76.61	77.29	+0.68	100.89
Excise	49.63	40.36	- 9.28	81.31
Stamps	23.88	22.54	- 1.35	94.37
Forest	5.58	4.88	- 0.75	87.37
Registration	3.20	2.81	- 0.38	87.98
Irrigation	- 4.34	- 4.23	+0.11	97.49
Miscellaneous	22.64	17.66	- 4.99	77.99
Total revenues	177.7	161.76	- 16.01	91.02

Source: *Letter Nos. 158 & 159 (Mis.) Finance Department*, 7 March 1931; G.O. *No. 15 (MS) Finance Department*, 12 January 1932.

The decline was very large under the headings excise and miscellaneous. But there was hardly any decline under land revenue and irrigation; in fact, there was an increase in both. This was because of the coercive measures of the government.

Despite the government's retrenchment measures, which we shall discuss later, the financial position of the Presidency continued to fluctuate as revenues under excise, stamps and registration continued to decline. Compared to the figures of 1930–31, in 1934–35 excise had decreased by Rs. 10.38 million, stamps by Rs. 0.66 million, registration by Rs. 0.09 million and miscellaneous by Rs. 2.24 million (table 5.2). Picketing of liquor shops, which was going on as a part of Congress agitation, brought social pressures on the prospective bidders for toddy shops, resulting in considerable fall in toddy revenue. Total prohibition of arrack (country liquor) and toddy had been enforced during 1930–33 in certain taluks of Salem district.[10] All these added to the Depression and contributed to the decrease of government revenue under excise. Owing to the Depression, there had been a steady fall in the number of suits instituted in all the courts other than revenue courts after

[10] *Report on the Administration of the Excise Revenue in the Presidency for 1931–32*, 5.

1932. This affected the income under judicial stamps. The receipt from the judicial stamps during the year 1934–35 was Rs. 13.36 million. It decreased to Rs. 12.73 million in 1935–36, a decline of Rs. 0.63 million. In 1936–37 it fell further, by Rs. 1.03 million, to Rs. 11.7 million.[11] The decrease under non-judicial stamps was due to the slump in trade, the slackness in the banking business, and the fall in the prices of immovable properties and agricultural produce. Table 5.2, compiled by Professor Narayanaswamy,[12] shows the figures of revenue under the various accounts for the whole period of the Depression.

TABLE 5.2: Tax Revenues for Madras Government, 1929–30 to 1936–37 (In Rs. million)

Year	*Land revenue*	*Excise*	*Stamps*	*Forest*	*Regis-tration*	*Miscel-laneous*	*Total*
1929–30	75.04	59.23	25.09	6.35	3.45	15.55	184.71
	(100)	(100)	(100)	(100)	(100)	(100)	(100)
1930–31	71.66	52.84	23.47	5.12	3.04	15.19	171.32
	(95)	(89)	(94)	(81)	(88)	(98)	(93)
1931–32	71.94	42.90	23.49	4.53	2.98	12.25	163.09
	(96)	(72)	(94)	(71)	(86)	(79)	(88)
1932–33	74.68	43.17	24.16	4.97	3.25	12.12	162.35
	(100)	(73)	(96)	(78)	(94)	(78)	(88)
1933–34	69.25	42.96	22.81	4.16	3.03	12.72	154.93
	(92)	(73)	(91)	(65)	(88)	(82)	(84)
1934–35	71.65	42.46	21.71	4.43	3.11	13.23	151.59
	(95)	(72)	(87)	(70)	(90)	(85)	(82)
1935–36	74.24	41.19	20.82	4.50	3.03	13.73	157.51
	(99)	(70)	(83)	(71)	(88)	(88)	(85)
1936–37	71.54	40.08	19.51	4.83	3.00	15.50	154.46
	(95)	(68)	(78)	(76)	(87)	(100)	(84)

Note: Figures in brackets give index number with 1929–30 = 100.
Source: B. V. Narayanaswamy Naidu, "Finance of the Madras Province 1920–40," *Indian Journal of Economics* 21, 1940–41, 884–85.

11 *Report, Administration of Madras Presidency*, 1935–36, 170.

12 There is discrepancy between the figures cited earlier and the figures given by Narayanaswamy, as the former are based on the budget estimates, while the latter are the actual figures.

GRAPH 2(a): Government Revenue by Major Heads in Madras Presidency
Land Revenue in 1929–30 = Rs. 75.04 million = 100

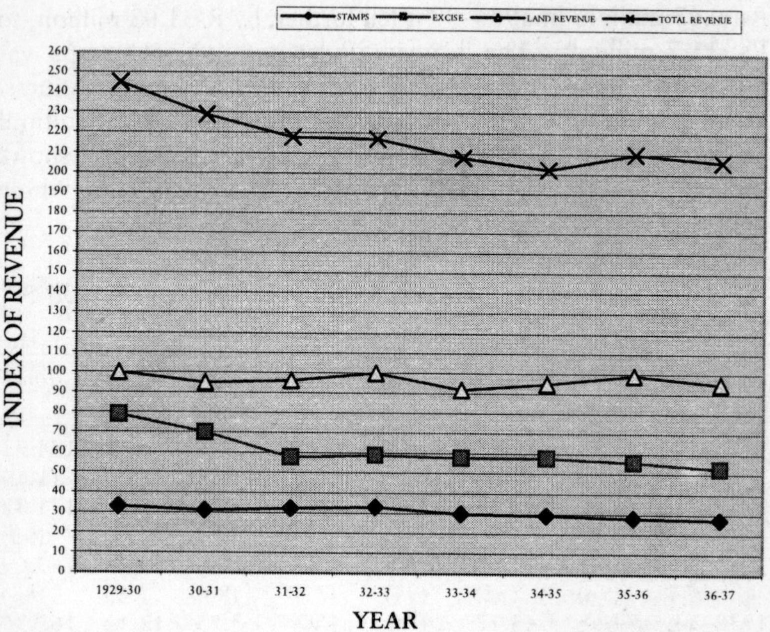

The government tried to meet the crisis by resorting to additional taxation. At the insistence of the secretary of state, Samuel Hoare, the finance member, George Schuster, presented a supplementary budget in the Legislative Assembly on 29 September 1931, involving increased taxation and drastic retrenchment of expenditure. Regarding taxation, a general surcharge of 25 per cent on all existing taxes was levied, with the exception of customs duties on exports. The existing import duties were increased on silk piece goods and silk yarn, on brown sugar, on boots and shoes, on camphor and on electric bulbs. In all these cases a surcharge was levied on the increased duty. An import duty of 10 per cent was levied on machinery and dyes, and of .5 anna per pound on raw cotton. The rate for inland postal letters was raised from 1 anna to 1.5 annas, and for postcards from 6 pies to 9 pies. The exemption limit for income tax was lowered from

Graph 2(b): Government Revenue by Minor Heads in Madras Presidency

Revenue From Forests In 1929–30 = Rs. 6.35 Million = 100

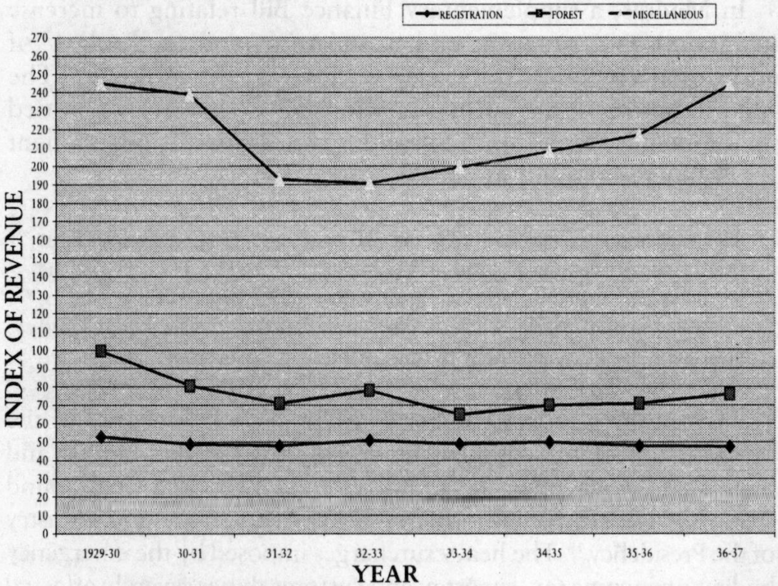

Note: Graphs 2(a) & 2(b) are drawn to different scales. And also note that the indices in both the graphs are different from the ones given in table 3.2, where the index for each head was calculated with its value in 1929–30 as the base.

Rs. 2,000 to Rs. 1,000 in a financial year. The tax imposed was raised from 2 pies to 4 pies in the rupee.[13]

The taxation measures of the government of India aroused deep resentment among all sections of people, and the Central Legislative Assembly rejected the supplementary Finance Bill. But the viceroy brought it into force through certification.[14] Even the pro-British newspaper *Justice* came out against the taxation proposals of the central government in its editorial dated 5 November 1931.

> However elaborate the defence might have been and however plausible the argument advanced in support of the bill [supplementary

[13] S. P. Sarma, *Indian Budgets 1921–1934* (Madras: G. A. Natesan, 1934), 196.

[14] *Justice,* 21 November 1931.

Finance Bill], he [finance member] has not succeeded in convincing the members of the Assembly as to the need for fresh taxation.[15]

In Madras, a supplementary Finance Bill relating to increase in income tax, supertax and postal rates and to the levy of additional customs and excise duties was introduced.[16] The Madras branch of the European Association vehemently opposed the supplementary Finance Bill and forwarded to the government the following resolution passed in its meeting:

> This meeting is of opinion that the proposals for increased taxation in the bill to supplement the Indian Finance Act of 1931 will be disastrous to the trade and commerce of this country at the present time and so, far from providing the increased revenues anticipated, are calculated effectively to decrease them by diminishing the source of taxation.[17]

The Southern India Chamber of Commerce disapproved of the introduction of the supplementary Finance Bill in Madras, and expressed the view that the additional taxes proposed were bound to be highly detrimental to the recovery of the trade and industry of the Presidency.[18] The heavy surcharges imposed by the emergency budget on income tax, supertax and customs duties severely affected the merchant community. Income tax, supertax, stamp duties, court fees, registration charges, excise and customs were now worth twice the quantity of goods that they had been formerly, due to the fall in prices. The mercantile class pleaded for introduction of the principle of carrying forward business losses against the profits of succeeding years, for the purpose of income tax calculation. They pointed out that a wealthy country like the United Kingdom had been enjoying the privilege of setting off losses against the profits of succeeding years. But the colonial government refused to concede the demand, on grounds of fiscal constraints.[19]

The agriculturists were unable to pay the land tax on account of their dwindling income, caused by the fall in prices. But land revenue

[15] *Justice*, 5 November 1931.
[16] *Report, Southern India Chamber of Commerce*, 1931, 80.
[17] *Justice*, 24 October 1931.
[18] *Justice*, 3 November 1931.
[19] *Report, Southern India Chamber of Commerce*, 1932, 7–8; *ibid.*, 1934, iii–iv.

was considered the mainstay of government finance and hence it was collected rigorously, by forcible means. The Madras government claimed that in 1930–31, 98 per cent of land revenue and irrigation taxes had been collected instead of 99 per cent, which was usually collected. The difference of 1 per cent was, as stated by the government, due to "a mere postponement of collection of *kist* [land tax] by one or two months in a certain limited area."[20] The finance member had budgeted for an increase of land revenue to the tune of Rs. 2.05 million for 1931–32.[21] The government gave the responsibility of collecting the land tax to the lower-level bureaucracy, who struck terror into the hearts of the peasants in rural areas. This was because of the pressure applied by their immediate superiors who were in turn pestered by the higher echelons of the officialdom. Complaints of harassment and intimidation by the revenue officials were highlighted in the Legislative Council. The Council was informed of the orders issued by the *tahsildar* (the chief administrative officer of a taluk) of Nannilam taluk in Thanjavur district, directing the peasants to pledge their jewels in the Imperial Bank in order to pay the kist if they failed to sell their paddy.[22] A member in the course of a debate narrated how the revenue inspector went about his job in Thanjavur district.

> The other day I had a letter from a friend of mine in Tanjore district stating that the Revenue Inspector while on duty to collect the land assessment went about harassing the people. I understand that he went to a village at mid-night, harassed the people, pulled down the tiles from the roof [*sic*] of houses, pulled away the clothes and the ear-rings that the people were wearing and worried them as much as he could.[23]

Another member of the Council alleged that the Salem collector had issued a circular instructing the village *munsiff* (headman) to make remittance of kist from his or her own pocket first and get it reimbursed by making collection from the peasants later. The member also stated that the village munsiffs were

[20] *Ibid.*, 1931, 99–100.
[21] *PMLC* 60, 1932, 183.
[22] *G.O. No. 82 (Press) Land Revenue Settlement Department*, 27 September 1934.
[23] *PMLC* 80, 1936, 322–23.

encouraged to collect by being given medals and certificates of merit.[24] These rewards served as an incentive to the petty village officers to apply duress to make the peasant pay his kist on time. In the Madras Legislative Council a member related how land revenue was realised in the Province.

> Sub-Divisional Officers go to the place with a posse of constables who are ready to beat the people and the police actually terrorise them and taxes are collected as if it were at the point of the bayonet; no collections are made without making the people sell their jewels and other belongings in order to see that they are not molested.[25]

A delegation sent by the League of Nations in 1932 to study the severity of the Depression in India noted that "attachment of property, usually a revenue process, had now become a police job. The police raided the villages, beat the foremost resisters, seized livestock, fodder, foodstuff from them, pulled down parts of houses and none of these can be questioned in a court of law."[26] The League delegation that recorded the posting of additional police forces in a number of Indian villages observed that in no tax areas of Madras had such forces been quartered.[27] The revenue officials adopted an attitude of extreme severity in attaching the personal belongings of the defaulters. But due to pressure in the Legislative Council, the government had to direct by departmental orders that "the implements of husbandry and one pair of ploughing cattle for each cultivator and such personal ornaments as in accordance with custom or religious usage cannot be parted with by a woman, for example a '*thali*' or 'wedding ring' should be considered to be exempted from attachment and sale for arrears of revenue."[28]

Land revenue collection became an arduous task as enhanced resettlement rates had come into operation in some districts on the eve of the Depression; in Thanjavur, land revenue had increased

24 *PMLC* 73, 1934, 251–52.

25 *PMLC* 61, 1932, 1: 42–43.

26 Quoted in A. R. Desai, ed., *Peasant Struggles in India* (New Delhi: Oxford University Press, 1982), 314.

27 *Ibid.*, 330.

28 *G.O. No. 82 (Press) Land Revenue and Settlement Department*, 27 September 1934.

by 18.75 per cent.[29] The government incurred the wrath of the cultivators by ordering resettlement operations which had become due in several districts during the Depression. It was the most inopportune moment for a revision of resettlement. Yet it was in progress in Salem in 1934. Other settlements due in Tamil districts before 1936–37 were two taluks in Nilgiris district and one taluk in North Arcot district.[30] The revenue member brushed aside any suggestion for change of land revenue policy, saying, "We are on the threshold of further reforms and it is better that the question is left to the new council."[31] In contrast to this, he was not prepared to leave the task of enforcing the resettlement rates to the government to be constituted under the "new reforms."[32] However, in the wake of a countrywide agitation the government had to finally abandon resettlements by 1936. The finance member, while presenting the budget for 1936–37, stated that the Province had sacrificed Rs. 1.5 million due to postponement of resettlement.[33]

The colonial government did not make any departure from its conventional financial administration even in the face of prayers, petitions and protests. The observations made by the accountant general in 1931 reflected the mind of the government: "The Government of Madras finds in the circumstances of the recent past and of the present time sufficient justification for now adopting a definitely conservative financial policy and while future prospects continue to be uncertain as they are at present there can be little doubt that this is a necessary course to pursue."[34] Presenting the budget for 1931–32, the finance member in Madras, Sir H. G. Stokes, dilated on the fiscal policy of the Province. He said, "We have entered a period of stagnation of trade and of general economic depression, the duration of which, it is impossible exactly to foretell," and that "to adjust more closely revenue receipts and

[29] *PMLC* 64, 1933, 214.

[30] *Ibid.*, 73, 1934, 38.

[31] *Ibid.*, 56, 1931, 26.

[32] *Andhra Patrika*, 5 February 1935, in *Report on Native Newspapers*, 1936, 2: 73.

[33] *Indian Annual Register*, 1936, 1: 194.

[34] *G.O. No. 35 (MS) Finance Department*, 20 January 1933.

revenue expenditure should be the main object of our policy, balances or no balances."[35] The Retrenchment Committee appointed by the government in 1931 echoed the government's economic philosophy in the preamble to its report.

> The greatest service that any Government can perform for its citizens during present economic crisis is to maintain equilibrium between revenue and expenditure; and the confidence that a balanced budget inspires is infinitely more important than any other consideration.[36]

Government's Retrenchment Measures

In pursuance of its policy to have a balanced budget, the government of India decided to appoint a Retrenchment Committee to suggest means of economy in public expenditure. Sir George Schuster, finance member of the government of India, referring to the desire of the government to appoint a Retrenchment Committee, stated that the primary task of this committee would be to investigate the possibilities of retrenchment in civil expenditure. He added that no substantial economies would be possible in military expenditure without changes in the composition and strength of armed forces, which had already received special consideration at the Round Table Conference.[37] In line with the government of India, the Madras government also appointed a Retrenchment Committee in March 1931, under the chairmanship of the finance member of the government of Madras, H. G. Stokes, I.C.S. (Indian Civil Service), with J. Kuppuswami Chowdary (raja of Bobbili), Mahmud Schammad (raja of Calicut), S. Ellappa Chettiyar, F. E. James, T. M. Narayanaswami Pillai, T. S. Ramaswami Ayyar, N. Sivaraj and C. S. Rathnasabapathi Mudaliyar as members. All the members were legislators. But the government chose to appoint only nominated members and close associates of the Justice Ministry. G. R. F. Tottenham was appointed secretary to the Committee.[38] Thus the Retrenchment Committee was virtually a committee of the government.

[35] *G.O. No. 327 (Mis.) Finance Department*, 13 May 1925.
[36] *Report of the Madras Retrenchment Committee* (Madras, 1931–32), 9.
[37] *Indian Annual Register*, 1931, 1: 152.
[38] *Report, Madras Retrenchment Committee*, 74.

In March 1929, R. N. Arogyaswamy Mudaliyar, M.L.C., had given a notice of motion in the Council to discuss the necessity for appointing a Retrenchment Committee. At the time, the government held that the necessity for such a committee had not arisen.[39] Within two years, due to the Great Depression, such a committee was necessitated. It was made clear that the government could for some years to come count on revenue of not more than about Rs. 165 million, and that the general level of expenditure would be regulated accordingly.[40]

The finance member announced in the Legislative Assembly on 29 September 1931 that the government of India, as a part of the retrenchment measures, proposed to make a cut "not exceeding 10 per cent in any individual case in the pay of officers under their control or under the control of Secretary of State."[41] In conformity with the announcement made by the finance member of the government of India, and in a bid to compensate for the revenue deficits of the current year (1931–32), the Madras government levied an "emergency cut of 10 per cent on pay and leave pay earned with effect from 1.12.1931 in respect of all government servants under the administrative control of the local government on pay exceeding Rs. 200."[42] In a press communiqué, the secretary of the Retrenchment Committee, G. R. F. Tottenham, stated: "Apart from the imposition of new taxation, a matter in which the field open to Local Government is limited, the only further possibility of securing the necessary savings is by making an emergency cut in salaries."[43] The salaries of the members of the All India Services under the government of Madras represented one-eighth of the total expenditure of the Presidency, and the cut helped save Rs. 0.8 million in a full year. The salaries of the provincial and subordinate services, as estimated by the Retrenchment Committee, accounted for about Rs. 60 million. At the time when the cut was introduced it was definitely

[39] *G.O. No. 315 (Mis.) Finance Department*, 5 May 1930.

[40] Meenakshi, "Finance of Madras Government," 56–79.

[41] *G.O. No. 345 (MS) Finance Department*, 28 May 1934.

[42] *Ibid.*

[43] *G.O. No. 4043 (Mis.) Land Revenue and Settlement Department*, 16 December 1931.

announced that it would be of a temporary nature, not extending beyond the needs of the exceptional emergency. The government order on the 10 per cent salary cut said that "the cut would be removed as a first measure of relief as soon as financial conditions improved, and there was no intention that it should remain in operation after the 31st March 1933."[44] Addressing the scheme of retrenchment in the Legislative Council the governor said:

> In order to assist the country to economise, a cut has been foreshadowed in the pay of the services and I should like to pay a tribute to the way in which they have accepted that which must necessarily be a grave inconvenience to them. In this connection, I may mention that the members of the Executive Council and Ministers have agreed to a voluntary cut of 10 per cent in their salaries, and there will be a similarly voluntary cut of 10 per cent in mine. Though, in my case, I am having a further examination made of commitments on my private purse, with a view to a possible further surrender of salary. The Hon'ble Chief Justice and the Judges of the High Court have also agreed to a voluntary cut, the amount of which will be announced later.[45]

In the Legislative Council three resolutions were passed seeking introduction of graded cuts in salaries of government employees, instead of a uniform cut of 10 per cent starting with salaries of Rs. 40 per month. The resolution moved by Swami A. S. Sahajanandam recommended to the government that in the matter of cuts in salaries of government employees, a graded cut between 2.5 and 10 per cent, commencing with salaries of Rs. 100 per month, be adopted. V. T. Arasu proposed that no cut be imposed on salaries of government servants who drew less than Rs. 100 per month, and that in the case of salaries of those who drew Rs. 100 or more per month, a graduated cut from 5 to 20 per cent be imposed. Diwan Bahadur M. Gopalswami Mudaliar pleaded that the salaries of non-gazetted officers or gazetted officers drawing less than Rs. 250 be not reduced. But the government rejected all these proposals.[46]

The efforts of retrenchment pursued by the Madras government followed two parallel lines. On the one hand, the Retrenchment

[44] *Ibid.*
[45] *PMLC* 58, 1931, 13.
[46] *G.O. No. 169 (MS) Finance Department*, 25 March 1932.

Committee appointed in March 1931 examined in detail all items of expenditure in various departments of the government, in order to reduce the recurring expenditure in future years to the level of the anticipated revenues. On the other hand, the need for immediate savings to reduce the gap between revenue and expenditure during 1931–32 made it necessary for all departments of government to examine their own expenditure independently and suggest "such savings as were possible without undue loss of efficiency." The Committee agreed to the issue of a circular asking all heads of department to make suggestions for economy up to 8 per cent of their budget allotments, of which not less than half should be of a recurring nature. In a press communiqué, the secretary of the Committee stated that they had set before themselves the figure of Rs. 12 million as the extent of recurring savings to be aimed at.[47] When R. N. Arogyaswamy Mudaliyar raised a question in the Legislative Council on the anticipated figure of revenue to which the government was preparing their retrenchment proposals, Finance Member Stokes, who was also the chairman of the Retrenchment Committee, replied that it might be roughly about Rs. 160 million.[48]

The Retrenchment Committee made a series of recommendations, based on which the government started issuing orders. On the grounds of financial stringency, the Retrenchment Committee recommended that a cut from 10 per cent to 15 per cent should be applied to all fixed travelling allowances. The government directed that all fixed travelling allowances be reduced by 12.5 per cent.[49] The Committee recommended an immediate cut in all compensatory allowances, including those granted to officers of All India Service stationed at Madras. The government ordered a 31.25 per cent cut on allowances above Rs. 50, a 25 per cent cut on all allowances above Rs. 20 but below Rs. 50, and a cut of 12.5 per cent on allowances below Rs. 20.[50] The Committee also suggested that

[47] *Press Communiqué of Secretary of Retrenchment Committee*, G. R. F. Tottenham, in *G.O. No. 4043 (Mis.) Land Revenue and Settlement Department*, 16 December 1931.

[48] *PMLC* 58, 1931, 373.

[49] *G.O. No. 631 (MS) Finance Department*, 6 October 1931.

[50] *G.O. No. 612 Finance Department*, 29 September 1931.

conferences and committees be curtailed as far as possible; the government implemented the recommendation.[51] The government, in accordance with the recommendation of the Committee, directed all heads of department and their subordinates to make considerable reduction in the cost of printing by reducing the size of their departmental administration reports and the statistical tables attached to them.[52] The indenting officers of departments were instructed to restrict their requirements under stores to the absolute minimum.[53] The government accepted the recommendation of the Committee that expenditure under charges for electricity should be reduced as much as possible, and the reduction of telephone connections might be a possible avenue of economy.[54] The use of cheaper materials in construction of government buildings, as recommended by the Committee, was also accepted.[55]

The recommendations of the Committee concerning the Department of Education were the closure of certain colleges, or discontinuation of affiliation in certain subjects, or reduction of the status of the staff employed. In Madras Presidency College, the Philosophy and Sanskrit Departments were wound up. A 5 per cent cut was made in all teaching grants during 1931–32. The special grant of Rs. 15 million for the improvement of pay of trained teachers in aided elementary schools was withdrawn. The grant to Boy Scouts and Girl Guides Associations was reduced by 25 per cent. The Committee recommended that all government grants for medical inspection in secondary and elementary schools, a scheme that had been made compulsory in compulsory education areas, should be suspended until "more prosperous times return."[56] The Committee considered the proposals made by the director of public instruction for the abolition of scholarships, and came to the conclusion that sufficient economy could be secured by reducing the number of instalments, so as to

[51] *G.O. No. 487 Finance Department*, 23 July 1931.
[52] *G.O. No. 2462 Public Health Department*, 29 November 1932.
[53] *G.O. No. 1546 (MS) Law (Education) Department*, 1 September 1931.
[54] *G.O. No. 3232 (MS) Public Works and Labour Department*, 22 December 1931.
[55] *G.O. No. 1769 (MS) Public Works and Labour Department*, 22 August 1932.
[56] *Report, Madras Retrenchment Committee*, 123.

limit the holding of scholarships to nine months a year. The government not only accepted this recommendation, but also granted no new scholarship during 1931–32.[57]

On the revenue side the Committee made various recommendations for the enhancement of fees in government arts and professional colleges. It accepted the proposal of the director that a registration fee of five rupees should be collected from each student admitted in the Presidency College, and three rupees in other government-run colleges.[58] The government implemented this recommendation. The retrenchment in the Department of Education was massive and Sami Venkatachalam Chetty complained in the Council that "The Education Department is practically reduced to its former position, probably earlier than 1920 or 1922. By one method or another, the Finance Member is so clever as to induce the Minister to fall in line with his proposals, so much so that a good deal of the Education Budget is cut away."[59]

The Committee recommended virtual abolition of the anti-drink grant. The government dispensed with the officially financed propaganda against drink and drugs carried on by the Central Propaganda Board, temperance publicity committees, and the district propaganda committees.[60] The government had ordered a large measure of retrenchment, amounting in all to over Rs. 0.7 million a year, by abolishing two survey parties and one settlement party in the Survey and Settlement Departments. Hence, the Committee concluded that there was not much scope for further retrenchment.[61] In the light of the Committee's view that the expenditure on public works provided "an obvious and probably the largest field for immediate retrenchment," provision for the maintenance of roads and buildings was reduced to even below the minimum required for efficient upkeep. No new works were undertaken in the department.[62]

[57] *Ibid.*, 125.
[58] *Ibid.*
[59] *PMLC* 69, 1934, 173.
[60] *G.O. No. 1583 Public Health Department,* 28 August 1931.
[61] *Report, Madras Retrenchment Committee*, 11.
[62] *G.O. No. 44 (MS) Finance Department*, 28 January 1933.

In certain types of offices the Committee recommended a reduction in the strength of the menial staff. Considerable staff reduction was attempted in the Labour Department. Officers of the grade of deputy tahsildars were replacing district labour officers of the grade of tahsildars. Labour schools with poor attendance were ordered to be closed. Two posts of clerks in the labour commissioner's office were abolished, and grants in aid to societies and institutions working for the uplift of the depressed classes reduced. The industrial centres in Madurai, Ramanathapuram and Thanjavur districts remained closed, and the revenue establishment employed in connection with the grant of land to *Kallar*s (an agricultural caste that was registered under the Criminal Tribes' Act) had been dispensed with. New building and repair works were kept in abeyance.[63]

The Corporation of Madras followed the principle of equity while imposing pay cuts. It exempted those who were drawing Rs. 75 or less from the pay cut. It inflicted a cut of 5 per cent on those who were drawing salaries up to Rs. 500, and 7.5, 10 and 12.5 per cent on the remaining higher-income brackets.[64] On the recommendation of the Retrenchment Committee, the University of Madras also imposed a salary cut of 5 per cent on the administrative and the teaching staff for a period of one year from 1 April 1932.[65] The government suggested that the universities surrender 8 per cent of the amount of the grant in 1931. The University of Madras agreed to this suggestion. The surrender continued till 1932–33. Besides a 5 per cent salary cut, a cut was made on the rates of travelling allowances. The number of meetings of the Academic Council and the boards of study was reduced. On grounds of financial stringency, the opening of new branches of research was deferred.[66]

The net effect of retrenchment measures was that in the revised estimate for the year 1931–32, the government was able to show a saving of Rs. 11.27 million under expenditure (table 5.3).

63 G.O. No. *735-L (MS) Public Works and Labour Department*, 24 March 1932.

64 G.O. No. *169 (MS) Finance Department*, 25 March 1932.

65 *History of Higher Education in South India, The: University of Madras (1857–1957)* (Madras: University of Madras, 1957), 1: 126.

66 *Ibid.*

TABLE 5.3: Account under Expenditure

	Budget estimate 1931–32 (b.e.) (in Rs. million)	*Revised estimate 1932–33 (r.e.) (in Rs. million)*	*Variation (in Rs. million)*	*Explanation for variations*	*r.e. as percentage of b.e.*
Direct demands on revenue	15.12	13.97	- 1.15		92.40
Irrigation and other expenditure	6.02	5.90	- 1.28	Due to measures of retrenchment	
Debt series					
Interest payable on Financial Loan Fund	6.81	6.81			100.00
Other items	3.04	3.04	Nil		100.00
Deduct interest transferred to commercial department	- 0.34	- 0.34			100.00
Civil administration	112.63	106.04	- 6.59		94.15
Civil works	22.31	19.79	- 3.02		86.78
Other expenditure	10.86	10.48	- 0.38	Due to measures of retrenchment	96.44
Total	176.45	165.68	- 11.27		

Note: The cut was the sharpest in civil works.
Source: *G.O. No. 15 (MS) Finance Department*, 12 January 1932.

The Retrenchment Committee formally presented its report in March 1932. According to a government estimate, their recommendations would effect a saving of Rs. 18.6 million per annum in expenditure, and an increase of Rs. 1.1 million per annum in revenue.[67] As the Committee summed up in its report,

[67] *Report, Madras Retrenchment Committee*, 8.

> The total saving for a full year comes to Rs. 14.35 million, which is increased to Rs. 18.30 million by the addition of Rs. 3.95 million from the emergency cut in pay. The proposals still under consideration account for a further saving of Rs. 4.85 million. Excluding the proceeds from the emergency cut in pay and the permanent revision of salaries, the sum total of our recommendations therefore reaches a figure of (Rs.14.35 million plus Rs. 4.85 million) Rs.19.2 million. This is Rs. 5.2 million more than the figure of Rs.14 million (Rs.10 million recurring and Rs. 4 million non-recurring) which we set before ourselves at our first meeting as the amount to be aimed at on the basis of a revenue of Rs.165 million.[68]

Criticism of Retrenchment Policy

In view of the massive retrenchment undertaken by the government during 1932–33 there was an actual surplus of Rs. 7.92 million against the budgeted deficit of around Rs. 1.6 million.[69] When the whole world was reeling under acute financial depression of an unprecedented nature, the Madras government's budget could not only be balanced but leave a surplus. The government's strict adherence to a policy of retrenchment had enabled it to maintain budgetary equilibrium. But it led to reduction in government spending on developmental activities. The government's drastic cut in their capital expenditure reduced the country's purchasing power. [70] The government of India's annual capital expenditure, which had run at an average of Rs. 270 million between 1920 and 1930, declined to an average of under Rs. 60 million between 1931 and 1939.[71] The total provincial (Madras) expenditure on civil works, which amounted to Rs. 93 million in 1928–29, fell by 41 per cent to Rs. 54 million in 1932–33; the expenditure not charged to revenue (excluding Burma) fell from Rs. 9.7 million to Rs. 0.6 million—a fall of 94 per cent.[72] The capital outlay on railways and provincial expenditure on civil works amounted to about Rs.100 million. After 1930–31, "capital expenditure on the

[68] *G.O. No. 65 (MS) Finance Department*, 4 February 1935.
[69] *Report, Southern India Chamber of Commerce,* 1933, 11–13.
[70] Thomas, *Growth of Federal Finance in India*, 363.
[71] Thomas, *Papers on Currency and Depression*, 449.
[72] Thomas, *Growth of Federal Finance in India*, 363.

railways nearly disappeared for a time, and even the provincial expenditure on civil works (charged to revenue) was reduced by one half."[73] P. J. Thomas observed:

> In a country where the Government is the largest single employer, a reduction of public works expenditure from an annual total of Rs. 50 crore [Rs. 500 million] to 12 crore [Rs. 120 million] was bound to have a very adverse effect on purchasing power. In most European countries, public works expenditure was increased during the depression with a view to maintaining purchasing power, and in most cases this meant unbalanced budgets. But the Government of India pursued an old fashioned "sound" financial policy and considered a balanced budget as of supreme importance.[74]

In the wake of the Depression the economist Keynes was advocating a public works programme. He was of the view that it would not only bring about full employment but also provide direct stimulus to the construction industry, which would in turn help absorb the idle labour.[75] Keynes hoped that other industries would indirectly be influenced as a result of the increasing purchasing power of the workers employed on the government projects. Speaking on radio in England in 1931, Keynes made a plea for increased spending to counteract the Depression. In his address he attacked thrift, the classical virtue. The housewife was urged to spend, and propaganda aiming to popularise the theory of increased public works expenditure was deployed.[76]

In India, on the contrary, the retrenchment hit the department of public works most severely. In Madras the retrenchment effected in public works amounted to more than 40 per cent, while in other departments it worked out to not more than 10 per cent.[77] P. J. Thomas pleaded for priority to the public works programme in an article titled "A Plan For Economic Recovery," which was published in *Economic Journal* in 1934.

[73] Thomas, *Papers on Currency and Depression*, 449.
[74] Tomlinson, *Political Economy of the Raj*, 90.
[75] Lawrence R. Klein, *The Keynesian Revolution* (London: Macmillan, 1968), 13.
[76] *Ibid.*, 32–33.
[77] *PMLC* 66, 1935, 975.

> A hundred years ago, 1825–1850, there was a prolonged depression on Southern and Western India. Prices fell rapidly, agriculturists suffered, weavers lost their occupation and public revenues diminished. After much hesitation, the Government of Madras launched on schemes of irrigation works and road making and as a result money circulated in the country, prices gently rose after 1850, public revenues improved and prosperity revived.[78]

Expenditure on irrigation was also expected to yield rich returns, leading to employment and agricultural improvement. But the government of India progressively reduced the capital outlay on irrigation too, and refrained from starting new projects. In Madras, after the Kauvery-Mettur Project no other major project was started during this period.[79] The members of the Madras Legislative Council quoted the views of economists such as Keynes and pressed for more allocation of funds under the head irrigation. But the finance member ignored their pleas and instead made a strong case for the curtailment of expenditure in irrigation.

> There is one method, which has often been mentioned in the house to stimulate purchasing power by undertaking expenditure on public works and other developmental projects. This method is worthy of consideration, but it must be directed mainly to purposes which will directly or indirectly increase the economic strength of the country and it must not be employed beyond what the credit and resources of the country will stand—for much expenditure means raising loans and paying interest upon them.[80]

The government's investment in development projects could have generated employment and accelerated future economic growth. But excessive contraction of the activities effected at the time of economic depression resulted in widespread unemployment and impoverishment. Delivering the presidential address to the nineteenth session of the Indian Economic Conference held at Dacca in 1936, Manohar Lal observed:

78 Thomas, *Papers on Currency and Depression*, 453.
79 *Indian Year Book*, 1934–35, 21: 86.
80 *G.O. No. 350 (MS) Finance Department*, 29 May 1934.

> It may be confidently asserted that in no country in the world, certainly in no large country, was Governmental endeavour to remedy depression and secure recovery so utterly non-existent as in India, for small efforts at improvement in our agricultural departments and the grant of discriminating protection to some industries constitute no part of any special programme to beat down the swelling tide of Depression.[81]

When retrenchment was proposed in Madras, it was enforced in transferred departments immediately. On the other hand, it was said that the reserved departments would not "lend themselves to the pruning knife" and hence retrenchment could be effected only step by step.[82] The government spent Rs. 30.4 million on education in 1930–31. For the year 1931–32 the budget grant under education was Rs. 26.48 million, but the actual expenditure was Rs. 24.33 million—a reduction of 12.90 per cent over one year.[83] The allotment of teaching grants for the Presidency in 1931–32 was Rs. 4,937,717, which represented a decrease of 11.6 per cent from the figures for 1930–31.[84] This was so when the number of institutions had increased. "Quite a sensation was caused," wrote *The Hindu*, "among the members of the District Educational Councils and the managers of aided elementary schools in the Presidency by the unexpected and drastic reduction in the allotment for teaching grant."[85]

As regards higher education, some block grants were given during 1929–30 to various universities; they were told in 1931 that for three years to come they would have to be satisfied with these. The block grants were meant for the day-to-day administration of the universities and hence there could be no further expansion of their spheres of activity. The University of Madras applied for a grant to open chairs for statistics, geography and physics, but the government said that they had no funds and hence the University had to be satisfied with the block grants.[86] The retrenchment effected in the Departments of Education and

[81] *Indian Annual Register*, 1936, 1: 434–35.
[82] *PMLC* 60, 1932, 375.
[83] *Report on Public Instruction in the Madras Presidency for 1931–32*, 14.
[84] *The Hindu*, 6 March 1932.
[85] *Ibid.*
[86] *PMLC* 76, 1935, 728–29.

Public Works clearly indicated that the transferred departments bore the real brunt of the economy drive of the government.

It was the lower-grade government staff that was most affected by the government's retrenchment measures. The officials and clerks who had been terminated from service by March 1932 numbered 2,993 (table 5.4).

TABLE 5.4: Government Servants Dismissed by March 1932

Category	*Number*	*Percentage of total retrenched*
Persons drawing over Rs. 500	NIL	–
Persons drawing between Rs. 250 and Rs. 500	22	0.77
Persons drawing between Rs.100 and Rs. 250	101	3.37
Persons drawing between Rs. 50 and Rs.100	262	8.75
Persons drawing between Rs. 15 and Rs. 50	1,674	55.93
Persons drawing Rs. 15 or less	933	31.18
Total	2,993	100.00

Source: *PMLC* 61, 1932, 1: 868–69.

The dismissal of lower-level servants came under fire in the press as well as in the Council. Mentioning the two armed sepoys (soldiers) on horseback standing at the gate of the Government House in Madras, a vernacular newspaper commented, "Why should not the axe of retrenchment fall on this sepoy show? Is it fair on the part of the Government who plead want of funds and advocate retrenchment to squander money like this? What right have they to let the axe fall on the poor peon, *duffador* [personal attendant of the district collector] and clerk instead of giving up vain show?"[87] It was charged that the Committee's recommendations did not impinge much upon the higher echelons of the bureaucracy. Some of the items of wasteful expenditure identified and prohibited by the Bombay Retrenchment Committee had been ignored by the Madras Committee, for which it was questioned. For instance, the Bombay Retrenchment Committee had recommended the "stoppage of the exodus of the Government to the hills" during

[87] *Sutandira Sangu*, Madras, 7 November 1931, in *Report on Native Newspapers* 47, 1931, 156.

the summer. The Madras Committee did examine this issue but resolved to permit the practice.

> The only other recommendation to which we need refer is on a subject that attracts possibly more general interest than the expenditure on it deserves, namely the annual move of Government to the hills. Our proceedings show that the total expenditure involved does not exceed about Rs. 85,000 per annum. Most of us are not among those who profess to maintain that the whole of this expenditure is unnecessary. The majority of us believe that a period spent in a congenial climate during the hottest months of the year tends to increase efficiency and also probably obviates considerable expenditure on leave allowances.[88]

The Bombay Committee had recommended that the salary of the ministers and members of the Executive Council should be reduced to Rs. 300. But the Madras Committee declined to interfere in this matter.[89] The axe of retrenchment did not fall on the police department either. On this, the Committee expressed the following view: "An efficient and contented police force is a primary necessity of good Governments. The present political situation does not, unfortunately afford a good opportunity for making large reductions and it is for this reason that we have refrained from making any recommendation in favour of a decrease in the strength of police force."[90]

The revocation of cuts in pay took precedence over all other measures of relief granted to government servants. While other economy measures continued, the 10 per cent salary cut on government servants was abandoned. The Cabinet considered the question of continuing the cut after 31 March 1933 on 4 February 1933, and it was decided to discontinue it in entirety from 1 April 1933 for all services "under the rule making powers of Local Government." As for services for which the secretary of state was responsible, like I.C.S. and I.P.S., the government of India issued orders extending the 5 per cent cut for a further

[88] *Report, Madras Retrenchment Committee*, 21.

[89] *India*, Madras, 3 December 1931, in *Report on Native Newspapers* 50, 1931, 1653.

[90] *Report, Madras Retrenchment Committee*, 30.

period of one year, i.e., up to 31 March 1934.[91] In 1933, during the budget session of the Legislative Council, the finance member made a long and laboured apologia for the refusal of the Madras government to honour the resolution of the Madras Legislative Council to give 12.5 per cent remission in land revenue. At the same time, he stoutly defended the decision of the government to lift the 10 per cent salary cut. It was urged by a majority of the members that the 5 per cent cut—which continued for All India Service personnel under the control of the government of India—should be extended to Madras state government employees. But the government turned a deaf ear to this plea. Condemning this policy of the government, *Indian Express* wrote, "We contrast the Finance Member's defense of the restoration of the salaries to his apologia against relief to people. The people might suffer and their standard of life might as well sink to nothing. But the kindly gates of the Fort St. George will protect all Government servants from the economic blizzard."[92]

It was widely felt that when the prices of foodstuffs and other articles had come down, there was no justification in keeping up the high salaries of government servants, which had been raised during the time of war when prices were high. Speaking in favour of levying a 10 per cent pay cut on a permanent basis, A. B. Shetty argued in the Council that "if there is one class of people who are today not only not affected by the present economic Depression but are even better off than what they were in previous years, it is the Government officials. Every rupee of the salary they are getting today is worth two times as much as what it was half a dozen years ago. So Government can without difficulty impose a pay cut on a permanent basis on the salaries of the servants."[93]

As the discussion for land revenue remission grew more intense, the issue of a salary cut on government employees was stressed again and again in the Legislative Council. A member argued in the Council as follows:

[91] *G.O. No. 345 (MS) Finance Department*, 28 May 1934.
[92] *Indian Express*, 25 February 1933, in *Report on Native Newspapers* 1, 1933, 61.
[93] *PMLC* 69, 1934, 179.

> Why should the ryot who was paying Rs.10 when the rice bag was worth Rs. 9 or Rs. 8 pay the very same amount of Rs.10 as kist now when the rice bag is selling at Rs. 2-8-0 or Rs. 3? Why should the receiver of Government money, I mean the Government official, receive the same sum of Rs.100 as before, now that the money value in terms of purchasing power has risen two-fold or three-fold?[94]

But the government rejected the views of the members, saying that the salary cut should be considered an extreme measure, and should be adopted only when all others failed.

Government's Monetary Policy

On 21 September 1931, the British government announced its decision to abandon the gold standard.[95] The government of India took immediate action by issuing an ordinance relieving themselves from the obligation under the Currency Act of 1927, and the three days 22, 23 and 24 September were declared public holidays under the Negotiable Instruments Act.[96] On 24 September the decision to link the rupee to sterling at the existing ratio, 1s. 6d., was announced and a new ordinance was issued, canceling the earlier ordinance.[97] Thus when the pound sterling was forced off gold, the rupee also went off; but it was kept tied to the pound. Had the rupee been left to itself, it might have fallen lower and caused loss to sterling capital. Hence the rupee was linked to sterling so that British capital might not suffer in India.[98] The nationalists stoutly opposed the sterling link, stating that India should have her freedom to regulate the currency in her own interest. They held the view that while the value of the rupee in terms of sterling remained intact, its value in terms of the currencies of countries that still remained on gold suffered diminution, and the benefit of that difference in value went to the British exporter in the Indian market.[99] The

94 *Ibid.*, 264.
95 Thomas, *Growth of Federal Finance in India*, 360.
96 *Ibid.*
97 *Ibid.*
98 Nehru, *Glimpses of World History*, 902.
99 Thomas, *Papers on Currency and Depression*, 237.

Congress Working Committee, which met at Delhi on 27, 28 and 29 October 1931, condemned the monetary policy of the government of India.

> The Working Committee is of the opinion that the currency and exchange policy recently adopted by the Government of India in complete disregard of Indian opinion and at the behest of the British Government, linking the rupee to the pound sterling, instead of leaving it to find its own level in terms of gold, is conceived solely in the interests of Britain so as to provide, inter alia, a back door calculated to work against the interests of the masses of India, in as much as it depletes the already too slender gold resources of this country and is bound to embarrass India both in regard to the early establishment of a Reserve Bank and the due settlement of foreign obligations. The Working Committee warns the British Government that the responsibility for pursuing such a selfish policy should rest entirely on its own shoulders and that the injurious results accruing to India therefrom would be duly taken into account in the settlement of financial obligations between India and England.[100]

The *Indian Annual Register* remarked, "The 18d. ratio had been at gold point. That had kept the poor rupee at least a dependable thing. Wedded to a gold standard it was respectable. But a simple decree from Whitehall divorced the Indian rupee from its natural and respectable alliance with gold and wedded it to the erratic sterling. The linking of the rupee with the fluctuating sterling made it lose its domicile, as it was called, its natural level in the world market."[101] But the secretary of state for India, Sir Samuel Hoare, defended the government's decision by saying, "Since the fixing of the rupee by Statute at 1s. 6d., sterling has until today been synonymous with gold and for all practical purposes the stability of the Indian exchange has been based on sterling. The Indian trade is financed through sterling. The greatest part of India's external obligations is in terms of sterling. . . . It has therefore been decided to maintain the present currency standard on a sterling basis."[102]

[100] Zaidi & Zaidi, *Encyclopaedia of Indian National Congress*, 10: 211.
[101] *Indian Annual Register*, 1931, 2: 57.
[102] Thomas, *Papers on Currency and Depression*, 237–38.

The suspension of the gold standard by the British government and the correlative action of the government of India caused "a good deal of excitement in commercial circles in Madras City; but there was no political reaction of any kind and no run on any bank."[103] In the conditions then existing, no country could remain in the gold standard unless it had abnormally large gold reserves like the USA. As a debtor country with large foreign obligations, with her export trade exposed to various trade barriers, and with no central bank, it would have been impossible for India to remain an independent standard.[104] Therefore the only alternative left to her was the sterling standard. But the sterling link would not necessarily mean the maintenance of an 18d. ratio. While fixing the value of the rupee in relation to the sterling, Britain had sacrificed the Indian interests to further her own interests in 1927. When the government wanted to fix the value at 1s. 6d., Indian opinion wanted it at 1s. 4d. In spite of the Indian opinion the government unilaterally fixed one-and-six as the gold-rupee value. An upward revaluation of Indian currency in relation to the British pound basically made Indian exports costlier and imports cheaper. This compounded the matter and the Southern India Chamber of Commerce highlighted this aspect in its annual report of 1930.

> Our trouble did not commence with October 1929 as some interested people would have us believe. They struck their roots several years ago, when in a fateful moment, a ridiculously narrow majority of the Legislative Assembly consisting of the solid Government phalanx of nominated members with a handful of elected members walked into the 18d. lobby against the vital interest of the millions of India.[105]

The available evidence suggests that the rupee was overvalued during the period of the Depression. Taking 1923 as the base year, the lowest level of the wholesale price index reached in England showed a fall of 36.3 per cent in 1932, whereas the lowest level reached by the wholesale price index in India showed a fall of 40 per cent. Again, whereas by 1936 the wholesale price

[103] *Fortnightly Reports,* second half of September 1931.
[104] Mukerjee and Dey, *Economic Problems, Modern India*, 2: 233.
[105] *Report, Southern India Chamber of Commerce,* 1930, 3–4.

index in England had recovered to the extent of 16.3 per cent, the corresponding figure for India remained 5.7 per cent.[106] M. Jamal Mohamad Saib, president of Southern India Chamber of Commerce and of the Federation of Indian Chambers of Commerce and Industry, wrote in *The Hindu* criticising the government's currency policy. This created widespread interest among the people in India, and the Associated Press of India therefore obtained a detailed interview from him on the currency situation. When the interviewer asked whether he objected to the linking of the rupee to sterling, Jamal Mohamad said:

> It is not the sterling-rupee link we object to, but to the unnatural artificial ratio at which it is linked at present. We do realise that the multifarious relationship between India and Great Britain does require the linking of the rupee to sterling, one of the greatest international currencies of the world. But the link should be at a rate suitable to the economic interests of this country.[107]

The press reporter shot back: "England having gone off the gold standard in 1931, sterling had depreciated by about 33 per cent, the rupee had also depreciated to the extent of being linked to sterling. Haven't you therein some depreciation of the rupee already and has not that done some good to us?" The president of the Chamber of Commerce then elaborated his point of view. "Yes, there was a depreciation and it did benefit us to some extent. But unfortunately its benefit was very much restricted for obvious reasons. In this connection it must be remembered that the rupee was appreciated by 12.5 per cent before England went off the gold standard. So the net depreciation of the rupee compared to countries still on the gold standard comes to only about 21 per cent as against the 33.25 per cent depreciation of the sterling."[108]

The countries which were directly involved in World War I had depreciated their currencies after the war. For instance, Australia and New Zealand had depreciated their currencies by

[106] Mukerjee and Dey, *Economic Problems, Modern India*, 2: 89.
[107] *Tragedy of the 18d Rupee*, 65.
[108] *Ibid.*

25 per cent. Since Britain's departure from the gold standard, Japan and United States of America had considerably depreciated their currencies (table 5.5).

TABLE 5.5: Depreciation of Currencies since the War, in 1933 (in percentage)

British pound	33.33
Australian pound	47
New Zealand pound	47
Canadian dollar	33
American dollar	33
Japanese yen	41

Source: *Tragedy of the 18d Rupee*, 67–68.

When nationalists were advocating a devaluation of the rupee, the colonial rulers argued that devaluation would be a dangerous step because "it would provoke counter-devaluation on the part of other nations, so that in the end it will, like a boomerang, recoil with double force upon the country that started the race of depreciation."[109] The economist H. L. Dey, professor and head of the Department of Economics and Politics, Dacca University, refuted this viewpoint:

> I don't think that this objection to devaluation is a well-founded one. For, if it is a fact that many countries followed each other in rapid succession in adopting the method of devaluation, it was done largely with a view to obtaining quick relief from the intolerable strain caused to economic structure of these countries by the heavy pressure of deflation during the period. Great Britain, U.S.A. and France—these three leading creditor nations—have devalued their currencies and yet the final verdict of world opinion has been that actions have been appropriate and even wise.[110]

In order to maintain the rupee ratio at 1s. 6d. the government of India adopted the policy of contracting the currency. By March

[109] H. L. Dey, "The Rupee-Ratio Controversy," *Modern Review* 61, no. 5, 1937, 558.
[110] *Ibid.*, 559.

1932 circulating currency was 82 per cent of its March 1929 level.[111] In 1928–29 total circulating currency had been Rs. 4,940 million.[112] The government withdrew Rs. 400 million in 1929–30, Rs. 330 million in 1930–31, and a further Rs. 250 million between April and August 1931. It was to aid the internal credit networks that the finance member of the government of India, George Schuster, suggested devaluation in September 1931 to reflate the internal money supply. But the imperial government in London did not accept the proposal of devaluation of the rupee.[113] It has to be noted here that Great Britain around this time was making all effort to reflate her currency. Withdrawal of money from circulation affected the rural credit system. P. V. Krishnayya Choudari spoke about it in the Madras Legislative Council:

> Now the banks are not giving any loans to the ryots. Even if we deposit paddy, the Imperial Bank gives only 14 annas or one rupee. They do not advance more. Though we have several co-operative banks in the last two years, they do not give any advance towards the maintenance of the land or towards the payment of land revenue.[114]

The prominent citizens of Madras held a meeting at the Gokhale Hall on 6 November 1933, to protest against the monetary policy of the government. There they formed an organisation called "Madras Currency League." The object of this organisation was "to work for the attainment of a national Currency and Exchange policy in the country." The Madras Currency League in one of its meetings held in the Gokhale Hall passed a resolution favouring devaluation of the rupee and forwarded it to the government.

> This public meeting of the citizens of Madras strongly disapproves the apathy and indifference shown by the Government of India on the question of devaluing the rupee in line with the other countries of the world and demands the immediate devaluation of the rupee in the best economic interests of the country.[115]

[111] Tomlinson, *Political Economy of the Raj*, 86.
[112] *Ibid.*, 85.
[113] *Ibid.*, 86.
[114] *PMLC* 64, 1939, 217.
[115] *Tragedy of the 18d Rupee*, 107.

The Madras Currency League mobilised public opinion in favour of lowering the exchange value of the rupee. As a result of the efforts taken by the League, Anantasayanam Iyengar of Madras moved an adjournment motion in the Legislative Assembly on 8 October 1935. The motion was left to vote and it resulted in a tie, with fifty-two voting on each side. The speaker of the Assembly, Sir Abdur Rahim, gave his casting vote in favour of the government.[116] So the motion was lost. Jamal Mohamad gave a press note explaining the reason for the defeat of the motion: "If any one takes the trouble to analyse the votes recorded for the contention of the government in both the cases, one would have no difficulty in assessing the true value to be attached to these votes. They are composed mostly of Government officials and nominated members who are in the nature of things obliged to vote with the Government."[117]

India compensated for the loss of export value not by devaluation, but by export of gold. The abandonment of the gold standard by India put a premium on gold. As the rupee fell in value with the pound, the internal price of gold went up. Gold could fetch more rupees now. The greatest hardship and privation in the country induced people to sell whatever gold they possessed. The peasant had always invested his savings in gold, and those reserves were intended for use in a lean time. When the lean times arrived in the form of the Depression, the stored gold was brought to the market for sale. Gold flowed from all over the country to the banks, who made a profit by selling it in the London market. The statutory price of gold in India was Rs. 21-3-10 per *tola* (a measure of weight, less than .5 ounce), much lower than the actual price. Owing to the depreciation of sterling, and consequently of the rupee, the actual price of gold was as high as Rs. 29-7-0 per tola. By exporting gold one could gain about Rs. 8-3-0 per tola (38 per cent).[118]

Many countries that had gone off the gold standard had put an embargo on the export of gold. It was the efflux of gold from the Bank of England that prompted England to abandon the gold

[116] *Ibid.*, 31 & 85.
[117] *Ibid.*, 85.
[118] Thomas, *Growth of Federal Finance in India*, 365.

standard. Since then it had taken measures to prevent the flight of gold. The United States of America, with more than seven billion dollars' worth of gold in its vaults, put an embargo on the export of gold.[119] But in India, the flight of gold was permitted without hindrance. A national government in India would have kept this gold in reserve, as gold was the only recognised medium of payment. But India's finance member characterised the distressing export of gold from India as "a pleasing phenomenon."[120] In his budget speech of March 1932, Sir George Schuster observed, "We are absolutely certain that in the present circumstances the best interests of India are being served by allowing free movement of gold to continue."[121] On the other hand, it was maintained by the nationalists that the export of gold was in the highest degree injurious to the nation, and they wanted the government to take measures to buy the gold. The Federation of Indian Chambers of Commerce and Industry gave expression to this view in a resolution passed on 26 March 1932. The Federation, while voicing its grave concern over the continuous and heavy exports of gold from India, warned that such a drain of the precious metal would seriously endanger India's future monetary reconstruction. It urged the government of India to place an immediate embargo on the export of gold and purchase gold in the open market at a price fixed on the basis of a day-to-day ruling rate.[122]

But the British could point to the doctrine of free trade, which always came in handy. The government defended itself against the Indian nationalists' criticism for not intervening to stop the flow of gold.[123] Justifying the government's refusal to restrict gold exports, Sir George Schuster explained that "India could not with exports at their present level support the present volume of imports simultaneously with meeting her external obligations

[119] *The Hindu*, 1 March 1932.

[120] Thomas, *Papers on Currency and Depression*, 242.

[121] *Indian Annual Register* 1, 1933, 211–12.

[122] Mukerjee and Dey, *Economic Problems, Modern India,* 2:249.

[123] Proceedings of the Federation of Indian Chambers of Commerce and Industry, quoted in B. R. Shenoy, "The Rupee-Sterling Ratio and the Export of Gold," in *Economic Problems, Modern India*, eds. Mukerjee and Dey, 249–50.

unless they are supplemented by gold exports."[124] According to Schuster, a reduction of imports meant loss of customs revenue, which as the mainstay of central government finance would hit the budgetary position.[125]

However, the contemporary scholars were critical of the government's monetary policy and pointed out the grave nature of the issue involved. H. L. Dey, for instance, observed: "Gold and land are two forms on which wealth is stored in India and they are sold only in the last extremity of the distress and not on account of the profit motive, though of course the profit motive stimulated the bullion dealers to collect and export this gold on a large scale."[126] The leading Tamil newspaper *Swarajya* wrote, "To private speculators, Sir George Schuster's policy is nothing short of a veritable godsend for making quick and easy fortunes. . . . The gold that is exported is not the gold that is usually brought to sale by the middle and higher classes, it is what the poor ryot is obliged to take to the market and sell, either out of private necessity, or to raise the revenue due to Government."[127] Contesting the claim of the finance member that the proceeds of gold realised by Indian sellers had been transferred to interest-bearing investments, the *Indian Annual Register* wrote:

> It seems he [finance member] has ignored the fundamental fact that the average Indian is not likely to bring into market his gold ornaments unless he is compelled by circumstances to meet daily wants. Thus a portion of the sum realised by the sale of gold must have gone to the moneylenders from the pockets of the agriculturists and small holders of gold articles, which the greater part of the remaining sum had to be exchanged for commodities. This process of forced sale of gold led to the increase of British imports in the country, which was wished for both by the Finance Member and the manufacturers in his country.[128]

[124] D. Rothermund, "British Foreign Trade Policy in India during the Great Depression, 1929–1931," *Indian Economic and Social History Review* 18, nos. 3 & 4, 1981, 371.
[125] J. C. Sinha, *Indian Currency Problems in the Last Decade, 1926–1936* (Delhi: University of Delhi, 1938), 119.
[126] *Ibid.*
[127] Mukerjee and Dey, *Economic Problems, Modern India,* 149.
[128] *Swarajya*, 8 October 1931, in *Report on Native Newspapers* 40, 1931, 1336; *Indian Annual Register*, 1933, 1:197.

The economist P. S. Narayana Prasad's pithy comment in the *Indian Journal of Economics* is worth quoting here: "The consumption of capital has been allowed and it should not be surprising at all if this bill, drawn on hope, is likely to be heavily discounted by experience."[129] The final outcome of all such protests is brilliantly summed up by H. L. Dey:

> So keenly did a section of opinion in the country feel on the subject that, seeing that the Executive was against them and the legislature beyond their control or powerless to assist them, they drew upon the technique of satyagraha (passive resistance) to prevent the shipping of gold from the country! But with police and the economic forces ranged against them, these attempts resulted in little more than traffic congestion.[130]

Fallout of Government's Policy of Balancing the Budget

The enormous flow of gold from India enabled Britain to reflate her currency in England. It also enhanced the creditworthiness of the government of India, enabling it to borrow at low rates of interest. The government could have used this opportunity to borrow money for investment. But the colonial government made no such effort. Instead, it resorted to a ruthless deflationary policy. This was at a time when most of the countries were making bold economic experiments with borrowed money to tide over the crisis. The finance member's statement on the floor of the Legislative Assembly in 1930, hinting at the broad principles to which the government was committed, continued to be the governing creed even in the midst of deepened crisis: "I feel, moreover, most strongly, on general grounds, that this is not the time when, keeping in view our credit in the world, we ought to attempt any substantial diminution in our provision for reduction or avoidance of debt. Anything that savours of a 'raid' on a public sinking fund is normally and I think, quite rightly, viewed with disfavour."[131]

[129] P. S. Narayana Prasad, "World Depression in India," *Indian Journal of Economics* 16, 1935–36, 121–44.
[130] Mukerjee and Dey, *Economic Problems, Modern India,* 238.
[131] Quoted in Bagchi, *Private Investment in India*, 46.

The government not only avoided debt but was able to reduce the burden of public debt in India. The government's floating debt fell from Rs. 840 million in September 1931 to Rs. 350 million in 1933.[132] Public debt to the tune of £35.7 million was repaid between 1934–35 and 1938–39.[133] The government of India prohibited the provinces from drawing from the provincial loan accounts for new schemes. However, it made an exception of the Kauvery-Mettur Project and allowed advances for its completion. Since the balance that had piled up during the remission of contributions was considerable, it was felt by the nationalists that it was justifiable to put it to use—instead of applying to the government of India for advances, or floating a loan for funding capital expenditure schemes.[134] The finance member of the Madras government, G. T. H. Bracken, however, argued that "national finance is not in essence different from the finances of individuals," because "both nations and individuals have to balance their budgets or they land themselves in difficulties."[135] So debt was avoided to a maximum extent in Madras during this period (table 5.6).

TABLE 5.6: Amount Borrowed by Madras Government, 1931–37

	Amount borrowed (In Rs. million)	*Amount repaid*	*Amount outstanding*
1. For the Kauvery-Mettur Project	61.33	0.24	61.09
2. For other purposes	74.04	65.10	8.95
Total	135.37	65.34	70.03

Source: Meenakshi, "Finance of Madras Government."

132 Thomas, *Growth of Federal Finance in India,* 364.
133 A. K. Banerji, *India's Balance of Payments: 1921–22 to 1938–39* (London: Asia Publishing House, 1963), 81, 171, 175.
134 Meenakshi, "Finance of Madras Government."
135 Budget speech of 1936, quoted in Meenakshi, "Finance of Madras Government."

The government's fiscal policy yielded the "desired" results. The heavy taxation and the government's financial policy unbalanced the budgets of private individuals, but the government budget closed with a comfortable surplus in the years after 1931–32 (table 5.7).

TABLE 5.7: Budgetary Position of Madras Government, 1930–31 to 1935–36
(In Rs. million)

Year	*Revenue*	*Expenditure*	*Surplus (+) or deficit(-)*
1930–31	168.39	178.97	- 10.58
1931–32	162.99	162.45	+ 0.54
1932–33	164.02	156.30	+ 7.72
1933–34	155.03	154.40	+ 0.63
1934–35	156.26	155.17	+ 1.09
1935–36	158.83	158.34	+ 0.49

Source: *Report, Administration of Madras Presidency*, 1930 to 1936.

A government review described the period from 1932–33 to 1935–36 as follows: "The final phase of financial administration under Dyarchy has been a period of suspense, sometimes hopeful and more often the reverse and though we have escaped serious mishap, the outlook has been growing more and more gloomy and whether there will be improvement or whether a period of strife and struggle is on the horizon, it is not easy to predict."[136] The accountant general's report on the appropriation accounts of the Madras government for 1933–34 said, "The finances of the Madras Government are in a better position than those of any other province."[137] In other provinces, with the exception of Punjab, there were budgetary deficits, indicating that there were attempts to offer relief to the people hit by the Depression (table 5.8).

[136] *G.O. No. 327 (MS) Finance Department*, 13 May 1935.
[137] *The Hindu*, 18 May 1935

TABLE 5.8: Revenue Surplus or Deficit of Each Province, 1921–22 to 1935–36

	Surplus (+) Deficit (-) (in Rs. million)				
	From 1921–22 to 1932–33	*1933–34*	*1934–35*	*1935–36*	*Total*
Madras	+ 54.5	+ 0.6	- 1.9	+ 0.5	+ 53.7
Bombay	- 58.2	+ 1.7	- 1.7	- 0.2	- 58.9
Bengal	- 57.6	- 17.6	- 2.7	- 6.8	- 84.7
United Provinces	- 34.2	- 0.3	- 0.9	- 3.0	- 38.4
Punjab	+ 6.5	+ 6.3	+ 4.3	+ 0.9	+ 18.0
Burma	- 106.5	- 13.7	+ 2.8	- 9.3	- 126.7
Bihar and Orissa	- 5.8	- 0.8	+ 0.6	- 1.7	- 7.7
Central Provinces	- 11.6	- 3.9	- 1.1	..	- 16.6
North West Frontier Province	+ 0.2	+ 0.5	- 0.6	- 1.2	- 1.1
Assam	- 4.1	- 3.5	- 4.2	- 5.6	- 17.4

Source: *G.O. No. 28 (MS) Finance Department,* 23 January 1936.

In 1935–36 the revenue anticipated was estimated at Rs. 158.24 million and accordingly the expenditure was moderated and fixed at Rs. 158.61 million.[138] The year 1936–37 was viewed by Finance Member G. T. H. Bracken with "hesitant hope." He said: "The trend of the provincial revenues has at last been arrested and we shall almost at once be on the upward curve."[139] While some of the provinces had been living beyond their income in the period from 1921–22 to 1929–30, the Madras government was able to accumulate a considerable balance, which placed it in a rather more favourable position to meet the crisis than any other province in India. The fact that land revenue had been arbitrarily fixed on a cash basis without any relation to prices also helped the provincial government to save itself from bankruptcy. It is noteworthy that land revenue had decreased from 1930–31 through 1933–34 only by Rs. 2.4 million, after giving special revenue remissions (table 5. 9).

[138] *G.O. No. 327 (MS) Finance Department,* 13 May 1935.

[139] Budget speech of 1936–37, quoted in Meenakshi, "Finance of Madras Government."

TABLE 5.9: Loss of Revenue on Account of Land Revenue Remission

Years	*Total loss (in Rs. million)*	*Distribution over financial years* 1932–1933	1933–1934	1934–1935	1935–1936	1936–1937
Fasli 1342	3.34	1.07	2.27			
Fasli 1343	6.16		4.15	2.01		
Fasli 1344	5.55			4.81	0.74	
Fasli 1345	5.47				4.59	0.88
Total	20.52	1.07	6.42	6.82	5.33	0.88

Source: *G.O. No. 28 (MS) Finance Department*, 23 January 1936

Summary

To summarise, the Depression hit the state exchequer, as income under revenue heads such as excise and stamps declined precipitously. The collection of land revenue in particular became problematic. The government counteracted the crisis by resorting to increased taxation and retrenchment. The economy measures recommended by the Retrenchment Committee resulted in drastic retrenchment in government departments. Retrenchment effected in the Departments of Public Works and Education clearly indicates that the development activities, which remained under the Transferred Half, were very much curtailed. The government's adherence to an orthodox policy of sound finance ran counter to the Keynesian doctrine that advocated stimulation of a depressed economy through capital investment schemes to provide employment. This foreclosed the option of introducing any major public works programmes, which might have mitigated the severity of the Depression.

It was the employees at the lower level who were most affected by the policy of retrenchment in pay and services. On the other hand, the 10 per cent pay cut imposed on government servants was revoked in Madras even before the central government withdrew its order of pay cut on its employees. The provincial government justified the decision on grounds of financial well-being, though the genuine reason was probably that the government, while functioning as a law and order administration, had to depend on the goodwill of the bureaucracy.

The heavy surcharges imposed by an emergency budget on income tax, supertax and customs duties strained the business community. At the same time, the agriculturists who demanded relief in the form of land revenue remission were treated unsympathetically. The forcible collection of land revenue and the rigid resettlement policy followed put them to misery. The government's financial policy, symbolised by overvaluation of the rupee and objection to devaluation, only added to the Depression and aggravated it. Most of the agricultural countries in the context of a worsening balance of trade seem to have reacted with a devaluation of currency to provide relief to agriculturists and traders. But in India the government's refusal to devalue the rupee to 1s. 4d., and its withdrawal of currency from circulation to maintain the rupee at 1s. 6d., deprived the Indians of such relief. The British government's decision that the rupee should be on a sterling standard at 1s. 6d. created a premium in the price of gold, leading to its export. The substantial gold exports enabled the government of India to make remittances and meet all its commitments in London. Despite nationalist opposition to the drain of gold, the government did not make any efforts to stop the flow of the precious metal since it served the imperial interests.

The governments in the West took to borrowing and deficit budgeting to combat the Depression. Contrary to this, the government of India refrained from borrowing and avoided loan expenditure. The policy of extreme financial stringency helped to restore budgetary equilibrium in the province, but it dealt a debilitating blow to the impoverished people and their country.

6

The Government's Remedial Measures

In several Western countries, governments had provided financial support to farmers in order to ease the burden of debt. Radical agrarian measures had been adopted to provide relief to the peasants. For example, the United States of America, through the Farm Relief Act, earmarked two billion dollars to give mortgage loans to farmers at 5 per cent interest. This enabled the farmers to settle mortgages carrying higher rates of interest.[1] Through the Agricultural Adjustment Act of 1933 the US government financially compensated farmers who came forward to restrict production and thereby help reduce the acreage under cultivation in the country.[2] In Germany a law was passed in 1933 to provide special assistance to the agriculturists, in order to clear debts contracted before 1931. In Italy, agriculturists' debts had been converted into twenty-five-year mortgages, while in Austria, encumbered agricultural property was protected from forced sale, under certain conditions. In several states of Australia, the right to sell mortgaged property had been restricted by legislation. Judicial courts were set up in Holland to negotiate between agricultural debtors and creditors.[3] In these and many other countries measures had been adopted to postpone debt claims, give priority to new loans, convert short-term obligations into long-term ones, negotiate rent reductions, and convert rents of fixed value into yearly payments depending upon the value of farm produce.[4]

1 P. J. Thomas, "The Problem of Rural Indebtedness," *Indian Journal of Economics* 14, 1933–34, 450–51.

2 Rothermund, *Global Impact of Great Depression,* 57.

3 *Ibid.*

4 *Ibid.*

George Schuster, despite his support for the drain of gold, showed undeterred enthusiasm for the development of a new economic policy, to meet the grave situation arising out of the Depression. Schuster's consultations with his colleagues on ways to tone up the economy, his communiqué to provincial governments calling for specific schemes of intervention, and finally his ardent plea for devaluation of currency, indicate that at least some of the well-meaning officers of the colonial administration were concerned about the need for remedial measures.[5] But as we have seen in chapter 5, the imperial interests prevailed over all other considerations. When Sir James Grigg succeeded Schuster even the fig leaf was absent.[6] In this chapter we assess the steps taken by the Madras government to combat the effects of the Depression.

Protests by Peasant Interests

The Madras government, relying on the reports of the district collectors, initially did not take a serious view of the Depression. The secretary in the Department of Commerce of the government of India addressed a letter to the chief secretary to the Madras government on 2 August 1930, calling for a report on the economic condition of the Presidency in the wake of the fall in prices. The government of Madras called for reports from district collectors. On the basis of their reports it wrote to the government of India, saying that "the reports received from the collectors of districts and the Director of Agriculture do not indicate that there is any ground for apprehending anything like a serious economic crisis in this Presidency owing to the fall in prices."[7] The report further stated that "the ease with which the land revenue has been collected, in spite of sharp decline of prices, suggests that the ryots have so far not been very seriously hit by

[5] Tomlinson, *Political Economy of the Raj,* 88–89.

[6] As one committed to the orthodox principle of balancing the budget, he started denouncing Keynesian concepts openly. See Tomlinson, *Political Economy of the Raj*, 88–89.

[7] *Proceedings of Board of Revenue, No. 3315 (Mis.),* 10 November 1930.

the low prices. The land revenue for 1929–30 was collected without any difficulty."[8] The fact, however, was that the agriculturists and traders were conveying their distress through numerous petitions and memoranda, while the legislators were articulating their alarm in the legislature.

Crushing burden of indebtedness, forcible collection of land revenue, and heavy incidence of railway freight were brought to the notice of the government by the peasant organisations and the trader associations. The responses of the government officials to their pleas and prayers were unsympathetic and dismissive. On the problem of indebtedness, the Tiruchirappally District Landowners' and Agriculturists' Association presented a memorandum to the provincial government.

> Coincident with the agricultural and financial Depressions, agricultural indebtedness has reached a crucial point when it is no longer possible for the ryots to meet their obligations from their agricultural income. Value of lands had become considerably deflated owing to the fall in the commodity prices and the absence of buyers; but the agriculturists' debt continues to reach mounting proportions. Agricultural indebtedness is inevitable, perhaps, in view of the fact that the capital invested in agriculture rarely brings in a three per cent return, while even the co-operative credit societies require nine per cent interest for the money which they loan out to the ryots. . . . It is scarcely an exaggeration to say that the entire agricultural population is on the verge of a serious collapse which if left unchecked would add hundreds of thousands to the ranks of the starving and the unemployed.[9]

In the memorandum, the Association had drawn the attention of the Madras government to the appointment of a committee of enquiry in the province of Burma to investigate the problem of agricultural indebtedness and suggest measures of amelioration. It wanted the government of India to set up such a committee in other provinces. The collector of Tiruchirappalli, through whom the memorandum was submitted, observed in his remarks to the government, "I personally think it [appointment of enquiry

8 *Ibid.*

9 Extract from the memorandum in *G.O. No. 1450 (MS) Development Department*, 9 November 1932.

committee] will have no useful purpose."[10] The Development Department also thought that it would be a waste of time and money to have a committee of enquiry on the subject of agricultural indebtedness.[11]

As a matter of fact the Royal Commission on Agriculture had recommended that each province might consider passing a simple rural insolvency act for waiving overdue loans. According to the proponents of this measure, when a person's debt was such that the yield of his or her land for about fifteen years was not sufficient to clear it, that person was a fit case for insolvency.[12] But the governor of Madras remarked that he "could not understand how a legislation would help people to wipe off their debts, as no one could legislate that a person should not pay his debts or that his debts should be free of interest."[13]

The government's inaction in the face of mounting incidence of indebtedness, despite growing public opinion for a comprehensive debt relief scheme to agriculturists, provoked a discussion in the Legislative Council. But the government remained stubbornly indifferent. While answering a call attention motion raised by a member, the revenue member replied that "No collector has recommended any special measure of relief."[14] Reacting to the suggestion that "where a man had paid twice the capital by way of interest, capital and interest should be wiped off," the finance member argued that "The problem of indebtedness is one of immense difficulty and has many reactions and I may say that our present view is that a solution is not likely to be found by any heroic attempts to equip India in the midst of the crisis with some entirely new credit system different to that which had grown up as a result of centuries of experience."[15]

The Southern India Chamber of Commerce addressed a petition in 1931 to the viceroy on the issue of land revenue remission.

10 *G.O. No. 1450 (MS) Development Department,* 9 November 1932.
11 *Ibid.*
12 V. L. D'Souza, "Agricultural Debts and Depression," *Indian Review* 35, no. 7, 1934, 462.
13 *Ibid.*
14 *PMLC* 66, 1933, 427.
15 *G.O. No. 350 (MS) Finance Department,* 29 May 1934.

> Ever since the world Depression . . . the prices that ruled more or less steadily throughout the period in respect of several commodities have been uneconomic and below cost of production, so that the agriculturists have had nothing left to maintain themselves with or to meet their ordinary monetary commitments in the shape of land revenue or educational expenses or interest charges and so on. . . . In order to help the people to tide over such a difficult situation several of the provincial Governments notably the Governments of the United Provinces, the Punjab and Bengal are reported to have given considerable relief to the ryots in the form of agricultural loans and remissions of land revenues and cesses. The Government of Madras have not so far provided any particular relief to the ryots of this Presidency who have sustained the heaviest loss in the whole of India by the decline in the prices of oil seeds, rice and grains which are their most important staples.[16]

It is evident from the above memorandum that the government of Madras was lagging behind other provinces in terms of initiating remedial measures. But the viceroy in his reply to the Chamber asserted that "In Madras, the prevailing rates of assessment are so moderate in proportion to the value of the crops that even with prices at their present low level the ryot has so far experienced little or no difficulty in paying his land revenue."[17] The viceroy concluded by saying that he was "confident that the Government of Madras is watching the situation with keen sympathy and anxiety, and that it is always ready to consider any measure likely to relieve distress wherever it prevails; but neither the Local Government nor the Government of India can do much of an effective nature to combat the world economic Depression which is a problem exceedingly difficult of solution."[18]

When George Schuster was the finance member, he had sought the opinion of his department about the desirability of granting land revenue remission to the agriculturists in the wake of the fall in prices of agricultural produce.[19] The unanimous opinion expressed by his colleagues was that remission of land revenue

[16] Text of the Memorandum in *Report, Southern India Chamber of Commerce,* 1931, 95–100.

[17] Text of the reply of viceroy in *Report, Southern India Chamber of Commerce,* 1931, 95–100.

[18] *Ibid.*

[19] Rothermund, "Great Depression and British Financial Policy in India," 2–3.

could be claimed only when the crops failed. It was further clarified that fluctuations in prices had always been taken into consideration at the time of settlements, and just as the government would not claim additional revenue when the prices were rising, it need not reduce its charge on land when prices were falling.[20] When there was a unanimous demand from the members of the Legislative Council for an increased remission to relieve the hardships of the agriculturists, the revenue member in Madras asked why the agriculturists had not saved enough in prosperous days so as to tide over a period of stress.[21] The Thanjavur collector for his part went on record, saying that "prompt and coercive measures against defaulters" were all that was necessary.[22]

Apart from debt relief and land revenue remission, the agriculturists also demanded reduction in railway freight. The existing rates of railway freight proved to be the chief handicap to the marketing of crops. The Tanjore Delta Mirasidars' Conference passed a resolution to that effect and forwarded it to the government of Madras as early as 1931.

> This Conference brings to the notice of the Government that in spite of the low prices prevailing there is considerable slump of paddy in this district and the Mirasidars have not been able to market the same at any reasonable price and as such the only way to give temporary relief will be to reduce the existing heavy Railway Freight for paddy and other agricultural produce and to afford special facilities for the transport of the same to Colombo, West Coast districts, Salem, Coimbatore and other places and as such requests the Government to interfere and the railway authorities to reduce the railway freight by at least 50 per cent and to give special facilities for transport.[23]

When the question of reduction of railway freight was taken up with the railway authorities, they asked whether the government would follow the practice prevalent in Punjab of guaranteeing the railway company any loss consequent on

20 *Ibid.*

21 *Swadesamitran,* 26 February 1935, in *Report on Native Newspapers* 3, 1935,165–66.

22 *Fortnightly Reports,* second half of February 1934.

23 *G.O. No. 2142 Ry. (MS) Public Works and Labour Department,* 24 August 1931.

reduction of freights. When this was referred to the Public Works and Labour Department, it was noted that "such a course was not possible in the present financial stringency."[24]

Government's Initial Response

In the wake of escalating economic crisis, the first positive action of the government of Madras was appointment of a committee of officials and non-officials to conduct an enquiry. On 16 January 1931, the Madras Oil Seeds and Ryotwari Association called on the governor, to represent to him the depressed condition of the groundnut trade. In response, the government decided to form a committee of officials and non-officials, to examine whether some system of co-operative marketing of the Madras groundnut crop could be devised and organised. At the same time, the government also wanted to know how far the economic conditions of the agriculturists of the Presidency had been affected by the fall of agricultural prices. It decided—in supersession of the earlier decision—to appoint an Economic Depression Enquiry Committee, to probe into the effects of the Depression and to report whether any measures should be adopted by the government to mitigate them.[25]

The Committee consisted of the following officials: Commissioner of Land Revenue (chairman) H. A. B. Vernon, Director of Industries A. Appadurai, Director of Agriculture G. R. Hilson, Chief Conservator of Forests R. D. Richmond, and Registrar of Co-operative Societies D. N. Strathic. The collector of Madras, H. M. Hood, was appointed to serve as secretary to the Committee. The non-officials of the Committee were: H. F. Carter from the Eastern Bank Ltd., Madras, and C. D. Priestly of the Imperial Chemical Industries (India) Ltd., Madras (a European banker and European merchant, respectively, nominated by the Madras Chamber of Commerce); M. A. Muthiah Chettiyar and Sami Venkatachalam Chetty, M. L. C.

[24] *G.O. No. 2142 Ry. (MS) Public Works and Labour Department,* 24 August 1931.

[25] *G.O. No. 328 Revenue Department* (Confidential), 11 February 1931.

(an Indian banker and Indian merchant, respectively, nominated by the Southern India Chamber of Commerce); raja of Paḷakimedi and raja of Ramnad (representing zamindars); T. K. Doraiswamy Ayyar, professor of economics, Annamalai University, K. P. Raman Menon, M.L.C.; A. Ranganatha Mudaliyar and M. R. Sethuraman (both ex–Justice Party ministers), Kumararaja of Chettinadu, C. V. Venkatarama Ayyengar, Srinivasan, M.L.C., M. S. Sreshta, M.L.C., Hota Suryanarayana and D. Seshagiri Rao Pantulu.[26]

The appointment of a committee to conduct enquiries, when the situation warranted radical action, came under severe criticism. The *Tamil Nadu* wrote: "We are glad at the Government taking such an interest in the matter. But no one can deny that when a person asks for water when he is about to die it is foolishness to offer it to him only after a committee has been appointed and it has made enquiry. Committees should of course be appointed for matters which need them. But when an emergency arises, action has to be taken to suit it also."[27] The composition of the Committee caused misgivings about the probable outcome of the enquiry. Referring to the Committee, the *Andhra Patrika* observed, "No good will result from such a committee as it will depend on the statistics furnished by Hood and not upon the evidence gathered from those who are directly affected by the economic crisis. It will be no wonder if this should prove useless as all other committees."[28] Paradoxically, even the recommendations made by such a pro-government committee were unacceptable to the colonial government.

The Economic Depression Enquiry Committee, amongst other things, recommended *(a)* a 10 per cent reduction in railway freight rates on agricultural products; *(b)* increased government grants to co-operative societies to provide loans to small farmers; *(c)* government investigation of the feasibility of growing sugar cane on sufficiently compact areas, and giving encouragement to peasants for cultivation of sugar cane instead of paddy;

[26] *G.O. No. 328 Revenue Department* (Confidential), 11 February 1931.

[27] *Tamil Nadu,* 16 February 1931, in *Report on Native Newspapers* 9, 1931, 302.

[28] *Andhra Patrika,* 19 February 1931, in *Report on Native Newspapers* 9, 1931, 308.

(d) regulation of land revenue so as to leave a small margin for the maintenance of the ryot's family; and *(e)* modification of the land revenue collection procedure in favour of small landholders.[29]

However, the orders of the government on the recommendations of the Economic Depression Enquiry Committee were disappointing.[30] On the question of reduction of railway freight the government addressed the railway administration. The agent of the Madras and Southern Mahratta Railway replied that such reduction would be solely at the expense of railway revenue. He pointed out that the implication of the Committee's recommendation would be a serious matter for the government of India, as a 10 per cent reduction in freight rates on agricultural produce during a year would result in a large decline in railway earnings.[31] The government used this as an alibi and relegated the recommendation to the dustbin. As regards allocation of more grants to co-operative societies, the government stated that the registrar of co-operative societies had reported that most of the central banks had ample funds and that there was no need, therefore, for the government to intervene with loans. The registrar was, however, asked to watch the situation and report if he considered action on the lines recommended by the Committee to be necessary at a later date.[32] As for sugarcane cultivation in place of paddy, the government in the course of the order pleaded inability to bring round the unwilling cultivator and observed that "under the circumstances, the government cannot do anything useful in the matter at present."[33] With regard to the suggestion that the land revenue be regulated, the government order said, "The existing rates are sufficient to leave a good margin to cover the maintenance of a ryot family."[34] Another suggestion, namely that the government show some lenience in collecting land revenue, was turned down by the government as "impracticable and contrary to the fundamentals

[29] *The Hindu,* 2 March 1932.

[30] *Ibid.*

[31] *G.O. No. 2142 Ry. (MS) Public Works and Labour Department,* 24 August 1931.

[32] *The Hindu,* 2 March 1932.

[33] *Ibid.*

[34] *Ibid.*

of land revenue system by which the land revenue was levied according to the potential yield of the land and remission was granted in certain affected tracts and never in favour of selected individuals or classes of people."[35] The editorial in *The Hindu* which criticised the government on this score concluded with the remark that "the Government was unwilling to commit themselves to any measure which might humanise their mechanical system."[36]

It was only in early 1934, when the government of India elicited information from provincial governments regarding the action taken or contemplated for reduction of rural indebtedness, that the Madras government began to take some initiative.[37] The government of India, for its part, was prompted to take this initiative by one curious factor. In 1934 the Civil Disobedience Movement had been officially called off, but the agitation had not died down in villages. Peasants' agitation and no-rent campaigns were going on with renewed vigour. The government of India suggested to the provincial governments that the best method of approaching the problems would be to convene a provincial economic conference—they could consult each other and know from the experience of one another how best economic crisis could be handled in rural areas. Accordingly, a Provincial Economic Conference was held in Delhi on 3 April 1934. Revenue Member Sir Archibald Campbell, Minister P. T. Rajan and H. M. Hood, now finance secretary to the government of Madras, represented the Province in the Conference.[38] The issues taken up for discussion at the Conference were *(a)* the problem of existing indebtedness and the possibility of scaling down debts; *(b)* the problem of finance in giving effect to such schemes; *(c)* the problem of providing suitable credit machinery for the future; and *(d)* restricting usurious practices.[39] The conference resolved that central and provincial marketing officers should be appointed, that marketing surveys should be undertaken, and that crop planning conferences should be held under the aegis of the

[35] *Ibid.*
[36] *Ibid.*
[37] *G.O. No. 971 (MS) Development Department,* 13 July 1934.
[38] *G.O. No. 333 Finance Department,* 24 May 1934.
[39] *Ibid.*

Imperial Council of Agricultural Research.[40] So far as the relief of agricultural indebtedness was concerned, the Provincial Economic Conference expressed the opinion that in view of the diversity of the conditions prevailing in the provinces, any legislative measure to afford relief must be primarily provincial. The Conference at the same time considered it highly desirable that each local government should know what other provincial governments were doing to fight the Depression and that there should be a regular exchange of information on it.[41] In a letter dated 18 October 1934, the deputy secretary to the government of India in the Department of Education, Health and Lands requested the Madras government to furnish information on steps taken to relieve agricultural indebtedness in the Presidency. The Madras government replied that since the issue of the letter, the Legislative Council had passed the bill for the Madras Land Mortgage Banks Act, which had come into force.[42]

Like the Provincial Conference, there was a Crop Conference in Simla. The outcome of the Conference was that the government of India advised the provincial governments to appoint marketing officers.[43] The Madras government in connection with the budget estimate for 1934–35 considered the proposal favourably, and decided to appoint a marketing officer and constitute a marketing board.[44] Before the formation of a marketing board, however, the government wanted to conduct preliminary enquiries and collect data with regard to the prices of rice and the marketing facilities available. C. R. Srinivasan of the Agriculture Department was appointed special officer to investigate the condition of production of rice and the rice trade in the Presidency.[45]

The special officer in his report noted that there was a disparity between the railway freight rates for rice from certain inland production centres to local consumption centers, and those from ports to the same consumption centres. He explained that the

[40] Anstey, *Economic Development of India,* 488.

[41] *G.O. No. 1662 (MS) Development Department,* 6 December 1934.

[42] *Ibid.*

[43] *PMLC* 83, 1934, 422.

[44] *Report, Southern India Chamber of Commerce,* 1934, iv–v.

[45] *PMLC* 69, 1934, 129.

freight rate from Tadepalligudam to Calicut, a distance of 748 miles, was Rs. 0-6-10 per *maund* (measure of weight used earlier in India, equivalent to 82.28 lb), while the charge from the same place to Coimbatore, a distance of 641 miles, was Rs. 0-10-0 per maund. It was this disparity in freight rates that encouraged merchants in Coimbatore, Tirupur and Erode to obtain their requirements in the form of imported rice from Calicut or Cochin at Rs. 0-4-8, Rs. 0-5-5 and Rs. 0-6-5, respectively, instead of paying Rs. 0-10-0, Rs. 0-13-0, Rs. 1-0-6 from Tadepalligudam for local rice. The special officer found that it was the nearness of the ports to those inland consuming centres and the lower transport charges that encouraged the movement of imported rice inland from various ports of the Presidency.[46] He recommended an increase of railway freight rates for imported rice from ports to inland centres, to offset their advantage of short distance and reduced rate, and thereby facilitate a free movement of local rice. The special officer's recommendation was "recorded but no action taken."[47] At a meeting held at Delhi in June 1935 between railway officials and "representatives of Chambers of Commerce, Agriculture and other interests," stress was laid on the bearing of railway freight charges on the prices of commodities. It was pointed out that the freight charges had not moved in conformity with commodity prices. The consensus arrived at this meeting was to reduce the railway freight rates.[48] But, as a rebuff to this collective opinion, the Madras and Southern Mahratta Railway announced enhancement of the rates for the traffic of certain commodities such as sugar, kerosene, tobacco and piece goods.[49]

The Madras government ordered an enquiry through a special officer into agricultural indebtedness in the Province. The special officer, W. R. S. Sathyanathan, suggested that the work of granting loans for all agricultural purposes except relief of distress be transferred from the Revenue Department to the Agriculture Department—according to him the latter was a specialised department, and would be able to gauge the needs of the

[46] *G.O. No. 217 Development Department,* 13 February 1936.

[47] *Ibid.*

[48] *Proceedings, Madras Chamber of Commerce for 1936,* 39.

[49] *Ibid.*

cultivators more correctly than the district revenue staff. But the Board of Revenue turned down the proposal, stating that the "District Revenue Staff would for a long time to come be the most suitable agency for doing this work."[50] The special officer critically reviewed the performance of the land mortgage banks that had been established to offer credit to small farmers on easy terms, repayable within a maximum period of twenty-five years.[51]

> I visited several land mortgage banks. What struck me forcibly was the enormous number of rejected loan applications as compared with sanctioned applications. I examined several cases in detail. I confess I was sometimes puzzled why some applications were rejected. In some cases, the titles were sound, the repaying capacities were good and the value of the hypothecation sufficient. They had been strongly recommended by the primary banks and Sub-Deputy Registrars and legal opinion held definitely that the title was good. Yet these applications were rejected, while others of no better position, as far as I could see, were sanctioned. I venture to suggest that greater attention be bestowed by the Central Land Mortgage Bank on the scrutiny of loan applications, which have been strongly recommended by Primary Land Mortgage Banks, the legal adviser and Sub-Deputy Registrars and that only the really unsatisfactory cases should be rejected.[52]

The special officer damned some of the practices in the co-operative system, provoking the registrar of co-operative societies to complain to the secretary to government. The registrar claimed that Sathyanathan's suggestions on the co-operative movement went beyond the terms of reference of the enquiry. He contended that Sathyanathan had had neither the time nor the facilities to make a thorough study of the issues raised by him.[53] The government, too, concurred with the view of the registrar, as the remarks of the special officer that the Central Mortgage Bank rejected valid loan applications had offended it.[54] Therefore, the government dismissed his recommendations.

[50] *G.O. No. 217 Development Department,* 13 February 1936.

[51] S. Krishnaswamy, *The Role of Madras Legislature in the Freedom Struggle, 1861–1947* (New Delhi: Indian Council of Historical Research, 1989), 250.

[52] Sathyanathan, *Report, Agricultural Indebtedness*, 67–68.

[53] *G.O. No. 694 Development Department,* 4 May 1936.

[54] *Ibid.*

The special officer's suggestions were either rejected by the director of agriculture as unwarranted and unjustified, or were not held worthy of consideration by the Board of Revenue, since the financial position was not such as to allow for the necessary increase in staff and other expenditure.[55] The government took no action on the recommendations of the special officer beyond the appointment of debt conciliation boards.

Agrarian Debt Legislation to Combat Depression

Faced with the obvious magnitude of rural indebtedness, the government of Madras enacted a series of debt acts to reduce the debt burden of agriculturists. C. Basudev, a nominated member of the Legislative Council, introduced the Madras Moneylenders' Bill on 31 October 1932. The chief features of the bill were: compulsory registration of moneylenders, restriction of interest rate to 18 per cent, a half-yearly statement of accounts to be sent to each borrower, accounts to be kept in a prescribed form and in the local language, and non-issue of receipt to be made a cognisable offence.[56] The bill underwent drastic changes in the select committee and was later called the Debtors' Protection Bill. The important provision in the Debtors' Protection Bill was that moneylenders could not charge interest exceeding 24 per cent annually on secured loans. When the clause relating to interest was taken up, the revenue member announced that intimation had been received from the government of India to the effect that the government of India itself was considering a comprehensive scheme for all the provinces, and accordingly suggested that the clause be deleted. But as we have seen, the government later decided against any such move for a uniform legislative measure. C. Basudev naively believed the government's version and accepted the suggestion for the deletion of the clause on interest charges. This roused a storm of protest from Sir A. P. Patro and Sami Venkatachalam Chetty, who disapproved of the acceptance of amendments which defeated the very object of the

[55] *G.O. No. 217 Development Department,* 13 February 1936.
[56] *Report, Southern India Chamber of Commerce,* 1933,18–19.

bill. They said, "The bill becomes useless, without fixing the maximum rate of interest leviable by the creditors."[57] The bill was passed by the council and came into force as the Madras Debtor Protection Act from 15 January 1936. The objective of the act was to regulate moneylending and pawnbroking carried on by private individuals.[58] Under the act, the creditor was obliged to furnish accounts to his debtor only if asked to by the latter, which proved to be a drawback. The act limited its scope to loans of the value of five hundred rupees or less. The penal provisions in the act were not sufficiently stringent to bring about the desired result. Therefore, the act was not of much help in solving the problem of rural indebtedness.[59]

Other attempts at resolving the problem of agricultural indebtedness were by means of amendments effected in the then existing acts. The first effort in this direction was an amendment to the Land Mortgage Banks Act. The Madras Co-operative Land Mortgage Banks (Amendment) Act, 1934, empowered the land mortgage banks to make payments to creditors directly, in discharge of debts incurred by their members belonging to the agricultural class.[60] In 1934–35, in 143 cases, a total debt of Rs. 368,889 was scaled down by Rs. 38,191, and in 1935–36 the banks prevailed on the creditors to write off a sum of Rs. 55,203 in 326 cases.[61]

The Agriculturists Loan Act, 1884, was amended in 1935 to grant loans to agriculturists, for discharge of their debts. The aim was to afford relief to a creditor. Special loan officers who were appointed to work the scheme were required to settle a debt at not more than twice the amount of the original principal, or the principal plus 5.5 per cent simple interest, whichever was less. All creditors had to agree to the amount fixed by the special loan officers. If any creditor refused, no loan was to be granted and the application was to be rejected.[62] This scheme of relief of

[57] *Indian Annual Register,* 1934, 2: 141.

[58] S. Y. Krishnaswamy, *Rural Problems in Madras* (Madras: Superintendent, Government Press, 1947), 371.

[59] *Ibid.*

[60] *Report, Administration of Madras Presidency,* 1934–35, xiv.

[61] *G.O. No. 528, Revenue Department,* 9 March 1937.

[62] S. Y. Krishnaswamy, *Rural Problems in Madras,* 371.

indebtedness was in force in Chengalpattu district during 1935–36; in the course of the next year, it was extended to eight districts. In the Tamil region, the act was in operation in South Arcot, Salem and Tiruchirappalli.[63] Under the act the government sanctioned Rs. 0.17 million in 1935–36, Rs. 1.69 million in 1936–37, and Rs. 0.74 million in 1937–38.[64] Considering the volume of debt in the Presidency, this was a meagre sum and therefore the relief afforded was minimal. "One gathers from the measures undertaken by the Government," wrote *The Hindu*, "that they recognise the need for granting relief to the debtors. This is welcome. But that the Government are prepared to earmark only 5 or 6 lakhs [500 or 600 thousand] under Agriculturists Loan Act is but regrettable considering the total indebtedness of the ryots."[65] It was officially stated in the Legislative Council in 1936 that the government had set apart Rs. 2 million for relieving the agriculturists of their debt burden. Commenting on this, *Indian Express* observed:

> Twenty lakhs of rupees to relieve a few debtors in a few taluks when the actual debt is Rs. 200 crores and the indebted are many millions is surely not the way to demonstrate that the officials are aware of the magnitude of the problem. The land value and income from land declined precipitously and the halving of pre-Depression debts is the minimum provision likely to give any effective relief.[66]

Another important legislative measure adopted by the government to provide relief to the debtor was the Debt Conciliation Act of 1936. Originally, when T. A. Ramalingam Chettiyar introduced the Debt Conciliation Bill, everybody looked upon it as a panacea for the sufferings of the peasants. But it was diluted by a number of amendments by the government, with the result that the act was "an effete measure incapable of doing the ryot any substantial good."[67] Even the very important

63 *Ibid.*
64 *Ibid.*
65 *The Hindu,* 7 August 1935.
66 *Indian Express,* Madras, 28 August 1936, in *Report on Native Newspapers* 8, 1936, 445–46.
67 *PMLC* 80, 1936, 261.

provision relating to government assistance to agriculturists by means of loans on proper security, that the special officer Sathyanathan had strongly recommended, was struck off.[68] The Madras Debt Conciliation Act provided for "voluntary and amicable settlement of debts by bringing together agriculturist debtors and their creditors through the medium of Debt Conciliation Boards constituted for the purpose in each district with a Deputy Collector, and two non-officials appointed by government on the board." The act applied to those whose debts had exceeded Rs. 100. According to the act, no creditor was allowed an amount greater than twice the principal due.[69] If the creditors came to an amicable settlement with the debtor, it was recorded by a debt conciliation board and registered, and then had the same effect as the decree of a civil court.[70] If there was no settlement the application was dismissed; but the board could issue a certificate to the debtor that the offer made by him to any creditor was, in its opinion, fair.

The working of the debt conciliation boards was by no means satisfactory. The creditors often refused to accept the terms of the boards. As a matter of fact, when the government sought the opinions of different agencies regarding rural indebtedness by circulating a questionnaire, the Southern India Chamber of Commerce made it clear that it was opposed to the debt conciliation scheme.[71]

> In the matter of rural indebtedness, the Chamber does not support any debt conciliation schemes, either voluntary or compulsory. They are bound to be a failure. The Chamber emphatically protests against the suggestion in the questionnaire that capital might be reduced, because it is opposed to all notions of contractual relationship and because the economic condition of the country does not warrant any such drastic and confiscatory measure. A reasonable reduction in the rates of interest where they are excessive might however be attempted. The Chamber desires to emphasize that the present Depression has affected the moneylender no less than the borrower. Nor is the

[68] *Ibid.*

[69] S. Y. Krishnaswamy, *Rural Problems in Madras,* 371–72.

[70] *Ibid.*

[71] *G.O. No. 350 (MS) Finance Department,* 29 May 1934.

Chamber in favour of more simple and facile insolvency law, which will still further reduce public morality.[72]

As the public opinion was also not in favour of any drastic measure to reduce the debt burden of the agriculturists, the conciliation boards failed to achieve anything substantial by way of scaling down rural indebtedness. *The Hindu* reported that even after the passage of a few acts in the Province, the general position of the agricultural classes did not materially improve.[73] In this context the working of the Usurious Loans Act, 1918, was reviewed. It was found that the powers conferred on courts by the act to examine the pro-notes or any registered documents of the government had not been exercised, as they were discretionary in nature.[74] The Usurious Loans (Madras Amendment) Act of 1936 was therefore passed on 23 November 1936, to make the powers of the courts mandatory. As the burden of loans at compound interest was unbearable, a provision was incorporated in the act to check the practice of charging compound interest on loans advanced to agriculturists.[75]

The Congress had pledged to tackle the twin evils of debt and drink.[76] So when it was voted to power in 1937 it desired to adopt a radical measure for the scaling down of agricultural debts. Until comprehensive measures were formulated for dealing with indebtedness, a bill intended to give temporary relief was brought forward. The Moratorium Bill was passed in the middle of September 1937. The bill laid down that for a year "no suits or proceedings could be instituted against agriculturists whose liabilities under the heads of land revenue, rent and taxes and liabilities to local authorities did not exceed Rs. 400, who had saleable interests in lands; and who derived three-fourths of his income from lands."[77] Payments due to provincial and central banks and land mortgage banks were excluded from the purview

[72] *Ibid.*
[73] *The Hindu,* 7 August 1935.
[74] S. Y. Krishnaswamy, *Rural Problems in Madras,* 372.
[75] *Ibid.*
[76] Thomas, *Growth of Federal Finance in India,* 425.
[77] Narayanaswamy Naidu and Vaidyanathan, *Madras Agriculturists' Relief Act,* 10.

of the bill. The Moratorium Bill stayed the proceedings of the courts between 11 October 1937 and 22 March 1938, the date of the enactment of the Madras Agriculturists' Relief Act.[78] In the case of sale of land effected during the said period, the sale was to be set aside and the auction purchasers were to be refunded the amount they had paid, provided the debtor applied to the court within ninety days of the commencement of the operation of the act. Any sale of immovable property by a debtor during this period was decreed invalid; further, no debtor was permitted to transfer any immovable property with the covert intention of affecting the rights of his or her creditor. There was widespread opposition to the bill from the moneylending class and hence the bill had to be withdrawn.[79]

In November 1937 another bill, called the Agriculturists' Relief Bill, was introduced. This came to be known as the Madras Agriculturists' Relief Act, that became operational in 1938. The act aimed at reducing the rate of interest on future debts, and at writing off the arrears of rent due to zamindars and other landholders.[80] Those who paid income tax or profession tax of more than a rupee a year, or property tax or house tax exceeding Rs. 600 a year, were excluded from the purview of this act. This became necessary in order to ensure that persons following occupations other than agriculture were not benefited by this act.[81] An agriculturist was defined in the act as one who had a saleable right on land under the ryotwari or other tenures. So the agricultural labourer could not be brought within the purview of the act.[82]

According to the provisions of the Agriculturists' Relief Act, all outstanding interest as on 31 October 1937 for the debts incurred before 1 October 1932 was to be waived, and only the principal or such portion of the principal that had not been repaid, was to be collected from the agriculturists. In cases where the repayments had exceeded the principal, but were less than

[78] *Fort St. George Gazette,* part 4, 23 September 1937.

[79] Narayanaswamy Naidu and Vaidyanathan, *Madras Agriculturists' Relief Act,* 10.

[80] *Ibid.*

[81] *Ibid.*, 11.

[82] B. Sitaram Rao, "The Madras Agriculturists' Relief Bill," *Indian Review* 39, no. 6, 1938, 81–85.

twice the principal, only such amount proportionate to twice the principal or the outstanding portion of the principal, whichever was less, was to be remitted.[83] In regard to debts incurred on or after 1 October 1932, the principal was to be repaid and interest was calculated at the rate of 5 per cent per annum.[84] No debt incurred by an agriculturist after 22 March 1938 was to bear interest at a rate exceeding 6.25 per cent per annum. Debt conciliation boards acted as tribunals to hear the disputes.[85]

The Madras Agriculturists' Relief Act scaled down the agriculturists' indebtedness to some extent. In the first fourteen months of the act's operation, over 100,000 cases were filed, involving debts to the value of Rs. 20 million.[86] However, by the operation of the act, the local credit market was adversely affected since moneylenders were not anxious to do business at low rates of interest. Professor Narayanaswamy Naidu noticed during the course of his survey in Cuddalore taluk that a good number of agriculturists had left their land fallow on account of their inability to get credit.[87] It was revealed in the course of an investigation in Chidambaram taluk that there was an unusual rush for unattractive government taccavi loans.[88]

Land Revenue Remission

The fall in prices of agricultural products, accompanied by heavy incidence of land revenue, caused decline in the profits of the big absentee landholders and rich peasants. As this landed gentry dominated the Legislative Council, they conducted a vigorous agitation against the government's land revenue policy. The question of land revenue remission overshadowed everything else in the Council during this period. The first outcome of the opposition of the Council was a resolution passed on 2 November

83 *PMLC* 3, 1938, 246.
84 *Ibid.*
85 *Ibid.*
86 V. V. Sayana, *The Agrarian Problems of Madras Province* (Madras: Book View Press, 1949), 165–66.
87 Narayanaswamy Naidu and Vaidyanathan, *Madras Agriculturists' Relief Act*, 23.
88 *Ibid.*

1931, to the effect that land revenue should be collected in six equal instalments.[89] Thereafter, the discussion on the land revenue policy of the government became a recurring phenomenon. The main task of the Council members in the years 1931 and 1932 was to pressurise the government not to raise land revenue through resettlement operations. The rate of increase that the resettlement promised was 18.5 per cent in the case of wet lands and 12.5 per cent in the case of dry lands. The members of the Council argued that the government had hitherto been raising the land revenue on the ground that the prices of agricultural produce kept increasing; but now that the prices were actually crashing, the government, using its own logic, should come forward to reduce the revenue.[90] On 23 January 1933 they succeeded in passing a resolution recommending a 12.5 per cent remission of land revenue. The government on 18 February issued a press communiqué refusing to accept the resolution of the Legislative Council. Sami Venkatachalam Chetty moved an adjournment motion on 24 February to discuss the issue. But the president disallowed the motion.[91] After that, cut motions and adjournment motions on land revenue remissions became the order of the day. The members who spoke on the subject repeatedly drew the attention of the government to the relief measures adopted in other provinces with regard to land tax.

T. A. Ramalingam Chettiyar argued in the Council that the Madras government was financially better off than other provinces, and could offer more meaningful relief to the peasants.

> The Government in the United Provinces allowed reduction in land revenue to the extent of 15 to 30 per cent in 1932. The Government in Burma did come to the relief of the ryots and they have reduced the taxation. Lately we saw in the papers that in the Punjab also the Government have come to the help of the ryots and they have reduced the rates there. In all provinces in India where this question was raised, the Governments have come to the relief of the ryots and they have reduced the land tax. I do not see why the Madras Government should stand in the way of the ryots getting

[89] *PMLC* 59, 1932, 295.
[90] S. Krishnaswamy, *Role of Madras Legislature in Freedom Struggle,* 245–48.
[91] *PMLC* 15, 1933, 146.

> what they are entitled to. It is the boast of the Madras Government that their finances are very much better off than those of other provinces. If any province is able to give the relief that is asked for, it is the Madras Government. In spite of the fact that the Madras Government are better off than other provinces, in spite of the fact that they will have a large balance—Rs. 100 lakhs more than what it was in the beginning of the year 1932–33—in spite of the fact that the Madras Government are able to give relief to the ryots, I beg to submit that it looks very unreasonable that the Government should take up their present attitude.[92]

The revenue member, however, expressed the view that the government was adhering to the policy of a balanced budget and ruled out the possibility of any further reduction of revenue on grounds of remissions.

> In the Budget debate of 1931 the Government laid down the policy that "balance or no balance" revenue expenditure should be kept within revenue receipts and the House gave ample evidence in that Budget debate that they endorsed the policy adumbrated. The principle followed and to be followed now is that we should not budget for revenue expenditure in excess of our revenue. . . . If therefore we are to follow the accepted policy of providing a balanced budget, expenditure must be reduced and brought within the more restricted compass of the revenue. When it is decided by what amount the revenue is to be reduced for the time being, the Government have to consider how that reduction is to be made and what items are to be restricted. It will most definitely however not be a sound policy to reduce the revenue and then to budget for a deficit.[93]

In spite of hectic campaigns and agitations in the Council for a remission of 12.5 per cent in land revenue, the government chose only to postpone the collection of 12.5 per cent of the land revenue in some districts until prices rose. In Tamil-speaking areas, collections were put off in Tiruchirappalli, Thanjavur, South Arcot, Tirunelveli, Chengalpattu, North Arcot and a portion of Nilgiris.[94] The collection for the year 1934 was to begin. Yet the

92 *PMLC* 66, 1933, 35–36.

93 *Ibid.*, 45.

94 *India*, Madras, 13 March 1933, in *Report on Native Newspapers*, 1933, 3:135.

Government had not announced that the suspension would be treated as remission. The governor in his Council address said: "The Government have suspended the collection of land revenue to the extent of some Rs. 33 lakhs and it is difficult to see what more the Government can do."[95] Yet the consistent fighting of the legislators bore fruit. The government announced 12.5 per cent remissions of land revenue for those districts in which revision of settlements had been made after the year 1919–20, and which therefore had been influenced by the trend of increasing prices at that time. There was overall acclamation for the government's gesture. *The Hindu* editorial aptly commented:

> The Madras Government's decision to remit the portion of land revenue the collection of which was suspended last year will be widely welcomed on two grounds. While nobody who knew anything of the agricultural situation seriously believed that the suspended amount could be collected in the present condition, the indefinite continuance of the suspension would have merely added to the uncertainties of the situation and deepened the worries and anxieties of the ryot who has been reduced to a condition of almost chronic dejection. The decision to remit the suspended amount forthwith is therefore all to the good because it may to some extent relieve the tension. It is to be welcomed, too, as indicating a realisation on the part of the Government that exceptional situations require exceptional remedies.[96]

The government looked at the question of reduction of land revenue purely from a financial angle and therefore it refused to yield to the pressure of the Council any longer. In consequence of its decision to grant a remission of 12.5 per cent of land revenue, it had reduced the financial outlay of certain ongoing projects and kept in abeyance certain schemes for which allocation had been made in the budget.[97] So when the Legislative Council passed a resolution on 31 January 1934 recommending 25 per cent remission of land revenue, the finance member gave this reaction: "The Government cannot allow these remissions because the utmost relief that an average Pattadar [one who holds a title

[95] *PMLC* 68, 1933, 13.
[96] *The Hindu,* Madras, 16 December 1933.
[97] *G.O. No. 612 (MS) Finance Department,* 4 September 1933.

deed] may get from a policy of remission will be about Rs. 2-1-0; will the agriculturist wish for this relief if, in consequence thereof, the Government has to abandon improvement on tanks, neglect irrigation works, close down schools and hospitals, let the village roads run to disrepair and otherwise give up or curtail their nation building activities?"[98] In a press statement issued on 10 January 1934, the government justified its stand on land revenue by maintaining that it received only a very small proportion of the profits made in the boom period, and the remaining portion was left in the pockets of the peasants.[99] But the Council did not give up. In the context of the continuing plight of the agriculturists, it recommended in 1935 to the government that a remission of not less than 33.33 per cent be granted in all the districts.[100] The government rejected this recommendation as financially unviable, arguing that acceptance of the resolution involved a loss of revenue of Rs. 37.14 million in one year alone.[101]

The Council members believed that the financial condition of the government was good enough to allow more than what was given in the form of remission. *The Hindu* impressively illustrated this viewpoint:

> So far as the financial position of the Madras Government is concerned, we feel that it is one that would justify a 25 per cent remission, which is the minimum that the agriculturists would consider to be adequate to relieve their distress. The Madras Government are in possession of large balances and it is believed that they will be in the position of having a realised surplus amounting to nearly a crore in the revised estimates of the present year. . . . The Government have been trying to keep a minimum balance of Rs. 125 lakhs which is an unnecessarily large figure. If minimum balances are intended not to be locked up but to be used when the urgency of a case requires it, there is no meaning in saying that balance should forever constitute an unalterable and unusable fund.[102]

[98] *The Hindu,* 2 February 1934.
[99] *PMLC* 71, 1934, 40–41.
[100] *Ibid.,* 74, 1935, 441.
[101] *G.O. No. 28 (MS) Finance Department,* 23 January 1936.
[102] *The Hindu,* 11 January 1934.

On the other hand, the reason adduced by the government for not conceding the demand for a 25 per cent remission was that they did not want to leave an impoverished treasury to the future government.[103] Echoing this sentiment, the finance member said: "If the state of things now existing is so terrible, as Hon'ble Members have described it, a remission of taxation by the Government on a scale commensurate to the needs of the case is not a practical proposition consistent with maintaining the solvency of the Government."[104]

Other Ameliorative and Protective Measures

The unprecedented distress in rural areas and the magnitude of privation and poverty reported from villages, however, alarmed the government. Therefore, in 1935 the government of India provided a non-recurring budgetary grant of Rs. 9.25 million for provincial schemes of rural development. The central government had suggested appropriate types of work—such as the improvement of water supplies, drainage, village roads and sanitation, and anti-malarial projects. The provincial governments submitted detailed proposals for projects of the type suggested.[105] While presenting the budget for 1936–37, the finance member of the government of India announced that a sum of Rs. 10.85 million would be distributed to provinces from the Rural Development Fund, and that Madras might receive Rs. 1.6 million. The grant actually received was Rs. 1.5 million, and it was in addition to a grant of Rs. 1.4 million previously given to Madras in 1935 for the development of rural areas.[106] The government of Madras sanctioned a scheme involving a capital expenditure of Rs. 5 million, for the repair of minor irrigation works on a three-year plan.[107] The amount earmarked was too meagre, considering the vast size of the Presidency. Therefore the belated rural development scheme did not help

[103] *PMLC* 70, 1934, 146.
[104] *Ibid.*, 71, 1934, 42–43.
[105] Anstey, *Economic Development of India*, 488.
[106] S. Y. Krishnaswamy, *Rural Problems in Madras*, 418–19.
[107] *PMLC* 78, 1935, 24.

substantially to stimulate the purchasing power of the people by providing employment.

The crisis of the Depression brought about some changes in government policies, resulting in the government extending selective protection in the agricultural sector.[108] The Wheat Import Duty Act of 1931 was passed to protect the Punjab wheat traders. The act provided for levying of duty of Rs. 40 per ton on imports.[109] This led to a demand from the rice dealers for similar protection against the increasing rice imports into the Madras Presidency. The issue was raised in the local Legislative Council. The officials concerned expressed their helplessness, saying that the matter came under the purview of the government of India. The legislators did not rest content with the reply and continued to attack the government. As a consequence, the Madras government was forced to take up the matter with the government of India. The government of India was first addressed regarding the matter in July 1933. It was reminded five times, and until February 1934 the Madras government received no response.[110] The government of India defended its policy of non-interference by stating that rice imports into India were very insignificant as compared to the total volume of rice production in the country.

The government, however, had to yield to the rice lobby. In 1935 import duty was imposed on broken rice, as it was a major item in the import bill.[111] But the import duty did not have much impact. The special officer, Sathyanathan, himself had to admit this frankly in his report: "The recent levy of a small import duty on broken rice will undoubtedly afford much relief; but it may not be high enough or comprehensive enough, I submit, to prevent paddy, whole rice and even broken rice from being imported in sufficient quantity to depress local prices seriously."[112]

The flooding of sugar from Java into the Indian market caused a furore and the government of India announced a protective duty of about Rs. 9 per cwt. from 1 April 1932. It has to be

108 Tomlinson, *Political Economy of the Raj,* 88.
109 Rothermund, "British Foreign Trade Policy in India," 3 & 4.
110 *PMLC* 75, 1935, 12.
111 Rothermund, "British Foreign Trade Policy in India," 363–64.
112 Sathyanathan, *Report, Agricultural Indebtedness*, 29.

noted that no British imperial interests were involved in the export of sugar to India—nor were any of the British colonies. The protective duty gave a great boost to the Indian sugar industry. Sugar factories came up in many parts of the Province. Similarly, the tea price had been affected. In order to maintain the price, the powerful European tea interests made an immediate move to restrict imports through an international agreement. The government of India helped the tea lobby by issuing a communiqué to check the export of tea by any unlicensed tea company. The authority to issue licences was delegated to the Tea Planters Association.[113]

The Japanese piece goods flooded the Indian market and depressed the Indian cotton industry. When the situation became worse, the government imposed high duties on these imports. In 1930–31, the duty on cotton piece goods was raised from 11 per cent to 15 per cent, with an additional 5 per cent on non-British goods, and the supplementary budget imposed a surcharge of 25 per cent on these rates.[114] Japan was the largest single consumer of all varieties of Indian cotton. When import duties were raised it embarked on a boycott of Indian cotton as a retaliatory measure. As a result, the government of India was forced to sign a trade agreement with Japan in 1934. The Anglo-Japanese agreement of 1934 permitted the Japanese to sell 325 million yards of cotton cloth annually to India, if they bought 1 million bales (where one bale is five hundred pounds of cotton) of Indian raw cotton.[115] Japan could skillfully increase her export of textiles by increasing her consumption of raw cotton while the agreement was in force (1935–37). The competition of Japanese textiles with Indian textiles therefore called for the revision of the first agreement in 1937. This time, the quota of Japanese exports of textiles was reduced from 325 million yards to 283 million yards, and her import of Indian raw cotton was fixed at 1.5 million bales.[116]

[113] Rothermund, "British Foreign Trade Policy in India," 357–65.

[114] Thomas, *Growth of Federal Finance in India,* 366.

[115] Rothermund, "British Foreign Trade Policy in India," 368.

[116] J. S. Ponniah, "The Production and Marketing of Raw Cotton in the Madras Presidency with special reference to the Districts of Bellary, Kurnool, Coimbatore, Madura, Ramnad and Tinnevelly" (D.Litt. diss., University of Madras, 1944), 2: 87.

A conference of British Empire countries, called the Imperial Economic Conference, was held in Ottawa in 1932. A lot of hope was pinned on this conference by the Indians. But the outcome of the conference caused only disappointment. Instead of giving concessions to its colonies, Britain tried to strike a business deal in furtherance of its own interests. At this conference, Great Britain declared which goods of each colony would be admitted free of duty, and which British goods should be granted access to each empire country.[117] Canada, Australia and South Africa refused to give up anything for the benefit of England. India alone was compelled to agree to give preferential treatment to British goods.[118] The Indian delegation was forced to conclude an agreement with the British representatives, giving preferences of between 7.5 and 10 per cent to a wide range of British goods over non-empire manufactures exported to India. In return, the British guaranteed free entry for some Indian goods.[119] At current volumes and 1928–29 prices, Indian preferences on British goods were worth about $55 million while British preferences on Indian goods were worth about $47 million.[120]

The Southern India Chamber of Commerce, in the course of a lengthy communication to the secretary of the Federation of the Indian Chamber of Commerce and Industry, said that the Ottawa agreement had tilted the scale against India. The Chamber complained that it was progressively subjecting India to helpless dependence on trade with the United Kingdom.[121] The Dominions and India hoped that currency policy would be fully discussed at the Ottawa Conference, and that the British authorities would commit themselves to a definite policy to raise the prices of primary commodities. But this expectation was belied and the British chancellor only expressed his wish to see world prices rise. Increased public works expenditure was ruled out and emphasis was laid on the control of production to raise prices.[122]

[117] Rothermund, *Global Impact of Great Depression*, 65.
[118] Nehru, *Glimpses of World History*, 906.
[119] Tomlinson, *Political Economy of the Raj*, 133.
[120] *Ibid.*
[121] *Modern Review* 56, 1934, 367.
[122] Tomlinson, *Political Economy of the Raj*, 136–37.

The Ottawa Conference turned out to be a business deal to grant preference to some special British commodities, as the gain accrued to India was small.

The Ottawa agreement came up for renewal in 1936. By then the Congress had lifted its boycott of legislature programme. The entry of Congressmen into the Legislative Assembly led to increasing attack on the Ottawa agreement.[123] A resolution for its rejection was carried in the Legislative Assembly by sixty-six votes to fifty-eight on 26 January 1935. Though this did not affect the validity of the Ottawa agreement, since the viceroy could ratify it through his certificate procedure, it was indicative of the attitude of the Congress Party to the imperial trade policy of the government of India.[124]

Summary

The initial response of the Madras government to the challenge of the Depression was not only minimal but even partly counter-productive. Instead of taking measures to stimulate economic activity, the government raised taxes and imposed retrenchment in an effort to balance the budget, and in the process contributed to further deceleration of the economy's development. The propositions of the agriculturists' and traders' organisations to resolve the problems by reduction in railway freights, remission of land revenue, and relief to debtors were scoffed at by the government officials, who instead adopted extreme stringency in financial matters. Madras seemed to have lagged behind other provinces in reacting to the situation. The Madras government, when the situation turned from bad to worse, preferred only to institute enquiries. But the enquiry committees' reports were put in pigeon-holes, and the recommendations of special officers who had held enquiry into agricultural indebtedness and rice trade in the Presidency remained only on paper.

After mid-1935, the government made passive attempts to provide relief to the suffering peasants. A series of legislative

[123] Rothermund, *India in the Great Depression*, 151.
[124] Anstey, *Economic Development of India*, 488.

measures was adopted. But these acts, ironically, had negative effects on the rural credit market. Moneylenders suspended their lending activities as debt legislation like the Debt Conciliation Act and the Agriculturists' Relief Act created apprehension in their minds about the possible recovery of their money loaned out to agriculturists. The government failed to cope with the situation, by refusing to distribute adequate funds through co-operative societies. Protective tariff given to wheat, sugar, tea and cotton by the central government, and the 12.5 per cent remission of land revenue granted by the Madras government from 1933, did not amount to any significant relief. Similarly, The Imperial Economic Conference held at Ottawa did not give much benefit to the Indian trading community. The measures taken by the government were totally disproportionate to the enormity of the crisis. Experimentation in economic affairs was a characteristic feature of the policies of European countries during the Depression. But this was not the case in India.

7

Society and Politics

The Depression worsened the living conditions of the people, both in urban and rural areas of the Presidency. As we have seen in the last chapter, the government did nothing concrete to combat the economic crisis. In fact, pay cuts and retrenchment resorted to by the government—an example the industrialists gleefully followed—demoralised the people thoroughly. This also led to greater unemployment, not only among skilled and unskilled workers, but also among white-collar employees. Agriculturists and weavers in particular faced acute unemployment; the former abandoned cultivation, while the latter lost their jobs on account of the dwindling demand for their products. Many of them moved out of their villages, seeking employment in the neighbouring towns. This led to urbanisation and increasing instances of crime in the Province. These changes in social life were also reflected in provincial politics.

This chapter has two sections. In the first section, the paralysing effect of the Depression on the social life of the Tamils is discussed. The second section will deal with its fallout in the politics of the time.

Impact on Society

Exodus from Villages to Towns

The "Slater villages" registered considerable decrease in population. In Gangaikondan (Tirunelveli district) the population fell by about 631 persons in ten years, despite the fact that there had been 392 births in excess of deaths in the decade.[1] In the case of

[1] Thomas and Ramakrishnan, *South Indian Villages*, 336 & 89.

Vadamalaipuram (Ramanathapuram district), the population had decreased by 14 per cent.[2] The study recorded that in Dusi (North Arcot district)

> the population increased from 1,266 in 1916 to 1,710 in 1932, but has since fallen to 1,316 in 1937. The striking fall is due to a large number of families having emigrated from this village. Families have moved to Conjeevaram, to Madras, to Tirupathi and to Thiruvottiyur and other places seeking means of livelihood.[3]

The exodus of rural artisans and agriculturists led to an increase in urban population. The populations of Coimbatore and Madurai increased by 45 per cent and 31 per cent, respectively, during 1921–31. The census of 1931 revealed a phenomenal increase in the population of Madras.[4]

TABLE 7.1: Population of Madras City, 1871 to1931

Year	*Population of Madras city*	*Absolute decennial increase*	*Percentage decennial increase*
1871	397,552	——	——
1881	405,848	8,296	2.1
1891	452,518	46,670	11.5
1901	509,346	56,828	12.6
1911	518,660	9,314	1.8
1921	526,911	8,251	1.6
1931	647,230	120,319	22.8

Source: Ranson, "Growth of Population of Madras," 320.

The remarks of C. W. Ranson on the cause of population increase in Madras city are illuminating:

2 *Ibid.*
3 *Ibid.*, 182.
4 C. W. Ranson, "The Growth of Population of Madras," *The Madras Tercentenary Commemoration Volume* (Madras: G.S. Press, 1939), 320.

> There is reason to believe that the rapid increase in the population of the city since 1921 has been, to a large extent, the result of migration of despair. Depressed agricultural conditions induced by the precipitous drop in prices appear to have driven large numbers of landless Adi-Dravida labourers towards the city.[5]

The increase of population posed a few urban problems in its wake. In order to mitigate the acute drinking-water scarcity new waterworks had been planned for Madras city. This was expected to cost the Municipal Corporation an estimated sum of Rs. 6.2 million. The Corporation engineer Madley designed the works for an estimated population of 700,000 in 1941. But in 1931 itself the population had reached 650,000, showing a phenomenal increase of 22.8 per cent from the level in 1921.[6] There was also an alarming increase in the number of slums, pavement dwellers, and vagrants in the city. The official census figure for "beggars and vagrants" was 1,578 in 1931. A Corporation census in 1933 counted 10,749 vagrants, beggars and homeless labourers in Madras.[7] There was also a considerable increase in the number of domestic servants—the census report of 1931 had recorded an increase of 30 per cent.[8]

Unemployment

Repatriation of labour from Ceylon and Southeast Asia, coupled with distress migration from rural to urban areas, aggravated the already prevailing unemployment in the Presidency. The colonial government had not compiled any statistics of the actual number of the unemployed. Sir John Simon asked Dr S. Radhakrishnan, who represented India in the International Committee for Cultural Relations that had its session in July 1932, whether it was a fact that in India there was no unemployment. Dr Radhakrishnan replied, "We had no record of the un-

5 V. D. Krishnaswamy, "The Problems of Water in Madras," *The Madras Tercentenary Commemoration Volume* (Madras: G. S. Press, 1939), 289.

6 *Ibid.*, 290.

7 Ranson, "Growth of Population of Madras," 322–23.

8 B. G. Gate, *Changes in the Occupational Distribution of the Population* (Delhi: Government of India, 1940), 7–9.

employed, but we had some calculations which showed that the gainfully employed in India largely numbered 1 per cent of the population while those just able to keep body and soul together scarcely numbered one in every three of the population."[9] A rough estimate put the number of unemployed in India at forty million in 1932.[10] The Madras government was totally ignorant of the actual number of the unemployed in the Province during the Great Depression.[11] But the speech of C. Natesa Mudaliyar of the Justice Party in the Legislative Council indicates the acuteness of the problem. He urged the government to set apart Rs. 100,000 from the provincial revenue to provide relief to the unemployed in Madras city and in rural areas: "The condition of the agriculturists is miserable. They have nothing to eat; most of them have come to Madras in the hope of finding some appointment. When they came here they were disappointed as they only served to swell the number of unemployed in the city."[12]

C. Natesa Mudaliyar presented in the Legislative Council figures for the educated unemployed in Madras city. He had taken these figures from the 1931 census. According to the census report, there were 485 graduates and 2,024 school finalists unemployed in the city itself in 1931. Taking into consideration the number of graduates passing out of university every year, and in view of the retrenchment of personnel in government services since 1931, the extent of unemployment among the educated should have caused grave concern then.[13]

The problem of unemployment was compounded by a rapid decline in the number of emigrants to Burma, Ceylon and Malaya, as the Depression had hit the rubber, tea and tin industries there. The number of persons emigrating from India rose to 137,910 in 1929, dropped to 31,720 in 1931, and to 10,043 in 1933.[14] There was near stoppage of emigration from Madras. The number

9 Shah, *World Depression*, 33–34.
10 M. Visveswaraya, *Unemployment of India: Its Causes and Cure* (Bangalore: The Bangalore Press, 1932), 6.
11 *PMLC* 82, 1936, 22.
12 *Ibid.*, 74, 1935, 144.
13 *Ibid.*, 82, 1935, 443.
14 Mukerjee and Dey, *Economic Problems, Modern India*, 2: 170.

of emigrants to Malaya fell from 42,279 in 1930 to 38 in 1933. The number of emigrants to Ceylon fell from 50,869 in 1932 to 32,898 in 1933.[15] This fall was accompanied by an unprecedented spurt in the number of immigrants returning to Madras. Those returning from Malaya and Ceylon numbered 51,775, exclusive of those who returned to India at their own expense.[16] The annual emigration from Thanjavur district was in the order of 4,420 persons a year. But the process was reversed in the Depression years. There was repatriation of 4,141 persons a year in 1931 and 1932.[17]

The resurvey done in Palakurichi, a Slater village in Thanjavur district, showed that due to repatriation of labourers from Malaya, Burma and Ceylon, the population had increased by 12.86 per cent.[18] The influx of repatriates led to an increase in the number of agricultural labourers. The number of agricultural labourers had increased from 4.62 million in 1921 to 5.09 million in 1931.[19] The increase in the ratio of agricultural labourers was a striking sign of economic ruin. As the 1931 census officer had recorded, in 1921 for every thousand ordinary cultivators there were 291 agricultural labourers, whereas in 1931 they numbered 429.[20] In eight Slater villages of Tamil districts, resurveyed by P. J. Thomas, the number of landless labourers and their proportion to the total population was "on the increase in three villages, more or less stationary in two others, while comparable figures were not available for the rest."[21] The unemployed took out a hunger march from Malabar to Madras in August 1936. On their way many unemployed persons joined them. The hunger march highlighted the acute unemployment problem in the Presidency.[22]

15 *Annual Report of the Director of Health*, 1933, 2.

16 *Ibid.*

17 Baker, *An Indian Rural Economy*, 189.

18 Thomas and Ramakrishnan, *South Indian Villages*, 56.

19 Sathyanathan, *Report, Agricultural Indebtedness*, 88.

20 Narayanaswamy Naidu, *Report*, *Committee on Co-operation in Madras*, 191; Narayanaswamy Naidu and Venkataraman, "The Problem of Rural Indebtedness," 203.

21 Thomas and Ramakrishnan, *South Indian Villages*, 347.

22 *Mathrubhumi*, Calicut, 19 August 1936, in *Report on Native Newspapers* 8, 1936, 83.

Agrarian Struggles

In agrarian tracts peasant struggles broke out. It was more pronounced in the zamindari areas as the Depression heightened the tension between zamindars and their tenants. The newly introduced clause to the Estates Land Act of 1908 had raised the cost of the procedure of bringing property to sale for rent arrears. This discouraged zamindars from moving the court for realising arrears of less than Rs. 200.[23] On account of it, the number of sales for arrears in the Presidency dropped from 34,132 in 1932, before the amendment of the act, to 11,362 in 1933, and to 5,548 in 1935.[24] Therefore, in the context of increasing instances of default, the zamindars had no option but to resort to force for collection of rent, or to evict the tenants. But the tenants had resolved to resist the high-handedness of the zamindars. In Sivagangai (Ramanthapuram district) the tenants stopped paying rent. The estate administration responded by initiating distraint proceedings against them. But the tenants had made up their minds to resist the coercive processes. In Mangalam village of the Sivagangai zamin, estate officials engaged in executing distraint proceedings with police support were attacked by the infuriated tenants.[25]

In Udayarpalayam (Thanjavur district) too, the collection of zamindari revenue became problematic. The zamindar and his tenants had become so estranged that when a haystack belonging to the zamindar was set on fire by some miscreants, it was suspected to have been the handiwork of the tenants. The situation became explosive enough to warrant promulgation of a prohibitory order. The district magistrate called a meeting of the zamindar and the representatives of the agitating tenants. The zamindar came forward to meet the demands of the tenants halfway. But the tenants were not satisfied and attempted to attack the zamindar when he was getting into his car. A party of reserve police was quartered at the zamindar's residence, as the zamin officials were frequently attacked by the tenants.[26]

23 C. J. Baker, "Tamil Nad Estates in the Twentieth Century," *Indian Economic and Social History Review* 13, no. 1, 1976, 26.

24 *Ibid.*

25 *Fortnightly Reports*, second half of May 1934.

26 *PMLC* 63, 1932, 192–95.

At Mamandur (Chengalpattu district) a dispute between landlords and their tenants over their respective shares of agricultural produce led to violent clashes and the police had to take "preventive action."[27] In Maniyachi (Tirunelveli district) the strained relationship between the zamindar and his tenants led to a riot. The zamindar's men shot dead two tenants and injured several others. The zamindar's son and ten others were convicted and the zamindar's privilege of exemption under the Arms Act was withdrawn.[28]

There was a violent clash in an "inaccessible village" situated on the top of the Kalrayan Hills (South Arcot district) in November 1934. The agent of the local *jagirdar* (holder of land assigned by the nawab) had gone there with two policemen to collect the rent. Suddenly, about a hundred people descended on them and attacked them with lathis (a long stick used as a weapon). The jagirdar's agent was killed. One of the policemen succumbed to his injuries later, while the other managed to escape with multiple injuries.[29] The tenants of the *inamdar* (a person who has been granted an inam) of Mallur (Salem district) rose in revolt against their oppressive landlord. In the course of the clash, an old woman was killed. "Sixteen of the tenants were convicted for causing riot, murder, etc., and sentenced to varying terms of imprisonment."[30] In Ramanathapuram, the zamindar had become bankrupt in 1934. As he could not pay the peshkush, the government attached his property. So the government had to face the consequences of the no-tax campaign launched by the tenants.[31] The government's indifference to the demands of the zamindari tenants for fair rent and security of tenure led to the emergence of anti-zamindari movements in the Presidency. The movement was particularly powerful in the coastal Andhra region, where many large zamindaris existed. In Tamilnadu, some Congressmen led movements for the abolition of the zamindari land tenure system.[32]

27 *Report on the Administration of the Police of the Madras Presidency* (hereafter *Police Report*), 1933, 15.
28 *Ibid.*
29 *Police Report*, 1934, 15.
30 *Police Report*, 1936, 15.
31 Baker, "Tamil Nad Estates, Twentieth Century," 26.
32 It was a betrayal that the central leadership of the Congress Party refused to include the abolition of the zamindari system in its manifesto during the 1937 elections.

Madras was a drought-prone province. The famines that broke out periodically impoverished the landless agricultural labourers who possessed no resources and led a hand-to-mouth existence. Therefore, when the Depression hit them they had nothing to fall back upon and suffered greatly. In the Kauveri Delta, those agricultural labourers who were paid in cash were getting from 3 to 6 annas if they were men, 2 to 4 annas if they were women, and 1.5 to 2 annas if they were children.[33] The increase in the number of agricultural labourers exerted downward pressure on real wages. Wage cuts were also inflicted on them. In the Thanjavur region, the daily wage was reduced from 3 Madras measures of rice to 2.5.[34] Kathleen Gough, who investigated the material condition of landless labourers in Thanjavur, wrote: "The wages of agricultural labourers had risen slightly in the 1920s, but had slumped in the Depression to lower than they had been before the boom, so that agricultural labourers and farm servants were unable to maintain their families and preferred their traditional roles as *panniyal*s [farm labourers]."[35] A similar observation was made in the study of the Slater village, Vadamalaipuram (Ramanathapuram district):

> Unemployment and underemployment have grown so serious that serfdom is not so much feared as the lack of any certain means of livelihood. No wonder, the Chakkilies [one of the lowest caste groups in Tamilnadu] of Vadamalaipuram are said to prefer serfdom to the freedom of the casual labourer.[36]

The agricultural labourers who were paid in kind were put to untold suffering. Four measures of paddy was worth about eight annas before the Depression. But during the Depression, the very same amount of paddy, given as wages, was worth only four annas. The rich peasants and landlords were fighting for relief in the form of tax remission in the Legislative Council. But they showed no sympathy for the demand of the landless labourers for a wage

[33] Thomas and Ramakrishnan, *South Indian Villages*, 349.

[34] Baker, *An Indian Rural Economy*, 189.

[35] Kathleen Gough, *Rural Society in Southeast India* (Cambridge: Cambridge University Press, 1981), 132–33.

[36] Thomas and Ramakrishnan, *South Indian Villages*, 351.

hike. In regions where the agricultural labourers had been organised on class lines, struggles broke out. In Mamandur (Chengalpattu district) about eight hundred agricultural labourers agitated for upward revision of their wages in 1933. In Korattur, near Madras, about seven hundred agricultural labourers struck work, demanding increase in cash wages. The issue figured prominently in the Legislative Council debates. But the whole body of landlords resented the demand of the agricultural labourers, and in the said two instances they had to return to work without achieving any of their demands.[37] Such attitudes of the landholders came in the way of organising all classes of agriculturists under a single banner. The South Indian Federation of Peasants had to work out a compromise whereby the peasants conceded to the minimum demands of the labourers regarding wages and other related issues, whereupon the latter agreed to co-operate with the former. It has to be remembered that up to 1939, the peasant parties and organisations in India represented the interests of middle peasants, rich and well-to-do farmers, and a substantial number of cultivating tenants. It was only when leadership was taken over by the communists that an agenda for the welfare of the landless labourers was incorporated into the agrarian programme.[38]

In the Slater village Palakurichi (Thanjavur district), the mirasidars complained that they were not able to extract work from Panniyals.[39] The striking feature of the Thanjavur situation was that the tenants and agricultural labourers jointly fought the oppressive mirasidars, an objective factor that enabled the Communist Party of India to organise them on class lines. At Palayam village in Nannilam taluk, Thanjavur, both tenants and agricultural labourers rose in rebellion against the mirasidar who set hirelings to intimidate them. A police sub-inspector, at the insistence of the mirasidar, went to the Dalit (the lowest or scheduled caste) quarters along with two constables and threatened them with dire consequences. The Dalits were not cowed down—they assaulted the policemen and kept

[37] *PMLC* 26, 1935, 52–53.

[38] See D. N. Dhanagare, *Peasant Movements in India, 1920–1950* (New Delhi: Oxford University Press, 1986), 144.

[39] Thomas and Ramakrishnan, *South Indian Villages*, 141.

them in detention.[40] It is worth mentioning here that the Communist Party made use of the situation, and formed the Agricultural Labourers Union with two hundred members in 1939. Many heroic struggles were fought in the later years that elevated the socio-economic status of the agricultural labourers in the region.[41]

In areas where the agricultural labourers were not organised on class lines, the issues assumed caste dimension and caste riots broke out. In Ramanathapuram and Tirunelveli districts the Dalits (mostly Pallars), as agricultural labourers, clashed with landholding Thevars, leading to the posting of police pickets. In Devakottai (Ramanathapuram district) the estrangement between Thevars and Dalits was total.[42] The Dalits of Ilavankottai near Devakottai refused to work for the Thevars under the old conditions. During the car festival in 1933 the Dalits attended the festival wearing shirts, in accordance with an agreement reached between the two groups some time earlier. Some diehards in the Thevar community considered it an infringement of caste norms and unleashed violence on the Dalits. The police arrested sixty-three of the persons belonging to the Thevar community and put them on trial. The tension continued and culminated in a group of Thevars vandalising the houses of the Dalits.[43]

A police report in the 1930s noted: "The movement among Adi-Dravidas for their emancipation was strengthened and consolidated . . . and in most districts there was evidence of growing resolve in this direction, which provoked the higher castes to the defence of their time immemorial privilege of domination and in some districts the inevitable clash of interests led to rioting."[44]

There was a violent clash between the Dalits and caste Hindus in Koothaparai (Tiruchirappalli district) on 17 June 1931,

[40] *G.O. 4030 Home*, 24 July 1939.

[41] Kathleen Gough, "Agricultural Labour in Thanjavur," in *Social Anthropology of Peasantry*, ed. John P. Mencher(Bombay: Somaiya Publications, 1983), 284; and K. C. Alexander, *Agricultural Labour Unions: A Study in Three South Indian States* (Hyderabad: National Institute of Rural Development, 1978), 27.

[42] *Fortnightly Reports*, 20 July 1933.

[43] *Ibid.*

[44] *Police Report*, 1939.

as Dalits refused to sign a declaration to the effect that they would wear clothes only above the knee, use no vessels except those made of clay, abstain from sending their children to schools, and not wear jewellery made of gold and silver.[45]

A census officer of 1931 attributed the growth of new-found consciousness among the "depressed classes" to emigration.

> Emigration is a great teacher of self-respect, for caste is to a large extent put away when the Indian emigrant crosses the sea. . . . One social effect of emigration has been . . . a growth in independence and self-respect on the part of the depressed classes. . . . A man, who little removed from praedial [*sic*] serfdom in Tanjore, finds himself treated on his own merits like every one else when he crosses the sea, paid in cash for his labours and left to his own resources, must in the majority of cases benefit from the changes, and it is probably the existence of the emigration currents that has contributed most to the growth of consciousness among the depressed classes in India.[46]

The Nadars who aggressively asserted their rights and clashed violently with the upper-caste people for entering temples for worship in the last quarter of the nineteenth century were lying low after the "Sivakasi riot" of 1899. In the context of widespread civil disturbances in the Depression years they renewed their agitation for realising their rights. In the village of Chintamani, in Sankarankoil taluk of Tirunelveli district, the Nadars rioted against non-Nadars. Nadars had not been allowed to take out religious processions in the streets of other upper castes, notably Brahmins, for a long time. On 24 March 1931, the Nadars decided to confront and take out a procession during Mariamman Festival along the Brahmin street. All the non-Nadars gathered together to stall the procession by violent means—resulting in rioting. The police opened fire, and five persons were killed and seven wounded.[47] In Tirunelveli district the provision of Section 30 of the Indian Police Act continued to be in force in the villages of Kalugumalai and Chintamani throughout the 1930s.[48] As for Ramanathapuram

45 *PMLC* 58, 1932, 347.
46 *Census of India*, 1931, 14, part 1, 93.
47 *G. O. 348 Public General (Mis.)*, 28 April 1933.
48 *Police Report*, 1939.

district, a police report noted that "constant vigilance and the frequent application of the provisions of the Indian Police Act were necessary to prevent untoward incidents in connection with the Nadar and non-Nadar factions" in Kallurni, Aruppukkottai and Kamudhi.[49]

Increasing Crimes

The growing social distress was also reflected in the crime rates of the Presidency.[50] The administrative report of the Madras Government for 1930–31 stated: "Crime in general increased by 1.73 per cent, murders increased by 17.3 per cent and dacoities and robberies by 14.8 per cent and 5.55 per cent respectively. The increase in these cases was most marked in the Southern Range especially in Madura, Salem and Tinnevelly."[51] The number of thefts increased every year in the Depression decade. The number of thefts during the year 1934 was 15,161, as against 14,866 in 1933—an increase of 295 cases—and the figure for 1935 was 15,936, an increase of 775 cases.[52] One type of crime which had shown a steady increase in the Depression years was cattle theft (table 7.2).

TABLE 7. 2: Cattle Theft during 1932–35

Year	*Number of cattle theft cases*
1932	2,743
1933	2,785
1934	2,864
1935	3,117

Source: Report, Administration of Madras Presidency, 1932 to 1935.

Cattle theft is always associated with famine conditions in rural areas, and the increased instances of that crime during the Depression years indicate the acute conditions of poverty.

49 *Police Report*, 1937.
50 *A History of the Madras Police, 1859–1959* (Madras: Inspector General of Police, 1959), 374.
51 *Report, Administration of Madras Presidency*, 1930–31, xx.
52 *Police Report*, 1933, 1934 & 1935.

The police administration noted increased burglary in the southern districts in 1932, and attributed it to "the Piranmalai Kallars and other criminal tribe members under economic pressure tending to revert to professional crime."[53] Liquor had always been a solace for people who were in a state of distress. But owing to wretched financial conditions, the regular consumer of liquor found himself unable to afford the price demanded for licit liquor. The illicit distillers met the demand for liquor at lower prices. The growth of illicit distillation was thus a vexing problem for the government. In 1931–32 the total number of cases booked under the Abkari Act (*Abkari* means excise duty) showed an increase from 19,839 to 20,255. The increase was mainly under the head of liquor offences. The increase in the cases of illicit distillation and allied offences was from 2,579 to 3,301.[54] The notable increase was in Salem town. The cases registered had risen from 242 to 502. In Sankagiri Circle the cases detected had risen from 225 to 513 during that year.[55] The call given by the Congress for picketing of liquor shops as a part of the Civil Disobedience Movement was timely, as it caught the imagination of the masses who responded to it enthusiastically. It will not be out of place to mention the fact that C. Rajagopalachari chose Salem district to enforce total prohibition as an experimental measure when he became the premier in 1937.

The breakdown of law and order in several parts of Tamilnadu came up for discussion in the Legislative Council. Basheer Ahmed Sayeed observed: "There have been recently grave offences, grave robberies and grave decoities [*sic*]. We know one or two advocates in Madras city lost their property in their houses in broad daylight."[56] T. A. Ramalingam Chettiyar complained in the Council that life was very insecure in some parts of the Coimbatore district.[57] The inspector general of police, in his letter dated 27 July 1933 to the chief secretary to Madras government, said, "A con-

[53] *Police Report*, 1933, 1934 & 1935.

[54] *Report, Administration of Excise Revenue*, 1931–32, 12.

[55] *Ibid.*, 20.

[56] *Ibid.*

[57] *PMLC* 67, 1933, 39.

spiracy has recently been unearthed in Madras city, the object of which was to commit decoity [*sic*] and robbery and murder officials. The conspiracy extended over a number of districts and up to date twenty three arrests have been made."[58] In the demand for a supplementary police grant for 1933–34, the minister Sir Mohamed Usman pleaded for further grant of Rs. 17,100 for additional police staff in the Criminal Investigation Department. This time the oppos-ition members approved the grant without any protest.[59]

Impact on Politics

The Depression changed the political conditions in several countries. In England, when a general election took place at the end of 1931, the Labour Party was thoroughly routed as it was held responsible for the financial collapse.[60] In South American countries like Argentina, Brazil and Chile, there was a change of government during the period of the Depression.[61] In the USA, the Republican Party, which had taken credit for the pre-Depression boom, was rejected by the people in successive elections for about twenty years after the Great Depression.[62] The Justice Party which shared power with the British during this period was trounced in the general elections of 1937.

When the available body of literature is surveyed, the final defeat of the Justice Party is explained as follows. R. Hardgrave claims that "The Justice Party had strangled itself on the rope it had woven: support of the British Raj had brought it to power, but with the impact of national self-consciousness and aspiration for Swaraj, its imperial connection brought its defeat."[63] However, Hardgrave has not elaborated his theory in convincing detail. D. A. Washbrook considers the elite nature of the Justicites to be the reason for their failure to capture the imagination of the masses. Even amongst

[58] *PMLC* 70, 1934, 504.
[59] *PMLC* 67, 1933, 28.
[60] Garraty, *The Great Depression*, 23–56.
[61] Eric Hobsbawm, *The Age of Extremes* (New Delhi: Viking, 1995), 105–06.
[62] *Journals of David E. Lilienthal, The* (New York: Harper and Row, 1964), xxiv–xxv.
[63] R. L. Hardgrave, *The Dravidian Movement* (Bombay: Popular Prakashan,1965).

their caste groups, the educated non-Brahmins stood socially isolated.[64] The sociologist Andre Beteille highlights this point with clarity: "The Justice Party was in a real sense an elite party dominated by urban, western educated landowning and professional people. It contained a formidable array of rajas, zamindars, industrialists, lawyers and doctors. It was by no means a mass party."[65]

Marguerite Ross Barnett attributes the decline of the Justice Party to two causes. First, the party lost the support of the Muslims and Dalits. Second, as the Justice Party did not adopt adequate legislative measures for social reform, the radical elements in the party moved to the Self-Respect Movement which had assumed radical postures then. Barnett has been unfair in not giving due credit to the radical nationalism of the Congress Party that put the Justice Party on the defensive. Barnett, however, observes correctly that the limited adult franchise restricted the voting right to the property-owning and educated section of the population, and hence backward non-Brahmins remained essentially unmobilised.[66]

For C. J. Baker the Justice Party was defeated "not so much by the strength of their opponents' campaign, as by the intrigues of their party colleagues."[67] Baker discusses the occurrence of the Depression in the Presidency, but the extent of its impact on Madras politics is not expounded in his study. N. Ram claims that it was the failure of the Justice Party to see the negative side of British imperialism which led to its collapse.[68] P. Rajaraman, whose doctoral dissertation on the Justice Party sounds like a rejoinder to D. A. Washbrook, sums up that "internal dissension, ineffective organization, inertia and lack of proper leadership led to the Justice Party along the path of decline."[69]

[64] D. A. Washbrook, *The Emergence of Provincial Politics: The Madras Presidency (1817–1920)* (New Delhi: Vikas Publishing House, 1977), 281.

[65] Andre Beteille, *Society and Politics in India: Essays in Comparative Perspective* (New Delhi: Oxford University Press, 1997), 101.

[66] Marguerite Ross Barnett, *The Politics of Cultural Nationalism in South India* (New Jersey: Princeton University Press, 1976), 23 & 47.

[67] Baker, *Politics of South India*, 242.

[68] N. Ram, "Dravidian Movement in Its Pre-Independent Phase," *Economic & Political Weekly*, annual number 7 & 8, 1979.

[69] P. Rajaraman, *The Justice Party: A Historical Perspective, 1916–1937* (Madras: Poompozhil Publishers,1988), 23.

According to Irschick, the 1919 act had left a great deal of patronage in the hands of Justice ministers, which sustained the party in the 1920s. In the 1930s, the ministers lost their powers to make appointments to the provincial establishment, which authority the Secretariat in Madras began to assume. The ministers had also been divested of their powers to deal with tenders and contracts. The final blow, he writes, came in 1933, when the authority to appoint executive officers (commissioners) in the municipalities was granted to the Secretariat.[70]

The phenomenal impact of the Great Depression—precipitating a serious economic crisis in the Presidency, and affecting the political behaviour of the masses—is a crucial aspect which the scholars did not take cognisance of, or elaborate on. In this chapter it will be shown how the co-operation of the Justicites to operate dyarchy associated them with the unpopular measures of the colonial government and discredited them in the eyes of the masses. Then, the emphasis of the Congress on the economic demands of the exploited masses in the context of the Great Depression is contrasted with the indifference of the Justice Party to the economic grievances of people of different sections. This, I contend, would explain the political fiasco of the non-Brahmin movement in the pre-Independence era.

The Indian ministers under the new political system, introduced by the 1919 act, were endowed with limited powers, whereas the governor as head of the provincial executive enjoyed enormous authority. He had the right to overrule his ministers. Even in the event of ministers resigning and the governor finding none to take their place, in view of the confidence of the local legislature they enjoyed, the governor was empowered to undertake temporary administration of a transferred department.[71] While the ministers were individually and directly responsible to the local legislature, the governor-in-council, for his administration of the reserve department was answerable only to the Parliament of England.[72] Therefore, working with the dyarchy was a severe handicap for the Justicites.

[70] Irschick, *Tamil Revivalism,1930s*, 149.

[71] E. A. Horne, *The Political System of British India with Special Reference to the Recent Constitutional Changes* (Oxford: Clarendon Press, 1922), 68–102.

[72] *Ibid.*

3

Realising the defects of the new political system, the Congress, under the leadership of Gandhi, decided not to co-operate with the Montford constitution. On the other hand, the Justice Party, on finding its demand for communal representation rejected, became apprehensive that the Montford reforms would strengthen Brahmin domination and therefore anxiously collaborated with the British. It could also come to power, thanks to the Congress boycott of legislatures.[73]

As the disinclination of the British to transfer power completely to Indians was evident, the Congress in its bid to attain total Swaraj embarked on the Civil Disobedience Movement in 1930. The British responded by resorting to repressive measures. Prohibition of public meetings, large-scale arrests and detention of political activists, dispersal of public meetings by "lathi charge" and shooting, were some of the means the government adopted to crush this movement.[74]

Resentment against Justicites' Attitude

Meanwhile, the depression that broke out in the Presidency manifested in the form of a fall in prices, of both food grains and commercial crops, resulting in an increasing debt burden on an already indebted peasantry. When the peasants ventilated their grievances by lawful means, they were all treated as political agitators and imprisoned. A member of the Legislative Council spoke about this in the House:

> The leaders of the peasants are prosecuted and sent to Jails as political suspects and political agitators. The Government has itself created an occasion for the civil disobedience movement. The Government is only responsible for the powerful way in which the civil disobedience movement is carried on in some of the districts of this province because it created discontent in the minds of a very large number of peasants.[75]

Even before Gandhi was interned in May 1930, the *Swarajya* remarked: "Events are taking a serious turn in Madras. . . . For

73 S. Krishnaswamy, *Role of Madras Legislature in Freedom Struggle*, 79.
74 *Ibid.*, 217–27.
75 *PMLC* 61, part 1, 1932, 42–43.

some days past, there has been a virtual rule by the police."[76] The *Hindu* wrote that "the violent assault by the police on the salt law satyagraha volunteers" in Madras would be viewed "with indignation and pain by all lovers of fair play and justice."[77] Condemning the repressive actions of the government, the *Andhra Patrika* observed: "The police highhandedness in Madras is exceeding all bounds. Both on the hartal day (April 23), as well as at the beach meeting (on the following day), the police resorted to lathi charge in order to terrorise people. Several prominent Congress leaders and women volunteers who broke the salt law were imprisoned . . . some were given rigorous imprisonment."[78] In the Madras Legislative Council, adjournment and cut motions were tabled by independent nationalists like Sami Venkatachalam Chetty and R. N. Arogyaswamy Mudaliyar against the repressive actions of the government. None of the Justice Party members spoke out or condemned the repression in the Council.[79]

Though repression was in force, the Justicites co-operated with the British, however much they encroached on "popular liberty," and the two sections got on amicably.[80] The ministers' attitude towards the Reserved Half became the subject of discussion in the Madras press during this period. Urging the ministers to assert their authority the *Swadesamitran* commented:

> Though the Reserved Departments are under the control of the Executive Council, the ministers have the right of acting as they like in the matter of determining the budget of the province. They are aware of the hardships suffered by the peasants and as their representatives they have a responsibility in the matter of securing justice for them. They can well offer to reduce the expenditure of the departments in their charge for this purpose. If, in spite of it, the executive councillors attach no value to their words, what is the use of their continuing in their posts?[81]

76 S. Krishnaswamy, *Role of Madras Legislature in Freedom Struggle*, 220.
77 *Ibid.*
78 *Ibid.*
79 *Ibid.*, 217–27.
80 *Andhra Patrika*, 17 March 1932, in *Report on Native Newspapers* 12, 1932, 383.
81 *Swadesamitran*, 30 January 1934, in *Report on Native Newspapers* 2, 1934, 79.

Satyamurthy repeatedly charged the Justice Party with responsibility for the passing of the repressive laws in the Province. P. T. Rajan's defence of his party's position was: "The elementary duty of every citizen would be first to help the authority to maintain peace in the land and to avoid chaos. Beyond that their party as such was neither directly nor indirectly responsible for such laws."[82] Such a reply could hardly be expected to convince the people. Further, the Justicites ridiculed political struggles and sacrifices. Addressing a meeting at Uthagamandalam in June 1935, S. Kumarasamy Reddiyar, the minister for education, said:

> Look at the record of the work of the Congress. It was nothing but non-co-operation and civil disobedience. They had refused to co-operate with the government in all things, both good and bad. They disobeyed the laws of the country and the legislatures and sent numberless youths to jail and wrought incalculable harm to the country without any profit, whatever.[83]

The Justice ministers brought disrepute to their party by their unresponsive attitudes and deeds in the context of economic measures initiated by the government for combating the Depression. One of the important recommendations of the Madras Retrenchment Committee was that the strength of the Cabinet should be reduced by one.[84] Not only was this recommendation ignored, but an unsuccessful attempt was made by the raja of Bobbili at creating a fourth minister's post to conciliate some of his colleagues.[85] For purposes of retrenchment two executive councillors and one minister had resigned their posts in Bombay. In Madras none of them offered to resign. The *India* scathingly remarked:

> Of the four executive councillors in Madras two are whites and two are Indians. We would not ask the whites to resign. The two Indians may resign. One of them Sir Muhammad Usman Sahib has been con-

[82] *Justice*, 15 July 1935.
[83] *Ibid*., 28 June 1935.
[84] *Report, Madras Retrenchment Committee*, 20.
[85] *Dravida Kesari*, Madras, 8 June 1935, in *Report on Native Newspapers* 6, 1935, 376.

> tinuing in service beyond his time and the other Sir M. Krishna Nayar has become old and cannot even write steadily. If these two resign they will not only expiate all their official sins but will also become eminent persons in the eyes of the people. Of the Ministers Mr. P. T. Rajan may well resign as he is spending his time pleasantly without any anxiety about the responsibility of his work. Why should not these three persons resign?[86]

Contrasting the conduct of the ministers of the Central Province, who had agreed to reduce their salaries to Rs. 2,250 per month from April 1931, with that of the ministers in Madras, who were drawing Rs. 4,333.60 per month, the *India* wrote: "Is not Rs. 2000 enough for Madras Ministers, who were only second rate vakils in the Muffassal [rural area]? When the poor are suffering for want of money, they are drawing fat salaries, what an injustice?"[87] The *Sutandira Sangu*, raising the question as to why the ministers in Madras should not reduce their salaries, remarked: "The government officials are reducing their salaries in different places. Even the heroes who have gone to the Round Table Conference have offered to reduce their allowances. But the Madras Ministers alone are averse to admit the retrenchment rat in their granary of pay. Can the administration of a province be left in the hands of these persons who are highly enamoured of money?"[88]

The *India* invited the attention of its readers to an instance which it considered not to be in keeping with the retrenchment policy of the government.

> When the country is on fire, when the axe of retrenchment has fallen on the poor and when the people are experiencing intense suffering under the heavy burden of taxation, the Madras Ministers have started on their tours immediately after passing of the budget. The tour of Honourable Mr. P. T. Rajan causes us heart-burning. We have to feel sorry that the Ministers have been reduced to such a deplorable state. Mr. Rajan is going to Hindupur today, which is at a distance of 400 miles from Madras for laying the foundation stone for a Taluk

86 *India*, 10 June 1932, in *Report on Native Newspapers* 20, 1932, 628.

87 *India*, 28 August 1931, in *Report on Native Newspapers* 36, 1931, 1199; *India*, 14 October 1931, in *Report on Native Newspapers* 8, 1415.

88 *Sutandira Sangu*, Madras, 17 October 1931, in *Report on Native Newspapers* 8, 1415.

> Board School. For this trivial affair a minister is squandering the money of the poor tax payer.[89]

The ministers remained indifferent to all the pleas and prayers of the nationalists, and questions which were put to them in the Legislative Council were answered in a fashion which would cause irritation. About this, the *Sutandira Sangu* wrote:

> In regard to certain questions, the wise ministers will keep silent. At times they will say that the Government are not prepared to reply. In the case of certain questions, they will plead the excuse that the Government can not state the facts openly. It will be funny indeed when they say that the Government have no information. In the local Legislative Council, Sir M. Krishnan Nayar and Sir Muhamad Usman Sahib are experts in stating that they have no reply to give or that they have no information.[90]

In zamindari tracts, the tenants were reeling under the accumulated burden of rent, and the zamindars were threatening them with eviction on grounds of non-payment of rent. A bill to provide security of tenure to the tenants in the estates was introduced when B. Muniswami Naidu was the chief minister in 1932. After Bobbili had replaced him as chief minister he managed to change the character of the bill completely, and the protective measures contemplated for the zamindari tenants were entirely "emasculated."[91] Muniswami Naidu had to lose the post of minister after evincing some sympathy for the zamindari tenants. He also antagonised Bobbili, who epitomised zamindari interests in the Presidency. In his statement presented to the Council on his resignation as chief minister, Muniswami Naidu said, "I did not provide a place in the ministry for a zamindar. I had no prejudice against any one, but in choosing my colleagues I had to be guided by the feeling in the party as a whole. . . . The choice that I eventually made was not agreeable to the Hon. the Raja of Bobbili and some of his friends and consequently they began giving trouble in the party."[92]

89 *India*, 25 March 1932, in *Report on Native Newspapers* 14, 1932, 439.
90 *Sutandira Sangu*, 28 January 1933, in *Report on Native Newspapers* 1, 1933, 87.
91 Baker, *Politics of South India*, 207.
92 *PMLC* 63, 1932, 545.

The raja of Bobbili incurred the antagonism of all sections through his abuse of authority. The *Sutandira Sangu* complained about it.

> The Local Boards Act has been recently amended, taluk boards have been abolished, a district board has been bifurcated and attempts are made to bifurcate other boards, which are hostile to him. . . . He is superceding municipalities, which do not bow to his authority, removing chairmen not liked by him and trying to forfeit the liberty of these bodies by the appointment of commissioners.[93]

Once a champion of the Justice Party, the European-owned *Madras Mail* had by the mid-1930s become impatient with its ineptitude and was sickened by the Justicites' preoccupation with patronage. In an editorial on 1 June 1935 it observed that "if the Justice Party is really determined upon reorganisation, it should be one of its first proclamations that, so far as it is concerned, the spoils system must go."[94] On 4 June 1935 *Madras Mail* carried a news item alleging that in a private meeting of the prominent members of the Justice Party, it was decided that the sum proposed to be set apart by the government of India for rural development should be spent through the party channels in order to boost its image.[95] Erskine, governor of Madras, reported in February 1937 to Zetland, the secretary of state for India, that the peasants were fed up with the Justice Party, particularly in southern India, "as every sin of omission or commission of the past fifteen years is put down to them."[96]

Congress Attitude in Contrast

The leaders of the national movement, in contrast to the Justicites, saw in the agrarian distress a great chance to draw the peasantry into the freedom movement. Rajagopalachari's choice of Thanjavur district for a civil disobedience programme shows that he was

93 *Sutandira Sangu*, 26 February 1935, 5 & 9 March 1935, in *Report on Native Newspapers* 3, 1935, 167.
94 David Arnold, *The Congress in Tamil Nad (1919–1937): Nationalist Politics in South India* (New Delhi: Manohar Book Service, 1977), 179.
95 Quoted in *Justice*, 5 June 1935.
96 Arnold, *Congress in Tamil Nad*, 177.

aware of the discontent among the landholders in the wake of the Depression. Rajaji hoped to mobilise all those who had grievances against the government.[97] In the Non-Co-operation Movement of the early 1920s, the number of prosecutions hardly crossed 600, but during the Civil Disobedience Movement of 1930s, between April 1930 and March 1931, around 4,754 had been imprisoned in the Madras Presidency.[98]

The Congress gave priority to the problems of peasants in the struggle for national liberation. It adopted a no-rent and no-tax campaign as part of its civil disobedience programme. Under the pressure of the Depression, socio-economic demands were more sharply articulated in its Karachi Resolution of 1931. A government report presented to Parliament in 1932 said, "The twenty fundamental objects of the Congress adopted at the Karachi session . . . included the reduction of land revenue by 50 per cent and total relief to small owners. Lured by this political chimera . . . Congress leaders were not able to resist the opportunity of exploiting so fruitful a field as agrarian distress."[99]

In the Andhra coastal regions, the Peasants' Protection League under the leadership of Professor N. G. Ranga organised several militant struggles.[100] But in Tamil districts there was no organised resistance of the peasants except in Thanjavur district, where the rich peasants were to some extent united under the Mirasidars' Association.[101] The South Indian Federation of Peasants, in Madras, was not struggle-oriented.[102] N. G. Ranga's sympathisers in the North Arcot district had formed a North Arcot Kisan Sangam. But that too was not active.[103] Thus, the resistance of unorganised land labourers in these districts fizzled out, and a union for fighting their cause was established only in 1939, in Thanjavur.

The Legislative Council, which was dominated by rich peasants, fought a relentless battle during this period. The Congress, led by Satyamurty, extended its support to the members of the

97 Irschick, *Tamil Revivalism, 1930s*, 119.
98 *Ibid.*, 134.
99 *India in 1931–32*, 5–6.
100 *Fortnightly Reports*, first half of November 1933.
101 *Ibid.*, second half of November 1933.
102 *Ibid.*, second half of November 1934.
103 *Ibid.*, first half of May 1937.

Council from outside the legislature. In response to the severity of the depression in the agricultural sector, the nationalists brought forward a resolution in the Legislative Council for 12.5 per cent land revenue remission in non-zamindari areas. The Justice ministers remained silent and voted against the resolution when representatives of all parties spoke and voted in favour of it. The Tamil newspaper *Tamil Nadu* burst out:

> It would not have mattered much if they had remained neutral. One has to presume from their having voted against the resolution that they forgot their responsibility to the council. They can hold office only as long as they have the support of the majority in the council and they are bound to act according to the wishes of the majority. If they insist upon the government reducing the kist as demanded by the majority, it will surely be reduced. If the government do not reduce the kist so desired, they should resign their posts. It is only then that they will prove their gratitude to the public through whose votes they entered the Council and secured the posts of ministers. The very fact that the resolution has been passed indicated that they are bound to give effect to it. If they do not like to do so, the resolution would amount to a vote of censure against them. If the ministers keep quiet, the members should move a motion of no confidence against them, as remission of kist does not seem to be possible unless they do so.[104]

When the agrarian conditions became worse, the Justicites also had to support the resolutions passed by the Council demanding increased remissions. But there was no struggle launched by them to defend the cause of peasants. The Congress, on the contrary, in the light of the resolution for 12.5 per cent remission passed in the legislature, gave a call to observe 26 November 1933 as Land Revenue Reduction Day.[105] The peasants convened meetings throughout the Presidency on that day and passed resolutions demanding reduction of land tax. Satyamurty addressed the meeting organised on the Madras beach, demanding that land tax be reduced by 33.33 per cent. He called for the formation of a land revenue reduction league

[104] *Tamil Nadu*, 1 February 1934, in *Report on Native Newspapers* 2, 1934, 79.

[105] *India*, 13 March 1933, in *Report on Native Newspapers* 3, 1933, 135.

which would carry on the agitation for the reduction of land tax.[106] The peasants, now finding their demand in the Congress' agenda, backed all of its programmes wholeheartedly. A resolution passed by the executive committee of the South Indian Federation of Peasants on the eve of the 1937 election reveals the attitude of the peasants towards the Congress.

> This federation resolves that in the coming Assembly elections the proper and class-wise course for peasants to follow is to vote for the Congress candidates in general and to utilise all their organisational and other resources to strengthen those Congress candidates who give their unequivocal assurance of support for implementing of the peasants charter of minimum demands through their work both within and without the Legislatures.[107]

The Congress in all its election meetings in the mid-1930s narrated one "thali incident" which showed the Justice Party in a bad light. A magistrate named Dodwell, while presiding in a court in Tellichery sentenced Mrs. Prabhu, accused of civil disobedience, to fine and imprisonment. He insisted on her paying the fine on the spot, and on her pleading inability, asked her to remove her *thali* (marriage pendant) and lay it on the table. An advocate present in the court explained the sacred nature of the thali to the magistrate and pleaded with him not to insist on her removing it. But the magistrate was adamant and the lady had to remove the thali with the help of some women present there. Satyamurty told the people wherever he went during election campaigns, that the Justice Party did not move its little finger over the incident. When Satyamurty won the election to the Legislative Assembly in 1934, he said that it was the "thali incident" that got him votes.[108]

All regulations and legislative measures, including the amendments to the Estates Land Act of 1908, failed to meet the demands of the peasants for fair rent and security of tenure. The government's callousness to the grievances of the zamindari tenants led to the emergence of a strong anti-zamindari movement in

[106] *Ibid.*
[107] *Letter No. 2320 (MS) Development Department*, 18 December 1936.
[108] *Justice*, 13 July 1935.

the Presidency. The movement was militant in the coastal Andhra region where many zamindaries existed. In Tamilnadu some Congressmen led movements for the abolition of the zamindari land tenure system.[109] On the other hand, Bobbili's class interests inhibited him from intervening in favour of tenants. The colonial administration treated the problem as a law and order issue. The police firings in the estates convinced the tenants in zamindari tracts that they could no longer trust the Justice Party.[110] The *Zamin Ryot* reflected the mood of the tenants in the late 1930s.

> The Justice Party has disgusted the people of this Presidency like Plague and engendered permanent hatred in their hearts. Everybody, therefore, is anxiously awaiting the fall of the Justice regime which they consider tyrannical and the inauguration of Congress rule. . . . Even old women in villages ask as to how long the ministry of the Raja of Bobbili would continue. The country would never like to hand over the Ministerships to the Justice Party and allow the Congress to sit in a corner.[111]

In the Madras Presidency the handloom-weaving industry ranked in importance and magnitude next to agriculture. The weaving industry played a significant role in absorbing the rural population not engaged in agriculture, or keeping the agriculturists occupied during lean seasons. It also provided a suitable part-time job for the families of the small peasants and the landless agricultural labourers. The Depression had a disastrous impact on weavers, on account of dwindling demand for handloom products in foreign countries. A large influx of Japanese *gadas* (linen), and mass production of cheap cloth from the mills of Bombay and Ahmadabad, and from the mills that had been established in the Presidency, accentuated the crisis.[112] The boycott of foreign goods that had been going on as a part of the political movement since the Depression further aggravated the crisis-laden

[109] S. Krishnaswamy, *Role of Madras Legislature in Freedom Struggle,* 260.

[110] K. A. Manikumar, "The Impact of Great Depression on the Social Life of Tamils," *Artha Vijnana* 38, no. 3, September 1996, 259–73.

[111] *Zamin Ryot*, Nellore, 25 October 1935, in *Report on Native Newspapers* 11, 1935, 658.

[112] *G.O. No. 2421 Development Department*, 1 November 1937.

situation. Owing to the boycott of foreign yarns, all those weavers who were weaving clothes of finer counts were thrown out of work, sincc the finer yarn was not procurable from Indian mills. In Coimbatore, for example, ten thousand weavers were thrown out of work. Previously, they had been engaged in a prosperous trade of supplying fine clothes of cotton with silk and gold-lace headings and borders to North India.[113] In Salem, the weavers who were doing work similar to that in Coimbatore were also put to misery. In Salem town, three thousand weavers were unemployed.[114] In Madurai, two thousand Sourashtra weavers were jobless.[115] In three Slater villages resurveyed by P. J. Thomas, the weavers had sold their small plots of land and migrated to town. The study recorded that "there has been a steady decline in the number of actual weavers and their economic condition. . . . Some of the weaver fold have left the village for town in search of casual labour and a few have gone out as factory hands in cotton mills in the district."[116]

The concentration of large numbers of weavers in certain centres united them, making their actions in defence of their interests more massive. They looked to the Congress for their betterment—Gandhi's hand-spinning programme had a particular appeal to the unemployed handloom weavers, who strengthened the Congress by enthusiastically responding to all its calls. In many parts of the Presidency, they enthusiastically took part in the programme of picketing the foreign cloth shops. The Congress volunteers who picketed the foreign cloth shops in Coimbatore district were mostly drawn from the weaving community.

Sundaram of the All India Spinners' Association, its director, P. Nachimuthu Gounder, O.K.S.R. Kumaraswami (Tiruppur Kumaran), Viswanatha Nair, Narayanaswami, Appukutti Raman Nair, Subbarayan and Nachimuthu formed the first batch of Congress volunteers in Tiruppur to take part in picketing. They marched in procession, carrying the national flag, singing national songs and defying the prohibitory orders. As they were

[113] *Economic Depression Enquiry Report*, 1930, 14 –15.
[114] Irschick, *Tamil Revivalism, 1930s*, 132.
[115] *Indian Annual Register* 1, 1932, 2–4.
[116] Thomas and Ramakrishnan, *South Indian Villages*, 336 & 389.

nearing the police station on the main road, a number of police constables prevented their march. The volunteers stopped, but refused to disperse. Thereupon the police conducted lathi charge and all the volunteers fell down on the road after severe beatings. Kumaraswami, whose skull was fractured, did not regain consciousness and died on 12 January 1932;[117] he eventually became a symbol of martyrdom. This incident gave the Congress an opportunity to emotionalise the weavers and involve them in the militant struggle for national liberation.

The Congress evolved a labour programme to win over the factory workers. The programme finalised at the Karachi session of the Indian National Congress (1931) included a living wage for industrial labour and the "right of labour to form unions to protect their interests with suitable machinery for the settlement of disputes through arbitration."[118] Towards the end of 1934, the Madras Labour Union began to move closer to Congress. During the 1936 Madras municipal election campaign, the Madras Labour Union urged the workers at its meeting to vote for Congress, and explained how their lot would be improved under Congress rule. The Congress had lifted its ban on entry into legislature by then. The publication of a Congress election manifesto, drawn up for the 1937 provincial election and published just before the municipal elections, spelt out in some detail how the Karachi Resolution would be implemented.[119]

On 7 October 1936, during an election tour of South India, Nehru addressed a meeting organised by the Madras Labour Union, which was attended by an enthusiastic crowd of seven thousand workers. In his speech Nehru told the workers that Congress was the only political party which would look after their economic interests. The Justice Party was unable to establish links either with the Madras Labour Union leaders or with the workers in the mills.[120]

[117] *Indian Annual Register* 1, 1932, 2–4.
[118] N. F. Dufty, *Industrial Relations in India* (Bombay: Allied Publishers, 1964), 48.
[119] Murphy, *Unions in Conflict*, 127–29.
[120] *Ibid.*, 129–30.

Indian businessmen were also now drawn closer to the Congress. In Madras the Indian business class had the Southern India Chamber of Commerce—formed in 1910 as a counterweight to the Madras Chamber of Commerce where European traders were organised—to lobby with the colonial administration and fight for the trading interests in South India. The Chamber sent memoranda and petitions to the government of Madras and to the central government, voicing its views on every factor affecting the interests of traders and industrialists in the Presidency. A study of the annual reports of the Chamber reveals that in most economic matters it invariably concurred with the Indian National Congress. Whether it was on currency exchange ratio, income tax, the issue of supertax, the land revenue question, import policy or the Ottawa Pact, the views of the Congress and the Chamber were identical.[121]

From 1927, the Southern India Chamber of Commerce began to participate in all agitation programmes announced by the Federation of Indian Chamber of Commerce and Industry (FICCI). It boycotted the Simon Commission and the first Round Table Conference, and supported the boycott of foreign clothes movement of the Congress launched in 1930.[122] In the wake of the Depression, the Indian business class suggested that the government help trade and industry by checking foreign imports. They demanded substantial reduction of railway freight on agricultural products, the imposition of import duty on foreign rice and wheat, a revision of land revenue policy to provide relief to agriculturists, and measures for facilitating marketing, warehousing, financing and movement of crops.[123] The government's failure to meet any of the demands of the Southern India Chamber of Commerce strengthened the tendency among South Indian traders to regard the Congress, rather than the government, as an ally.

[121] K. A. Manikumar, "Role of Capitalists in India's Freedom Struggle: South Indian Scenario,1937–1947," in *Last Decade of India's Freedom Struggle*, ed. K. K. N. Kurup (Thiruvanathapuram: Centre for Inter-disciplinary Studies, 1994), 67–70.

[122] K. A. Manikumar, "Tamil Traders in the National Movement, 1900–1947," unpublished paper, 1998.

[123] See *Annual Report, Southern India Chamber of Commerce,* from 1930 to 1937.

1937 Elections

Meanwhile, the Government of India Act of 1935 abolished dyarchy and granted provincial autonomy. A bicameral legislature, consisting of an Assembly of 215 members and a Council of 54 to 56 members, came into existence under the new act. Both the Congress and the Justice Party started making preparations for the elections under the new constitutional scheme. On the Congress' side, Satyamurty was the most effective campaigner. The only person who could match him on the side of the Justice Party was A. Ramaswamy Mudaliyar. The Congressmen could criticise the Justicites for their acquiescence to the repressive laws of the British. They prided themselves on their sacrifices during the Non-Co-operation and Civil Disobedience Movements, and placed definite programmes before the people on the national issues. On the other hand, the Justice Party could only be on the defensive: it had no definite policy or programme on most vital matters affecting the nation. The Justicites continued their usual attacks on Congress, criticising it as being dominated by Brahmins.

The Justicites sought votes, claiming that they had better training and traditions than the Congressmen, and had a greater ability to undertake administrative responsibilities under provincial autonomy. The Congress told the people that "Conditions would change for better only when a government with a national outlook, and not subservient to the exigencies of interests foreign to those of the country, was established by the sanction of the masses of the people, by an administration constituted and controlled by the people."[124] The local Congress leaders like S. Satyamurty and C. Rajagopalachari told the voters that they should return to the Legislative Council those who would represent their grievances and fight for them.

The preamble to the Congress election manifesto of 1937 succinctly summed up the situation and stressed the need for demanding total independence.

> These years had seen the development of economic crisis in India and the world which had led to a progressive deterioration in the constitution of all class of our people. The poverty-stricken masses

[124] *The Hindu*, 19 July 1930.

> are today in the grip of an even more abject poverty and destitution and this growing decease urgently and instantly demands a radical remedy. Poverty and unemployment have long been the lot of our peasantry and industrial workers; today they cover and crush other classes also, the artisan, trader, the small merchant, the middle class intelligentsia. For the vast millions of our countrymen the problem of achieving national independence can give us the power to solve our economic and social problems and end the exploitation of our masses.[125]

"Pending the formulation of a fuller programme," ran the election manifesto, "the Congress reiterates its declaration made at Karachi that it stands for a reform of the system of land tenure and revenue and rent and an equitable adjustment of the burden on agricultural land, giving immediate relief to the smaller peasantry by a substantial reduction of agricultural rent and revenue now paid by them and exempting uneconomic holdings from payment of rent and revenue. The question of indebtedness requires urgent consideration and the formulation of a scheme including the declaration of a moratorium, an enquiry into and scaling down of debts and the provision of cheap credit facilities."[126]

In regard to industrial workers, the election manifesto said, "The policy of Congress is to secure them a decent standard of living, hours of work and conditions of labour in conformity, as far as the economic conditions in the country permit, with international standards, suitable machinery for the settlement of disputes between employees and workmen, protection against the economic consequences of old age, sickness and unemployment and the right of workers to form unions and to strive for the protection of their interest."[127]

As the *Indian Annual Register* commented, "The promises made in the election manifesto by the Congress, while seeking suffrage, roused hopes, that the Congress government, if voted to power, would give relief to them. Perhaps agrarian distress forced the Indian National Congress to give up the policy and programme of

[125] *Indian Annual Register* 2, 1936, 188.

[126] R. Coupland, *Indian Politics, 1936–1942: The Constitutional Problem in India* (Oxford: Oxford University Press, 1944), 2: 137.

[127] *Indian Annual Register* 2, 1936, 188.

non-co-operation and to undertake the responsibility of government under a hated act."[128] It was said that the Congress rule would usher in a positive millennium of high wages and low rents. In some districts, canvassers put down in their notebooks the names of individual peasants and the amount of their rent that would be cancelled if the Congress won the election.[129] "A vote to a non-Congressman is a power of attorney to him to sell you and your children into perpetual serfdom to Britain. It is a warrant committing the nation to political purgatory,"[130] as a Congressman commented at the time of electioneering.

In the elections held under the 1935 act the Congress polled 64.5 per cent of the votes in Madras. It won 159 out of the 215 seats in the Assembly, and 27 out of the 46 elective seats in the two houses put together, representing 73.8 per cent of the seats. The Justice Party got only 18 seats in the Assembly and 7 in the Council.[131] Justicite stalwarts like P. T. Rajan, the kumararaja of Venkatagiri, and A. P. Patro were defeated. Even the leader of the party, the raja of Bobbili, was defeated by a margin of 6,000 votes.[132] It was the most striking Congress victory in any of the provinces.

As we have seen, the Indian National Congress fully realised that the economic crisis was an opportune moment to intensify its struggle for the freedom of the country. At a time when the incidence of the Depression was severe, and the colonial state preferred to function as "law and order administration," the Congress seized the opportunity to tell the people that the remedy lay in retrieving the country from the colonial yoke. All-out efforts were made to win over every section. On the other hand, the Justice Party, which was the only other prominent party in the Presidency, earned the reputation of collaborating, and failed to evolve any definite policy or programme as the Congress had in regard to peasants, factory workers, handloom weavers and the business class. They harped on the same theme that the

[128] *Ibid.*, 2, 1937, 25.
[129] Coupland, *Indian Politics*, 126.
[130] Zaidi and Zaidi, *Encyclopaedia of Indian National Congress*, 10: 355.
[131] S. Krishnaswamy, *Role of Madras Legislature in Freedom Struggle*, 260.
[132] N. Perumal, *Bobbili* (Coimbatore, 1960), 128. Quoted in Rajaraman, *The Justice Party.*

Brahmins dominated the Congress, which had lost its relevance in the context of severe repression and serious economic crisis. Representing economic nationalism in the 1930s, the Congress emerged as a mass organisation, and the contribution of the Depression to this striking transformation was not insignificant.

Conclusion

The worldwide depression of the 1930s turned out to be a decisive influence on Tamilnadu, affecting all sectors, urban and rural, agricultural and industrial, public and private. Few were left untouched. Several classes of people—agriculturists, industrialists, weavers, artisans, moneylenders, traders, industrial and agricultural labourers, and employees in government and private establishments—underwent unprecedented experiences in the period of the Depression. But the nature and magnitude of impact on the above sectors and classes varied a great deal. The Depression, aggravated by British colonialism, also led to some striking changes in the political behaviour of people.

In the initial phase of its onslaught, the Depression was manifested in disastrous trade returns and a fall in prices of agricultural commodities. In Madras, by 1932 the value of imports and exports of merchandise had been practically balanced. In the Indian colonial context, the value of exports had to be much greater than that of the imports in order to cover Home Charges, British Commercial Services, and the like. As the export surplus showed an enormous decline in the wake of the Depression, provincial governments had to look for other resources to pay the Home Charges. This payment was made by the export of gold. Between 1932–33 and 1934–35, Madras exported gold to the value of Rs. 86 million.

A proper study of internal trade during the Depression is handicapped for want of regional statistical data. However, the slump in internal trade was reflected in the income of the railway companies. In order to overcome the financial crisis the railways had to retrench labour and expenditure, suspend their contribution to the general revenue, and enhance their fares.

The collapse of export markets led to a fall in the prices of agricultural and commercial products. The prices of cash crops fell more steeply than the price of rice. During 1929–31 the price of rice fell by 28 per cent, while the prices of groundnut and cotton fell by 45 per cent and 38 per cent, respectively. On the whole, Tiruchirappalli suffered greatly in terms of a fall in prices.

The fall in prices hit the agricultural class in particular—while their incomes were reduced, their obligations remained. To them, meeting obligations such as clearance of debt and payment of land revenue dues to the government was a heavy burden even in normal times. The fall in prices of agricultural commodities increased the real burden of indebtedness by as much as 50 per cent. Both peasants and the government initially hoped for an early recovery, but the prices continued to decline until 1934. And although the decline was arrested after 1934, there was no significant recovery. Consequently, the peasants became heavily entrenched in debt.

The increased burden of land revenue, in real terms, hit the peasantry very hard. But the government chose to forcibly collect land revenue, despite peasant protest. Peasant struggles led by the Congress in the ryotwari tracts were less militant than the revolts of the tenantry in the zamindari areas of both Andhra and Tamilnadu. The agricultural labourers who had been organised on class lines agitated for wage increase. Unorganised labour either resorted to grain looting or clashed with their oppressive landlords —which often assumed a caste dimension.

Neither the government nor the co-operative societies made any great effort to alleviate the hardship of the indebted peasants. Banks stopped lending money. Even moneylenders suspended their lending activities, and were concerned only with recovering their loans. The co-operative societies faced a liquidity crisis, and resorted to drastic measures to recover their loans. Depressing features such as mortality in the number of societies, overdue repayments, increase in the number of "moribund societies," and liquidation became prominent in the working of co-operative organisations.

The Depression exerted a great strain on the resources of the government, as public revenue under customs, excise, stamps and registration fell. From 1930 onwards, the budget was out of balance, and the government's orthodox and defensive policy of "a balanced budget" necessitated an increase in taxes and reduction in spending. The measures initiated by the government in pursuance of this policy only made matters worse. Two instances show how disastrous the government's taxation policy was to the Indian business interests. One was the imposition of fresh taxes by the government through an emergency budget, when the economy was already reeling under the impact of the Depression. The other was the levying of excise duty by the government, as a part of its effort to make good the loss of revenue from customs. This crippled the small-scale and cottage industries totally.

The monetary policy pursued by the colonial state during this period proved detrimental to Indian business interests. In September 1931 Great Britain abandoned the gold standard. Subsequently, the rupee was linked to sterling. Indian currency was thus made subservient to sterling, appreciating or depreciating along with it. The main consideration of the government in doing so was to prevent a "flight from the rupee." Indian opinion was in favour of decoupling the rupee from the pound; therefore, the change in the monetary system made by the British, without consultation of the Indian legislature, aroused deep resentment in the country. Currency leagues were formed by the nationalists to organise a countrywide agitation. This brought the business class close to the Congress.

Most of the European countries combated the Depression through inflation of the money supply. The "New Deal" policy of President Roosevelt of the US provided for substantial loan expenditure, increasing the money supply. But India was experiencing the most ruthless deflation during the Depression. Money was withdrawn from circulation to maintain the eighteen pence rate. At a time when the country was expected to ease the credit situation by increasing the circulation of money, the colonial government did the very opposite. Given the government's fiscal policy and a general feeling of insecurity, the banks constricted credit. In every country currency was devalued; but in the Madras Presidency the government, under pressure from London, rejected devaluation. The advice for increase in public works expenditure to tackle the problem of unemployment was also dismissed as economically unsound. The cut in the expenditure under public works was the largest, nearly 40 per cent, during the Depression years.

Initially, the provincial government's response to the Depression was a policy of no action. The government contended that the Depression was a worldwide phenomenon, and it had nothing to offer which would alter a global situation. Subsequently, when the situation worsened, it instituted enquiries. Yet, no action was taken on the basis of the recommendations of the Economic Depression Enquiry Committee, and on the reports of W. R. S. Sathyanathan and C. R. Srinivasan. The nationalists used the legislature to agitate against the government's land revenue policy. Resolutions demanding 25, 33.33, and, in some cases, 50 per cent land revenue reduction were passed. After much delay, the government granted 12.5 per cent remission to those districts where revision of settlements had been completed after 1918, and therefore had been influenced by the high prices ruling at that time.

When the crisis in the agricultural market deepened, the government of Madras belatedly appointed a marketing board. But before it started to function, the Depression dealt a mortal blow to a vast section of the agricultural population. Similarly, the government, in an attempt to tackle rural indebtedness, enacted debt legislation such as the Madras Debtor Protection Act (1936), The Agriculturists Loan (Amendment) Act (1935), The Madras Debt Conciliation Act (1936) and Agriculturists' Relief Act (1937). The Madras Debtor Protection Act, which sought to regulate the moneylending business in the Province, did not in any way help to reduce the burden of agricultural indebtedness. The money earmarked under the Agriculturists Loan Act worked out in average to Rs. 8 million per year, and when the actual debt of the Presidency was Rs. 2,000 million, the relief afforded by such a sum was minimal. The Madras Debt Conciliation Act provided for voluntary settlement of debts through debt conciliation boards. But as the creditors often refused to accept the terms of the boards, the act failed to achieve its objective of scaling down rural indebtedness.

Though the Madras Agriculturists' Relief Act helped scale down the agriculturists' indebtedness to some extent, the operation of this act adversely affected the local credit system. As the rates of interest to be charged under the act were considered low, the moneylenders showed no inclination to do business according to the new terms. The series of acts passed with the intention of giving relief to the agricultural debtors demoralised the creditors, who finally suspended their moneylending activities. Therefore, the government's legislative measures only helped constrict the money circulation. The fragility of the credit system stood exposed during the Depression. The government could have floated funds through co-operative credit societies to revamp the flow of money supply. But the deflationary policy of the government stood in the way of taking such a bold initiative. Throughout this period the government did not realise the potential of the co-operative societies.

In Western countries protectionism had been adopted to check the inflow of foreign goods. In India, the colonial government did little in this direction. Cheap rice from Burma displaced the local rice in many places. Burma rice was even transported from Tuticorin to Thanjavur, the rice bowl of Tamilnadu, resulting in further accumulation of stocks in Thanjavur. The Madras government did nothing to prevent such imports. The Imperial Economic Conference held at Ottawa evoked a lot of expectation from the Indian community. But the outcome of the conference was disappointing to the Indian traders, as the Indian delegation was forced to conclude an agreement which gave preference to some British goods over the manufactures of non-Empire countries. The British representatives' refusal to discuss the Indian currency question at the conference also upset the Indian trading community, because the prevailing exchange ratio made Indian exports costlier and imports cheaper.

The conditions of depression made rural moneylending an eminently unprofitable proposition. On the other hand, the impact of the Depression was not as severe on industries such as cotton textiles, sugar and cement, since the breakdown in international trade had reduced competition from abroad. Such consequences of the Depression as falls in the rates of interest, availability of raw materials at lower prices, wage reduction, and unemployment provided stimulus to industries. Not surprisingly, the moneylending capital found its way into industry. Cotton mills were started in and around Coimbatore. The textile industry in Madras developed proportionally to those of Bombay and Ahmadabad during this period. Similarly, the sugar industry expanded. The moneylending capital was diversified into banking institutions, and there was an unprecedented expansion of banking. In order to monitor and regulate the functioning of those banks the Reserve Bank of India finally came into being in 1935.

However, the industries that depended on foreign markets, like leather and jute, floundered. Small-scale and cottage industries such as hosiery, matches and handlooms faced a severe crisis during this period. While the proprietors of these enterprises were ruined, the workers in these concerns were rendered jobless.

Industrialisation was later accompanied by urbanisation. Madras, Madurai and Coimbatore recorded remarkable demographic change during this period. Similarly, all centres of industrial activity developed into urban centres later. There was phenomenal increase of population in all the industrial centres. In Madras, the increase of population, which was mostly due to "migration of despair" from rural areas, created problems such as growth of slums, increasing burglary, beggary and vagrancy. On the other hand, due to the large-scale exodus from rural areas there was a decrease of rural population. A re-survey done by P. J. Thomas and K. C. Ramakrishnan in 1937, of some South Indian villages originally surveyed by Slater in 1916, observed this trend in at least three villages.

The rates of crime in the region as a whole increased during this period. Normally, cattle theft is considered to be an indicator of acute poverty in rural areas. The increasing instances of cattle theft suggest the acute condition of depression in the Presidency. The increase in the cases of illicit distillation and related offences indicate that the depressed living conditions of the weavers and of agricultural and industrial labourers prompted them to take to liquor. But finding that the licit liquor was not within their reach, they went in for much cheaper illicit brew.

The people who had lost their lands in the aftermath of the Depression became agricultural labourers. The emigrant Tamil labourers who had lost their jobs in Southeast Asian countries returned to their native villages and looked for agricultural work. Consequently the number of agricultural labourers in the Madras Province shot up—a phenomenon that deserves further study. With an increase in the number of landless labourers, accompanied by an alarming proportion of unemployment, the social fabric was being eroded. The large-scale return of emigrant labourers from Ceylon, Burma and Malaya also had its social effect on rural Tamilnadu. The emigrants of depressed castes, who had not been discriminated against on the basis of caste while overseas, felt very aggrieved on their return, when they had to face discrimination again. The result was communal clashes between upper castes and lower castes, who constituted land-owning and labouring classes, respectively.

The government set the trend for wage-cutting when it inflicted a 10 per cent cut in the salaries of its employees. Soon industries and business concerns gleefully followed it. As we have seen, there were already unemployed and underemployed agriculturists. In the wake of export markets for handloom products being wiped out, there was a mass of unemployed weavers as well. Added to these sections were unemployed industrial labourers and retrenched persons from government and private sectors. There must have been an acute problem of unemployment and woeful deterioration in the standard of living of people. But the absence of reliable data on these aspects is a handicap in making a precise assessment.

It is generally expected of labour to agitate and protest in such a situation. But the working class, facing retrenchment, widespread unemployment and attack on money wages, was entirely on the defensive. This was due to a variety of reasons. The proportion of the workforce employed in factories was numerically small. Much of this workforce was in small factories. Of the remaining workforce belonging to the large factories, a considerable portion was unorganised. Therefore, although strikes broke out in mills, railways and some other industrial establishments, they were of short duration and generally fizzled out. The fear of unemployment sent the striking workers back to work within a few days.

As socio-economic conditions varied greatly, different classes and areas were affected very unequally by the Depression.[1] How different classes of people came to be affected is reported in the contemporary records and writings. The census officer in Madras observed that notwithstanding the difficulty in securing employment, the labouring classes came off best, since the prices of necessities of life had fallen more than the diminution in their wages.[2] The special officer, W. R. S. Sathyanathan, expressing a

1 Anstey, *Economic Development of India*, 488.
2 *Census of India*, 1931, 14, part 1, 23–24.

similar view in his report, argued that the labourer generally earned the same money as before but had to spend less on the necessaries of life as prices had fallen.[3] The director of industries in his report for 1937 wrote that the cultivators suffered much more during the Depression than the industrial labourers, and suggested that the key to the problems of raising the standard of life of the people was to industrialise the country.[4]

But from chapter 5, it is evident that the labourers faced severe retrenchment and wage cuts. They attempted to resist, but could not sustain their resistance. The workers thrown out of employment in private factories and government services were probably less in number than those distressed in the agrarian sector. But there is no basis to conclude that the labourers were in an enviable position or better off than the agriculturists.

Practically the whole class of agriculturists suffered, but the extent of suffering varied. Vera Anstey, speaking of the country as a whole, observed that the peasant who sold only a small proportion of his crops was less hit by a fall in prices than one who sold a larger proportion, as the former hired no labour and paid a small amount of land revenue. She further explained that the small farmer could adjust by cutting down his consumption of things that he did not produce. Whereas for the cultivator who normally sold a substantial proportion of his crops, the value of his produce fell catastrophically whilst there was no proportionate reduction in his cultivation cost.[5]

In the case of Tamilnadu two contrary opinions had been expressed, one given in *Season and Crop Report of the Government of Madras* for 1933–34, and the other put forth by the Special Officer W. R. S. Sathyanathan. The observation found in the *Season and Crop Report* was that the rich peasants, in particular absentee landlords, had difficulty in securing suitable tenants for their lands at fair rents, and hence they were the worst sufferers. The report concluded that the cultivating tenants and landless labourers were somewhat better off, although they had to face

3 Sathyanathan, *Report*, *Agricultural Indebtedness*, 31.
4 *Report of the Department of Industries*, 1937, 9–10.
5 Anstey, *Economic Development of India*, 488.

the problem of low prices.[6] However, Sathyanathan asserted that small and medium landholders, including cultivating tenants, were the hardest hit of all the agricultural classes.[7] The present study reveals that the special officer's observation is correct because it was the marginal farmer who had to lose land at the time of the Great Depression.

The Indian National Congress saw the economic crisis as an opportunity to intensify its struggle for the freedom of the country. At a time when the incidence of the Depression was severe and the colonial state preferred to function as "law and order administration," the Congress seized the opportunity of telling the people that the remedy lay in retrieving the country from the colonial yoke. All-out efforts were made to win over every section. At its Karachi session in 1931, a well-defined programme was formulated for peasantry and industrial labour. The Congress made it known that through its labour programme it stood for the right of labour to form unions, and that it supported a living wage for them. In regard to peasantry, it made a declaration that it would strive for reduction of land revenue, scaling down of debt, and the provision of cheap credit facilities. Gandhi's hand spinning programme had a particular appeal to the unemployed handloom weavers; they strengthened the Congress by enthusiastically participating in its programme of picketing the foreign cloth shops. The manipulation of the currency system —resorted to by the British government to transmit the impact of the Depression to India—united the business and trading interests against the colonial rule. The Indian businessmen who were organised in the Southern India Chamber of Commerce participated in all programmes of the Congress in the late 1920s and the 1930s.

The Justice Party, the only other prominent party in the Presidency, which had earned the reputation of playing the role of collaborator, failed to evolve any definite policy or programme in regard to industrial workers and peasants. They harped on the same theme of Brahmin domination, which lost its relevance

6 Quoted in Sathyanathan, *Report, Agricultural Indebtedness*, 31.
7 *Ibid.*, 43.

in the context of acute economic crisis. So when the Congress gave up its "no-council-entry" stand and contested elections under the new constitutional system in 1937, the electorate, which included a substantial number of peasants and labourers, returned a huge majority of Congress candidates, and placed a Congress ministry led by C. Rajajgopalachari in power in Madras. Historically, the Depression provided an opportunity for new bases in politics to emerge in the region.

Glossary

abkari	excise duties
anna	unit of money; 16 annas = 1 rupee; 12 pies = 1 anna
arrack	an alcoholic spirit made from the sap of the coco palm or rice
benami	illegal ownership under a false name
candy	a bazaar weight; 20 maunds = 1 candy; 1 candy =500 lbs
cholam & *cumbu*	varieties of millet
Dalit	member of the lowest or scheduled caste
dharna	demonstration
dhoti	a loincloth worn by male hindus
duffador	personal attendant of the district collector
fasli	an Indian agricultural calender
gada	linen (clothing)
garce	a measure of capacity; 400 mercauls = 1 garce or 1 garce = 185 cubic feet, 320 cubic inches
inam	a prebendal estate gifted by the king
inamdar	a person who has been granted an inam
jagir	land grant from a nawab
jamabandhi	the annual settlement of land revenue with the cultivators
kalam	a dry measure, usually of paddy, amounting to half a bag; weighing about 63.69 lbs
Kallar	people of agrarian caste in the south and southeast Tamilnadu registered under Criminal Tribes Act
kist	land tax
kuthagai	lease
lathi	a long stick used as a weapon
lungi	length of cloth worn around the waist
manyam	a land exempt from tax
maund	a measure of weight followed in India before the decimal system; equal to 82.28 lb or 37.12 kg.

mirasidar	holder of a heritable and transferable right to land
muffassal	rural area
munsiff	head of village
Nattukottai Chettiyars	a caste of traders and bankers
panchayatdar	persons forming court of arbitration in a village
panniyal	farm labourer
peshkush	land revenue collected from a zamindar
ragi	a kind of millet
ryot	a tenant farmer
ryotwari	land revenue system under which assessments are made on individual land holdings
satyagraha	non-violent civil disobedience
sepoy	soldier
shandy	market
shroff	moneylenders belonging to the Marwari, Multani and Sindi communities
sowcar	a moneylender originating from Rajasthan
taccavi	government agricultural loan
tahsildar	chief administrative officer of a taluk
taluk	an administrative district for taxation purposes
taram	quality
thali	marriage pendant
tola	measure of weight—less than .5 ounce
vakil	lawyer
zamindari	a type of landed estate governed by the system of revenue farming

Bibliography

PRIMARY SOURCES

Madras Government Annuals

Administration Report of the Labour Department. 1929 to 1939. Madras.
Administration Report of the Registration Department. 1929 to 1939. Madras.
Administrative Report of the Co-operative Department. 1929 to 1939. Madras.
Annual Report on the Working of the Madras Co-operative Societies Act. 1929 to 1939. Madras..
Annual Report of the Department of Industries. 1929 to 1939. Madras.
Annual Report of the Director of Public Health. 1929 to 1939. Madras.
Report of the Operations of the Department of Agriculture. 1929 to 1939. Madras.
Report on the Administration of the Madras Presidency. 1920 to 1939. Madras.
Report on the Administration of the Excise Revenue in the Presidency. 1929 to 1939. Madras.
Report on the Administration of the Police of the Madras Presidency. 1929 to 1939. Madras.
Report on Public Instruction in the Madras Presidency. 1929 to 1939. Madras.
Report on the Settlement of the Land Revenue of the Districts in the Madras Presidency. Fasli 1338 to Fasli 1345. Madras.
Season and Crop Report of the Government of Madras. 1929 to 1939. Madras.

Madras Government Files

The proceedings and orders of the government of Madras (1929–1939) in the departments of:

Board of Revenue
Development
Education
Finance
Law (General)
Public
Public Health

Public Works & Labour
Revenue
Land Revenue and Settlement

Madras Government Reports

Economic Depression Enquiry Report. Madras, 1930.
Madras Provincial Banking Enquiry Committee Report. Vol. 2. Madras, 1930.
Narayanaswamy Naidu, B. V. *Report of the Economist for Enquiry into Rural Indebtedness*. Madras, 1946.
Report of the Committee on Co-operation in Madras. Madras, 1939–40.
Report of the Madras Retrenchment Committee. Madras, 1931–32.
Sathyanathan, W. R. S. *Report on Agricultural Indebtedness*. Madras, 1935.
Srinivasan, C. R. *Report of the Rice Production and Trade in the Madras Presidency*. Madras, 1934.

Other Madras Government Records

A Statistical Atlas of the Madras Presidency (Revised up to the end of Fasli 1340). Madras, 1936.
Fortnightly Reports sent by chief secretary of Madras government to secretary of government of India in Home Department. 1929 to 1939. Madras.
Madras Legislative Assembly Debates. 1937 to 1939. Madras.
Proceedings of the Madras Legislative Council. 1929 to 1939. Madras.
Fort St. George Gazette. 1937 to 1939. Madras.

Gazetteers

Baliga, B. S. *Madras District Gazetteers: Coimbatore*. Madras: Director of Stationary and Printing, Government of Madras, 1966.
Krishnaswamy Ayyer, K. N. *Madras District Gazetteers: Tanjore*. Madras: Superintendent, Government Press, 1933.
Ramaswamy, A. *Madras District Gazetteers: Salem*. Madras: Director of Stationary and Printing, 1967.

Annual Reports of Chambers of Commerce

Annual Report of the Southern India Chamber of Commerce. 1928 to 1939. Madras.
Proceedings of the Madras Chamber of Commerce. 1928 to 1939. Madras.

Newspapers

The Hindu. 1930 to 1936. Madras.

Justice. 1931 to 1935. Madras.
Confidential Report on Native Newspapers Examined in the Fort St. George Secretariat. 1929 to 1936. Madras.

Journals

Asiatic Review. 1929 to 1937. London: East and West.
Indian Annual Register, The. 1929 to 1939. Calcutta: Bennet, Coleman and Co.
Indian Review. 1929 to 1939. Madras: G. A. Natesan.
Indian Year Book, The. Calcutta: Bennet Coleman, 1929 to 1939.
Modern Review. 1929 to 1940. Calcutta.

Government of India Annuals

Annual Statement of the Sea-Borne Trade of British India with the British Empire and Foreign Countries. 1929 to 1937.
British India Agricultural Statistics. 1929–30 to 1936–37.
India in 1928–29 to 1938–39 (Statement prepared for presentation to Parliament in accordance with requirements of Section 26 of the Government of India Act).
Review of the Trade of India. 1929 to 1939.
Report of the Railway Board on Indian Railways. 1929 to 1937.
Statistical Abstract for British India. From 1927–28 to 1936–37.

Reports of Government of British India

Census of India 1931. Madras volume XIV, parts I & II.
Report of the Fact-Finding Committee (Handloom and Mills). Calcutta, 1942.
Report of Royal Commission on Agriculture in India. Madras, 1928.
Report of Royal Commission on Labour in India. Calcutta, 1931.

SECONDARY SOURCES

Dissertations (unpublished)

James, Joseph. "Urbanisation and Economic Change in Tamil Nadu." Ph.D. diss., University of Madras, 1982.
Krishnamurty, R. "India through Slump and Recovery, 1929–1937: Being a Study of the Trade Cycle in relation to India." M.Litt. diss., University of Madras, 1940.
Meenakshi, T. "The Finance of Madras Government since 1919." M.Litt. diss., University of Madras, 1950.

Natarajan, K. V. "Economic and Financial Condition of the Residuary Madras State." M.Litt. diss., University of Madras, 1956.

Ponniah, J. S. "The Production and Marketing of Raw Cotton in the Madras Presidency with special reference to the Districts of Bellary, Kurnool, Coimbatore, Madura, Ramnad, and Tinnevelly." D.Litt. diss., University of Madras, 1944.

Rukmani, R. "The Process of Urbanization and Socio-economic Change in Tamilnadu." Ph.D. diss., University of Madras, 1994.

Books and Articles

Albertini, Rudolf Von. *European Colonial Rule, 1880–1940: The Impact of the West on India, South East Asia and Africa.* Connecticut: Greenwood Press, 1982.

Alexander, K. C. *Agricultural Labour Unions: A Study in Three South Indian States.* Hyderabad: National Institute of Rural Development, 1978.

Anstey, Vera. *The Economic Development of India.* London: Longman, Green and Co., 1936.

Arndt, H. W. *The Economic Lessons of the Nineteen Thirties.* London: Oxford University Press, 1944.

Arnold, David. *The Congress in Tamil Nad (1919–1937): Nationalist Politics in South India.* New Delhi: Manohar Book Service, 1977.

Bagchi, Amiya Kumar. *The Political Economy of Under Development.* Cambridge: Cambridge University Press, 1982.

———. *The Presidency Banks and the Indian Economy, 1876–1914.* Calcutta: Oxford University Press, 1989.

———. *Private Investment in India (1900–1939).* New Delhi: Orient Longman, 1982.

Baker, C. J. *An Indian Rural Economy (1880–1955): The Tamil Nad Countryside.* Delhi: Oxford University Press, 1984.

———. *The Politics of South India (1920–1937).* New Delhi: Vikas Publishing House, 1976.

———. "Tamil Nad Estates in the Twentieth Century." *Indian Economic and Social History Review* 13, no.1, 1976.

Baker, C. J., & D. A. Washbrook. *South India: Political Institutions and Political Change.* New Delhi: Macmillan, 1975.

Balachandran, G. *John Bullion's Empire: Britain's Gold Problem and India Between the Wars.* London: Curzon, 1996.

Baliga, B. S. *Compendium on History of Handloom Industry in Madras.* Madras: Controller of Stationary and Printing, Government of Madras, 1960.

———. *Studies in Madras Administration.* 2 vols. Madras: Controller of Stationary and Printing, Government of Madras, 1960.

Banerjea, Premathanath. *Provincial Finance in India.* London: Macmillan, 1929.

Banerji, A. K. *India's Balance of Payments, 1921–22 to 1938–39.* London: Asia Publishing House, 1963.

Barnett, Marguerite Ross. *The Politics of Cultural Nationalism in South India.* New Jersey: Princeton University Press, 1976.

Beteille, Andre. *Society and Politics in India: Essays in Comparative Perspective.* New Delhi: Oxford University Press, 1977.

———. *Studies in Agrarian Social Structure.* New Delhi: Oxford University Press, 1974.

Boag, G. T. *The Madras Presidency, 1881–1931.* Madras: Superintendent, Government Press, 1933.

Bogendranath, N. C. *Development of the Textile Industry in Madras (Up to 1950).* Madras: University of Madras, 1957.

Brunner, Karl, ed. *The Great Depression Revisited.* The Hague: Martions Nijhoff, 1981.

Buchanan, D. H. *The Development of Capitalistic Enterprise in India.* London: Frank Cass, 1966.

Chandavarkar, A. G. "Money and Credit, 1857–1947." In *The Cambridge Economic History of India, 1757–1970,* eds. Dharma Kumar and Tapan Raychoudhari. New Delhi: Orient Longman, 1984.

Chandra, Bipan. "Indian Peasantry and National Integration," *Social Scientist* 5, no. 50, 1976.

———. *The Rise and Growth of Economic Nationalism in India: Economic Policies of Indian National Leadership (1880–1905).* New Delhi: People's Publishing House, 1982.

Charlesworth, Neil. *Peasants and Imperial Rule: Agriculture and Agrarian Society in the Bombay Presidency, 1850–1935.* Cambridge: Cambridge University Press, 1985.

Chisthi, Sumitra. *India's Terms of Trade.* New Delhi: Orient Longman, 1974.

Coupland, R. *Indian Politics (1936–1942): The Constitutional Problems in India.* Oxford: Oxford University Press, 1944.

Coyajee, J. C. *The World Economic Depression: A Plea for Co-operation.* Madras: Huxley Press, 1933.

Dantwala, M. L. *Poverty in India: Then and Now (1870–1970).* Madras: Macmillan, 1973.

de Cecco, Marcello. *The International Gold Standard: Money and Empire.* London: Frances Pinter, 1984.

Desai, A. R., ed. *Peasant Struggles in India.* New Delhi: Oxford University Press, 1982.

Desouza, F. *The House of Binny.* London: Inchcape, 1969.

Dewy, Clive, and A. G. Hopkins, eds. *The Imperial Impact: Studies in the Economic History of Africa and India.* London: University of London, 1978.

Dey, H. L. "The Rupee-Ratio Controversy." *Modern Review* 61, no. 5, 1937.

Dhanagare, D. N. *Peasant Movements in India, 1920–1950.* New Delhi: Oxford University Press, 1986.

Digby, William. *Prosperous British India.* New Delhi: Sagar Publications, 1969.

Dobb, Maurice. *Political Economy and Capitalism.* Connecticut: Greenwood Press, 1975.

———. *Studies in the Development of Capitalism.* New York: International Publishers, 1970.

D'Souza, V. L. "Agricultural Debts and Depression." *Indian Review* 35, no.7, 1934.

Dubey, D. L. *The Indian Public Debt.* Bombay: D. B. Taraporevala and Son, 1930.

Dufty, N. F. *Industrial Relations in India.* Bombay: Allied Publishers, 1964.

Dutt, Rajni Palme. *India To-day.* Calcutta: Manisha Granthalaya, 1983.

Dutt, Romesh Chandra. *The Economic History of India.* 2 vols. New Delhi: Publication Division, Ministry of Information and Broadcasting, Government of India, 1970.

Feurer, Lewis S. *Marx and Engels: Basic Writings on Politics and Philosophy.* New York: Anchor Books, Double Day, 1959.

Findlay Shirras, G. "The Situation in India: A Rejoinder." *The Economic Journal* 42, 1932.

Gadgil, D. R. *The Industrial Evolution of India in Recent Times.* London: Oxford University Press, 1954.

Galbraith, John Kenneth. *The Affluent Society.* Bombay: Lalvani Publishing House, 1970.

———. *The Great Crash: 1929.* Australia: Penguin Books, 1969.

Garraty, John A. *The Great Depression.* Florida: Jovanovich, 1986.

Gate, B. G. *Changes in the Occupational Distribution of the Population.* Delhi: Government of India, 1940.

Goldsmith, Raymond W. *The Financial Development of India, 1860–1977.* Delhi: Oxford University Press, 1983.

Gough, Kathleen. "Agricultural Labour in Thanjavur." In *Social Anthropology of Peasantry,* ed. John P. Mencher. Bombay: Somaiya Publications, 1983.

———. *Rural Society in South East India.* Cambridge: Cambridge University Press, 1981.

Haberler, Gotfried. *Colonialism and Development: Britain and Its Tropical Colonies, 1850–1960.* London: Routledge, 1993.

———. *Prosperity and Depression.* Geneva: League of Nations, 1941.

———. *The World Economy, Money, and the Great Depression.* Washington: American Enterprise Institute for Public Policy Research, 1976.

Habib, Irfan. "Colonialisation of the Indian Economy (1757–1900)." *Social Scientist,* no. 3, 1975.

Hardgrave, Robert L. *The Dravidian Movement.* Bombay: Popular Prakashan, 1965.

———. *Essays in the Political Sociology of South India.* New Delhi: Usha Publications, 1979.

History of Higher Education in South India, The (1857–1957). Vol. 1. Madras: University of Madras, 1957.

History of Madras Police, The (1859–1959). Madras: Inspector General of Police, 1959.

Hobsbawm, Eric. *The Age of Extremes.* New Delhi: Viking, 1995.

Horne, E. A. *The Political System of British India with Special Reference to Recent Constitutional Changes.* Oxford: Clarendon Press, 1922.

Irschick, Eugene F. *Politics and Social Conflict in South India: The Non-Brahmin Movement and Tamil Separatism (1916–29).* Berkeley: University of California Press, 1969.

———. *Tamil Revivalism in the 1930s.* Madras: Cre-A, 1986.

Jain, L. C. "Economic Depression in India." *Indian Journal of Economics* 13, 1932–33.

Journals of David E. Lilienthal, The: 1917–1939. Vol. 1. New York: Harper and Row, 1964.

Justice Party Golden Jubilee Souvenir, The. Madurai, 1968.

Kannankunhi, K. *A Civilization at Bay: India—Past, Present, Future.* Madras: Natesan, 1936.

Karwal, G. D. "The Political Factor in Indian Economic Depression." *Indian Journal of Economics* 13, 1932–33.

Keynes, John Maynard. *The General Theory of Employment, Interest and Money.* London: Macmillan, 1964.

Kidron, Michael. *Foreign Investments in India.* London: Oxford University Press, 1965.

Kindleberger, Charles P. *Manias, Panics and Crashes: A History of Financial Crisis.* New York: Basic Books, 1970.

Klein, Lawrence R. *The Keynesian Revolution.* London: Macmillan, 1968.

Krishnaswamy, S. *The Role of Madras Legislature in the Freedom Struggle, 1861–1947.* New Delhi: Indian Council of Historical Research, 1989.

Krishnaswamy, S. Y. *Rural Problems in Madras.* Madras: Superintendent, Government Press, 1947.

Krishnaswamy, V. D. "The Problems of Water in Madras." *The Madras Tercentenary Commemoration Volume.* Madras: G. S. Press, 1939.

Kumar , Dharma, & Tapan Raychoudhari, eds. *The Cambridge Economic History of India, 1757–1970.* Cambridge: Cambridge University Press, 1982.

Leontiev. *A Political Economy.* Calcutta: National Book Agency, 1977.

Levkovsky, A. I. *Capitalism in India: Basic Trends in Its Development.* Bombay: People's Publishing House, 1966.

Loganathan, P. S. *Industrial Organisation in India.* London: George Allen and Unwin, 1935.

———. "Major Industries in India: An Examination of Their Structure," *Justice*, 30 August 1935.

Ludden, David. *Peasant History in South India.* New Jersey: Princeton University Press, 1985.

Madras Tercentenary Commemoration Volume, The. Madras: G. S. Press, 1939.

Mahadevan, Raman. "The Development of Modern Entrepreneurship in the Chettiyar Community of Tamil Nadu, 1900–1930." In *Essays in Modern Indian Economic History*, ed. Sabyasachi Bhattacharya. New Delhi: Munshiram Manoharlal, 1987.

Manak, Elizabeth. *Formulation of Agricultural Policy in Imperial India, 1872–1929: A Case Study of the Madras Presidency.* Hawaii: University of Hawaii, 1979.

Manikumar, K. A. "The Impact of Great Depression on the Social Life of the Tamils." *Artha Vijnana* 38, no. 3, 1996.

———. "Role of Capitalists in India's Freedom Struggle: South Indian Scenario, 1937–47." In *Last Decade of India's Freedom Struggle*, ed. K. K. N. Kurup, 67–78. Thiruvananthapuram: Centre for Interdisciplinary Studies, 1994.

———. "Tamil Traders in the National Movement, 1900–1947." Unpublished paper, 1998.

Marx, Karl. *Capital.* 3 vols. Moscow: Progress Publishers, 1978.

Marx, Karl, & Friedrich Engels. *Pre-Capitalist Socio-Economic Formation.* Moscow: Progress Publishers, 1979.

Medovoy, A. I. *The Indian Economy.* Moscow: Progress Publishers, 1984.

Mencher, John P. *Agriculture and Social Structure in Tamil Nadu.* New Delhi: Allied Publishers, 1978.

Menshikov, S. *The Economic Cycle: Post-War Developments.* Moscow: Progress Publishers, 1975.

Mukerjee, Radha Kamal, & H. L. Dey, eds. *Economic Problems of Modern India.* Vol. 2. London: Macmillan, 1941.

Mukherjee, Aditya. "Indo-British Finance: The Controversy over India's Sterling Balances, 1934–1947." *Studies in History* 6, no. 2, 1990.

———. "The Rupee Question, 1926–28: Rupee Sterling Ratio and the Gold Standard." *Studies in History* 5, no. 1, 1989.

Murphy, Eamon. *Unions in Conflict: A Comparative Study of Four South Indian Textile Centres, 1918–1939.* New Delhi: Manohar, 1981.

Naoroji, Dadabhai. *Poverty and Un-British Rule in India.* Delhi: Publication Division, Ministry of Information and Broadcasting, Government of India, 1962.

Narain, Lakshmi. *Price Movements in India, 1929–1957.* Meerut: Shri Prakasham Publishers, 1957.

Narayanamurthy, N., ed. *The Modern Indian Peasant: A Collection of Addresses, Speeches and Writings of Professor N. G. Ranga.* Madras: Kisan Publication, 1936.

Narayana Prasad, P. S. "World Depression in India." *Indian Journal of Economics* 16, 1935–36.

Narayanaswamy Naidu, B. V. *The Co-operative Movement in the Madras Presidency.* Annamalai Nagar: Annamalai University, 1933.

———. *The Economics of Indian Agriculture.* Madras: Rochouse and Sons, 1943.

———. "Finance of the Madras Province, 1920–40." *Indian Journal of Economics* 21, 1940–41.

———, ed. *Indian Trade.* Annamalai University Economic Series No. 9. Annamalai Nagar: Annamalai University, 1942.

Narayanaswamy Naidu, B.V., & V. Venkataraman. "The Problem of Rural Indebtedness." *Journal of the Annamalai University* 4, no. 2, 1935.

Narayanaswamy Naidu, B.V., & P. Vaidyanathan. *The Madras Agriculturists Relief Act: A Study*. Annamalai Nagar: Annamalai University, 1939.

Nehru, Jawaharlal. *Discovery of India*. Bombay: Asia Publishing House, 1967.

———. *Glimpses of World History*. London: Lindsay Drummond, 1949.

Patnaik, Utsa. "The Process of Commercialization under Colonial Conditions." *Proceedings of the Seminar on Commercialization in Indian Agriculture*. Thiruvananthapuram: Centre for Development Studies, 1981.

Rajaraman, P. *The Justice Party: A Historical Perspective, 1916–1937*. Madras: Poompozhil Publishers, 1988.

Ram, N. "Dravidian Movement in its Pre-Independent Phase." *Economic and Political Weekly*. Annual Number 7 & 8, 1979.

Ramakrishna Ayyar, V. A. "India's Agricultural Incomes." *Indian Review* 38, no. 6, 1938.

Ranga, N. G. *The Kisan Speaks*. Madras: Kisan Publication, 1937.

Ranson, C. W. "The Growth of Population in Madras." *The Madras Tercentenary Commemoration Volume*. Madras: G. S. Press, 1939.

Robbins, Lionel. *The Great Depression*. New York: Macmillan, 1935.

Robert, Bruce L. Jr. "Agricultural Credit Co-operatives in Madras, 1893–1937: Rural Development and Agrarian Politics in Pre-Independence India." *The Indian Economic and Social History Review* 16, no. 2, 1979.

Rosen, George. *Industrial Change in India: Industrial Growth, Capital Requirements and Technological Change, 1937–1955*. Bombay: Asia Publishing House, 1959.

Rothermund, D. "British Foreign Trade Policy in India during the Great Depression, 1929–1939." *The Indian Economic and Social History Review* 18, nos. 2 & 3, 1981.

———. *An Economic History of India*. USA: Croom Helm, 1988.

———. *The Global Impact of the Great Depression*. New York: Routledge, 1996.

———. "The Great Depression and British Financial Policy in India, 1929–1934." *The Indian Economic and Social History Review* 18, no. 1, 1981.

———. *India in the Great Depression*. New Delhi: Manohar Publications, 1992.

———. *Indian Economy under British Rule and Other Essays*. New Delhi: Manohar Publications, 1983.

Santhanam, S. S. "Rural Co-operation in Madras." *Indian Journal of Economics* 22, 1941–42.

Sarada Raju, A. *Economic Condition in the Madras Presidency, 1800–1850*. Madras: University of Madras, 1941.

Sarma, S. P. *Indian Budgets, 1921–1934*. Madras: G. A. Natesan, 1934.

Sayana, V. V. *The Agrarian Problems of Madras Province*. Madras: Book View Press, 1949.

Sen, Sukomal. *Working Class of India: History of Emergence and Movement, 1830–1970*. Calcutta: K. P. Bagchi, 1979.

Sen, Sunanda. *Colonies and the Empire*. Calcutta: Orient Longman, 1992.

Shachtman, Tom. *The Day America Crashed: A Narrative Account of the Great Stock Market Crash of October 24, 1929*. New York: G.P. Putnam's, 1975.

Shah, K. T. *World Depression*. Madras: National Literature, 1933.

Singh, V. B. *Economic History of India, 1857–1956*. Bombay: Allied Publishers, 1965.

———. *From Naoroji to Nehru*. Delhi: Macmillan, 1975.

Sinha, J. C. *Indian Currency Problems in the Last Decade, 1926–1936*. Delhi: University of Delhi, 1938.

Sitaram Rao. "The Madras Agriculturists' Relief Bill." *Indian Review* 39, no. 6, 1938.

Slater, Gilbert. *Some South Indian Villages*. Oxford: Oxford University Press, 1918.

———. *Southern India: Its Political and Economic Problems*. London: George Allen and Unwin, 1936.

Stokes, Eric. *The Peasant and the Raj*. Cambridge: Cambridge University Press, 1978.

Subramanyam, C. S., and N. Sundaram. "The Moratorium Bill." *Indian Review* 38, no.10, 1937.

Swaminathan, Padmini. "State Intervention in Industrial Development: A Case Study of the Madras Presidency." *Proceedings of the Seminar on South Indian Economy, 1914–1945*. Vol 1. Tiruvananthapuram: Centre for Development Studies, 1985.

Sweezy, Paul M. *The Theory of Capitalist Development*. New York: Modern Reader Paperbacks, 1942.

Thomas, P. J. "Agricultural Depression in Madras Presidency." *The Hindu*, 28 January 1938.

———. *The Growth of Federal Finance in India: Being a Survey of Indian Public Finance from 1833 to 1939*. Oxford: Oxford University Press, 1939.

———. "The Indian Budget: Prospect of Federal Finance." *Asiatic Review* 32, no. 10, 1936.

———. *India's Basis Industries*. Bombay: Orient Longman, 1948.

———. *Papers on Currency and Depression*. Madras: University of Madras, 1938.

———. *Papers on International Trade*. Madras: University of Madras, 1933.

———. *Papers on Rural Debt*. Madras: University of Madras, 1934.

———. "The Problem of Rural Indebtedness." *Indian Journal of Economics* 14, 1933–34.

Thomas, P. J., and K. C. Ramakrishnan. *Some South Indian Villages: A Resurvey*. Madras: University of Madras, 1940.

Thorner, Daniel, and Alice Thorner. *Land and Labour in India.* Bombay: Asia Publishing House, 1962.

Tomlinson, B. R. *The Political Economy of the Raj, 1914–1947: Economics of Decolonization in India.* London: Macmillan, 1979.

Tragedy of the 18d rupee: Speeches and Writings on the Currency and Exchange Question of M. Jamal Mohamed Saib. Madras: R. J. Ram, 1937.

Transition from War to Peace Economy, The: Report of the Delegation on Economic Depression. Part 1. Geneva: League of Nations, 1943.

Venkataraman, K. S. *The Handloom Industry in South India.* Madras: University of Madras, 1940.

Visveswaraya, M. *Unemployment of India: Its Causes and Cure.* Bangalore: The Bangalore Press, 1932.

Wadia, P. A, and K. T. Merchant. *Our Economic Problem.* Bombay: New Book Company, 1943.

Washbrook, D. A. "Economic Development and Social Stratification in Rural Madras: The Madras Region, 1878–1929." In *The Imperial Impact: Studies in the Economic History of Africa and India,* eds. Clive Dewy and A. G. Hopkins, 68–74. London: University of London, 1978.

———. *The Emergence of Provincial Politics: The Madras Presidency, 1870–1920.* New Delhi: Vikas Publishing House, 1977.

Zacharias, C. W. B. *Agricultural Planning for Madras.* Madras: University of Madras, 1953.

Zaidi, A. M., & S. G. Zaidi, eds. *The Encyclopaedia of the Indian National Congress, 1930–1935.* New Delhi: Chand, 1968.

Index